Scrap Quilts
Using
Fast Patch®

Other books available from Chilton:

Scrap Quilts Using Fast Patch®

Anita Hallock

Chilton Book Company
Radnor, Pennsylvania

Copyright ©1991 by Anita Hallock

All rights reserved

Fast Patch® is a registered trademark of Anita Hallock

Published in Radnor, Pennsylvania 19089, by Chilton Book Company

No part of this book may be reproduced, transmitted, or stored in any form or by any means, electronic or mechanical, without prior written permission from the publisher.

Photography by Walter A. Biddle

Designed by Martha Vercoutere

Illustrations by Anita Hallock

Manufactured in the United States of America

LC #90-55876

ISBN 0-8019-8116-6 paperback

ISBN 0-8019-8186-7 hard cover

1 2 3 4 5 6 7 8 9 0   9 8 7 6 5 4 3 2 1 0

To Del and Marlene Matheson

Cover photo: *The large quilt, made with the Nifty Nine-Patch block, is "Come Fly with Me," by Wilma Williams of Marysville, CA. (Courtesy of owner, Marnell Nicknig.) The Log Cabin lap robe and Flying Geese wall hanging were made by the author. Photographed at the Lane County Historical Museum.*

Contents

Introduction

Like other working mothers, I have many demands on my time and have to make priorities for how I spend it. I decided long ago that I would continue to take time to do creative things that fascinated and challenged me. I give that decision credit for the fact that I have no problems with high blood pressure and ulcers and feel twenty years younger than I am. (Unfortunately, I have too many fascinating and challenging things going on most of the time, and that explains my husband's high blood pressure, ulcers, and graying hair.)

To interest me, a project needs to move along at a reasonable speed and needs to create something that lasts. Quiltmaking was out of the question for a long time. It created something which lasted, but it took too long. Then I read Robbie and Tony Fanning's *The Complete Book of Machine Quilting* and started thinking of ways to make quilts with speed techniques.

In 1982, I tried to save an ugly quilt top by cutting it apart diagonally and sewing it back together. That experience led to some to-tally new ideas for piecing triangles with strips. In the years that followed, I did more experimenting, then self-published a series of books, using the trademarked name "Fast Patch" to describe my special techniques. In 1988 Robbie Fanning invited me to write for the Chilton Book Company, and in 1989 *Fast Patch: A Treasury of Strip Quilt Projects* was published, combining ideas from several of our small books.

Scrap Quilts Using Fast Patch includes material from two other self-published books, along with many new ideas. Like my first book, it is written especially for people who have more ideas than time and don't mind learning more ideas if it saves them more time. It's also for people with more plans than *money*, because most projects can be made from scraps and recycled fabrics.

Again, I thank everyone who helped prepare this book, especially the quiltmakers who lent their projects for us to photograph and the staff at the Lane County Historical Museum in Eugene, Oregon, where most of the photography was done.

Anita Hallock
Springfield, Oregon

This book is for you

What is your personal attitude toward fabric and scraps? Do you fit in one of these categories?

"Scrap fanatic"

I once heard about a frugal art student who had no money for paints but kept painting by retrieving and flattening empty tubes other students threw out. Scrap fanatics could almost make their quilts from the fabric scraps others throw out. I'm not close enough to anyone wasteful that I could do that, but I'm definitely a scrap fanatic.

You might not have much yardage; fabric "burns a hole in your pocket" and you have to make it into something. But you save all the pieces: scraps as small as 3" square and long strips as narrow as 1" wide. You organize them once in a while, eventually make them into something or, after much soul-searching, give them away. (While you're at Goodwill to donate them, you spot a cotton skirt and buy it to recycle the fabric.) Your house is cluttered, but you feel secure, knowing you can make a quilt from what you have on hand if a blizzard strikes. A scrap fanatic probably invented "charm quilts" (quilts where every piece is a different fabric—unless a duplicate was used somewhere and folks spent months trying to spot it).

This book is for you. Most projects in this book are speed-pieced from strips, but these strips can often be quite narrow and short, so genuine scraps can be used. Though there are no charm quilts in this book, you can often work quite small pieces into a project.

"Fabric collector"

You buy pretty fabric when you spot it, and as a result, your shelves are bulging. You'll be the one who wins by "dying with the most fabric." (What does the winner get? A sewing room up in heaven?) Just looking at fabric and handling it can give you great pleasure. It's almost like looking through a photo album and remembering favorite people and wonderful vacations. You can spend many hours organizing your fabrics, but that's your business. Tiny scraps are disposed of properly, just as wilted flowers are, but larger scraps are your dear friends.

This book is for you. A great way to start virtually every project in this book is to cut strips from yardage. You can dig out dozens of pieces, cut one strip off from each and have another pleasant experience with your fabrics as you refold them and stack them again.

"Fabric user"

You have a reasonable supply of fabric, but it hasn't taken over your house. You strike a nice balance between saving useful pieces and keeping your sewing room orderly. (I used to try to be like that, but I gave up.)

This book is for you. You'll probably find yourself cutting off 44" strips from the yardage you have, plus buying some special fabrics to supplement them.

"Fabric-free"

Journeyman level. You make plenty of quilts, but clean up leftovers and give them to Goodwill immediately so your house is clutter-free. I don't know any quiltmakers like this personally, but there are probably some.

Beginner level. You haven't been sewing long enough to collect much fabric (or just don't have room to store it). If you want to make a scrap quilt, you cooperate with fellow quilters to buy and share yardage, or you "borrow" it from relatives.

This book is for you. Directions for most projects in this book include ways you can get a scrappy look from new yardage, often from fat quarters.

"Fabric killer"

It's perfectly acceptable to be any of the types above. But if you throw pieces of pretty fabric over 6" wide in the trash to fill up the landfills, that's not acceptable.

This book is not for you. Return it for a refund.

How to use this book

As in my earlier book, *Fast Patch*, how you use this book depends on your experience. I'll tell you what's in the book and you can decide for yourself how to proceed. I suggest you read the whole book (except Chapter 9) before doing any sewing.

Chapter 1

If you haven't done many quilts, study Chapter 1 thoroughly and use it to buy supplies and to survey basic quiltmaking techniques.

Even if you're experienced, scan the chapter. If I say to do things one way, but you prefer another way, keep doing it the way that works for you. I've drawn on my experience as an art teacher to work up some design principles on pages 6 to 9 that might be new to you, so look those over at least.

Chapter 2

This chapter has lots of ideas for organizing your fabrics and scraps. If you are perfectly happy with your fabric management already, just skim over that chapter, but do look at the chart at the end. It summarizes projects by fabric types and sizes of strips and will help you make the best use of your fabric.

Chapter 3

These projects introduce the idea of strip quilting. Most are fairly easy and straightforward. Some are also good for thinning down your supply of fabrics that aren't suitable for projects later in the book.

Chapter 4

This is a showcase of quilt layouts for two-tone blocks such as Log Cabin. You'll refer to this chapter many times when doing projects in Chapters 5, 6, and 7.

Chapter 5

Even if you've done Log Cabin before, you probably haven't done it the way I describe. There's also a Log Cabin look-alike which is faster, but has much of the charm of the traditional Log Cabin.

Chapter 6

Study this chapter before doing projects in the last three chapters of the book, unless you have already used my other books and are familiar with my ideas about turning checkerboards on the bias.

Chapters 7 and 8

These chapters deal with triangles made with strips. They are based on small books I published earlier, *The Mock Log Cabin and Other Scrap Quilts* and *Flying Geese,* but there are many new things too.

Chapter 9

This is high-level stuff. Don't even read this chapter unless you have done some other projects with strips of triangles and thoroughly understand my special Fast Patch technique. Otherwise, you'll be confused! You should understand rules before you break them, and some ideas in that chapter don't follow the rules. Read this chapter about five years from now.

Appendix

The Appendix has cut-apart sheets that would be useful to photocopy, as well as charts, a glossary, and other handy things. Look it over before you start sewing.

1. The Basics

Tools and supplies

All projects in this book are machine-pieced, so obviously you'll need a sewing machine and standard sewing supplies.

Projects are usually made with strips so special cutting tools are needed:

1. A rotary cutter. It can make straight cuts much faster than scissors because it cuts through several layers of fabric at a time and no guidelines are needed. It's also more accurate because you cut on a flat surface with your blade guided by the straight edge of the ruler or grid. Get the large-blade type and replace the blade when it gets dull (which might be several months with normal use, or immediately if you run over a pin).

2. A cutting mat. A special mat is needed for accurate cutting and keeping the blade sharp. Get the largest mat you can afford and have room for. A smaller one to use by your sewing machine or to take to classes is also handy.

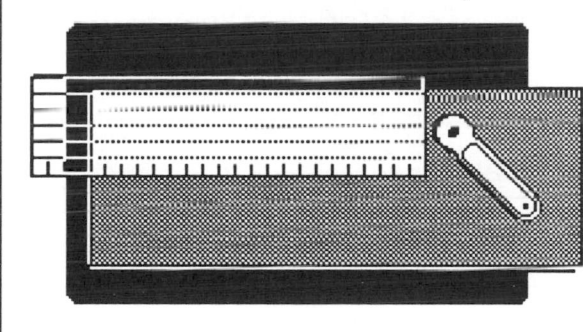

3. Transparent rulers and grids. These heavy acrylic grids are thick and durable so you can cut against them without your blade slipping up onto the ruler and getting dull. They are marked off in inches and have a 45° angle mark. Choose a style with 1/8" marks in both directions.

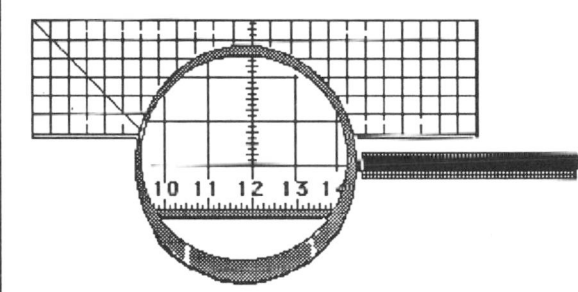

Most projects need the **6" x 24"** size and some also need a grid **12"** or **15" square**. If you have only a 3" x 18" ruler, you can do many projects, but put the larger sizes on your wish list.

These grids tend to slide out of place when you cut against them, but you can prevent most of that. Just put blobs of clear nail polish on the back in several spots and immediately sprinkle with salt. When it's dry, brush off the excess salt and you have transparent sandpaper.

Cutting techniques

How to cut 4" strips

1. Arrange the stack. Have your cutting mat at the end of a table that you can walk around if possible. Spread out layers of fabric on the mat, with two edges aligned as much as possible. Align the edges on the *right*, if you're right-handed.

Caution: *If you're cutting long strips from folded-over fabric, first square up the edge and the fold line with a large square grid. Otherwise, when you open up the strip, you may find it bends at the folds.*

2. Trim the first edge. Place the ruler over the stack just inside that edge. Spread out one hand to hold the ruler firmly. Cut with the other hand, pushing against the edge of the ruler, and trim off the edges. Even up the ends too, if necessary. If ends are aligned quite well already, you can just trim them after you sew the strips together.

3. Change your position. Now you must have the other side of the stack on your right, so walk around the table or turn the mat. Don't try to cut with the wrong hand or cross one hand over the other to cut.

4. Cut the other edge. Move the ruler over so that the edge you just trimmed is at the 4" line. Cut. You have a stack of perfect 4" strips. If you need more strips from those fabrics, move the ruler over to the 4" mark again and cut more strips without disturbing the stack.

5. Cover the blade. These blades are razor sharp and can give you a nasty cut if you're careless. Even if you plan to arrange more fabrics and repeat the process right away, keep the blade covered (or use a brand of cutter with a guard that automatically pops back over the blade).

How to cut large squares

The steps for cutting squares with the large grid are much the same: Arrange fabrics with two edges even, trim the edges (*two* sides of the square this time), and change your position. Move the grid so it *covers* a square the size you need and cut the other two edges. The diagram shows how you would cut 10" squares using a 15" grid.

How to use the ruler as a T-square

After sewing strips into a panel, trim ends to even them up before cutting cross sections. Keep seams parallel to the straight lines on the ruler. After cutting a few cross sections, you may need to trim off the end again to keep things squared up. Take advantage of the 45° angle marks on the ruler whenever appropriate.

Sewing and pressing

All projects in this book are machine-pieced, so I'm assuming you have basic sewing machine skills. If you don't, now's the time to learn. There are some easy projects like Rail Fence in Chapter 3 to practice on.

Here are some suggestions to make your sewing more satisfying:

1. Use the highest quality thread available. Find what works best with your machine (check your instruction book, ask your dealer, or experiment). Cheap thread can take the fun out of sewing by breaking or fouling up your tension. For economy, buy large cones of thread and a thread stand to lift the thread and feed it in evenly. Fill several bobbins of thread ahead of time when doing a large project.

2. Use a size 70 (10/11) needle unless your machine works best with another size, or you're sewing heavy fabric.

3. Sew with 1/4" seams. Most people line up the fabric with the presser foot, which may or may not be 1/4" from the needle. If not, some machines allow you to de-center the needle so seams are 1/4" wide. If a 5/16" seam works better for you, that's okay for most projects. Keep all seams exactly the same width.

4. Use a medium-length stitch. Seams aren't secured by backstitching when working with strips, but there's usually no problem with a seam coming unstitched unless you pick out a seam that crosses it later. Avoid tiny stitches which make it too hard to correct seams; 10 to 12 stitches to the inch is fine.

5. Chain your pieces as you sew. When you finish one seam, immediately feed in the next piece instead of cutting the thread. If you have no more pieces to sew, sew onto a "thread catcher," a scrap of fabric that you leave in the machine when you clip off the other work. This simple habit prevents the needle from coming unthreaded and saves a lot of time and thread.

6. Keep tension balanced. The one thing that makes most people enjoy or dread sewing is tension adjustment. If you have trouble, get your machine repaired or have your dealer give you some pointers.

7. Press seams before crossing with another seam, or at least finger-press to keep from having tucks. Press seams to one side, toward the darker fabric when possible. To avoid creating unnecessary bulk, press seams on the top layer in one direction, those on the bottom layer in the other direction.

8. If working on the bias:
(a) Use spray starch to stiffen fabric before making bias cuts.

(b) Do stay stitching (either before or after cutting) if that helps.

(c) Press with the grain and avoid pressing bias edges. You can easily distort fabric by careless pressing.

Enhancing the scrap look

Whether you use scraps or buy new yardage, you'll usually work with strips. You'll often make sections which are identical instead of getting a random look. That's okay in a large project, but it might bother you in a small project. Here are three easy ways to enhance the scrap look:

1. Use "switchers." This is my term for odd pieces inserted here and there in the final assembly of the quilt. Suppose your quilt will have 2-1/2" squares in it, and you've used strip-piecing techniques to make the chains. Cut several 2-1/2" squares of totally different fabrics ahead of time. As you start assembling chains into blocks, you'll occasionally find you have to pick out a seam to get a better alignment. Replace the piece you remove with a new piece in a different color.

2. Substitute shorter strips sometimes. For example, here's a panel for Rail Fence blocks made from 44" strips. Normally, you'd trim off one end, then move across the panel cutting off blocks.

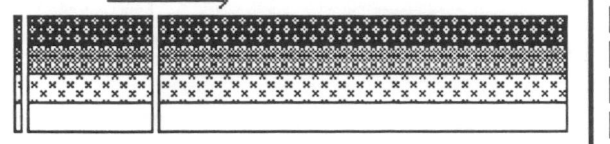

To work in smaller scraps and get a scrap look, substitute shorter strips:

(a) Cut lengths that allow you to cut an even number of blocks.

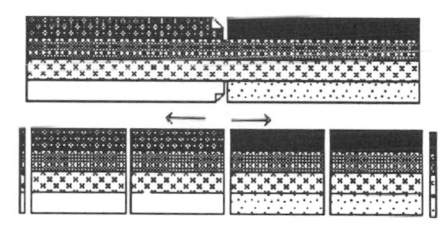

(b) Use the shorter lengths as the outside strips.

(c) Don't join the ends of the pieces; just leave them flapping.

(d) When cutting off your finished blocks, start where you switch fabrics and work both ways.

3. Work with a friend and trade blocks.

Accuracy

If you're young or a beginning quilter, scrap quilts are great to practice on. You don't need to fret about ruining expensive fabric, and mistakes have a primitive charm. As you get more experienced, you become more critical, especially when you press. (Strange how errors show up when pressing. They were there all along; you just didn't notice.)

Look for quality work at all stages:

1. Were strips cut exactly the same width?

2. Are seams the same width?

3. Are cross sections cut exactly the same width as first strips? (If you're making blocks like Rail Fence, do cross sections create a perfect square?)

4. Are cross sections cut at right angles to the seams? Did you use your ruler as a T-square?

5. Do seams line up well? (They should, if you answered yes to the first two questions.)

6. Are squares perfectly square in your checkerboards? When making projects in Chapters 7 and 8, checkerboards are turned into triangles. If squares aren't perfectly square, triangles will be skewed. To check, place a ruler diagonally across the checkerboard. It should start exactly at a corner and cross each intersection. If it doesn't, that's a warning flag. Squares are wider in one direction than in the other on those rows (see the arrows).

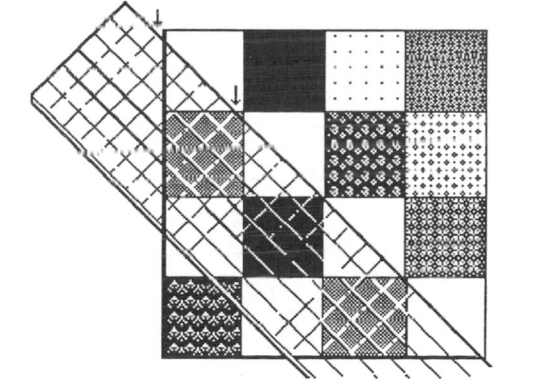

7. Are blocks the same size and do seams line up when you assemble the quilt top? Blocks are often a little longer one direction (the direction of the final seams), so keep them all turned the same way unless you have to have them turned on their sides for design purposes.

Keep things in perspective. Scrap quilts are usually for everyday use, so don't get fanatical. If you look at old quilts, you'll probably see plenty of mistakes. Don't do a lot of picking out or you'll take the fun out of your project. If seams don't line up too well, you might plan on tying the quilt with yarn at those intersections to hide the misalignment.

Designing your quilt top

With traditional blocks (which I used in *Fast Patch*), each block usually has symmetry, pleasing shapes, and enough detail to be interesting. In this book, most quilts have overall designs rather than individual blocks. Sometimes you'll look at the entire quilt in the same way you looked at one single block before, especially with the two-tone blocks. Here are some ideas for making the total effect pleasing.

Design principles

Old scrap quilts were sometimes quite haphazard, made to turn materials on hand into something useful; beauty was secondary. They had odd blocks, chopped-off pieces, a hodgepodge of fabrics, and things out of balance.

If you have plenty of blankets and make quilts for sentimental and decorative purposes, take a little time to apply some design principles. You don't need a perfect color scheme, but you can avoid results that jangle your nerves or depress you. Even if you have given yourself the challenge of using only what's on hand, you probably have a lot more fabric to choose from than Grandma did. Make a project you'll enjoy seeing.

For many years I taught art and emphasized that some basic design principles applied to all creative arts and crafts. When I started writing this chapter, I wondered how I could apply the most important design ideas to fabric in a few brief paragraphs.

The key seems to be a balance between serenity and excitement. A quilt can be pleasant and stress-reducing, as peaceful as a family reading quietly in a circle. But maybe you want your quilt to cheer you up rather than lull you to sleep. (Some quilt artists nowadays want quilts to shock or make social statements. This is the wrong book for them—my projects have a traditional look even if the working methods are surprising.)

Let's call the two quilt moods "restful" and "dynamic," and see how elements in the quilt affect it.

Predictability

Restful: A sense of order, of things being under control is created by repetition of basic shapes, colors, and lines. Symmetrical designs are comforting.

Dynamic: No obvious pattern to shapes and lines can be exciting, but is more likely to be disturbing. Having a general pattern but some surprises makes a quilt more interesting and fun.

Color

Restful: Cool colors like blue and green are generally restful. Pastels are more relaxing than intense colors. Related colors are restful, especially when they gradually blend into each other as colors of the rainbow do.

Dynamic: Warm and bright colors like reds, purples, and oranges are more lively. You can create excitement (or maybe chaos) with strongly contrasting colors or a wide variety of colors.

Caution: *Printed fabric is different from paint. See the notes under "Colors in fabrics," below.*

Colors in fabrics

If there are even two different colors in a fabric, you can no longer just look at the background color and say, "That's a basic green." Your eye blends all the colors and creates a new shade of green.

The subtle color differences in fabric are part of the charm, but they also make it hard to apply textbook color theories. There is no substitute for your own sense of whether two particular fabrics look pretty next to each other. Forget rules—if the colors look good to you (both close up and from a distance), use them.

One spin-off benefit of scrap quilts is that you often accidentally create in one part of the quilt a fantastic color scheme that you can later use for a whole quilt. If you give the quilt away, get a good color photograph first, or make another block of those same fabrics and pin it to your bulletin board to inspire you.

A special warning: *Small prints containing both red and green can be hard to use; from a distance they might be a muddy brown or gray! The same thing happens with small prints containing blue and orange, purple and yellow, or other colors opposite each other on the color wheel.*

Value (dark and light)

Restful: Low-key values (little contrast between darks and lights) are restful. Subtle contrasts can grow on you; you see more in them as time goes by. However, having nothing but light colors might be weak or boring, and having all dark colors might be depressing.

Dynamic: Strong dark/light contrast is bold and exciting. But it's not as relaxing, and you might grow tired of it quickly.

Fabric type

Restful: Solid colors or small prints are safe and comforting.

Dynamic: Large prints with high contrasts are more interesting but risky.

Lines

Restful: Lines that circle and tie things together are restful. Parallel lines are orderly. Horizontal zigzag lines suggest comforting natural things like mountains and valleys.

Dynamic: Lines that radiate from the center suggest explosions. Lines going at many different angles can be chaotic. Vertical zigzag lines are more active, suggesting lightning.

A wall hanging might have a different mood if hung a different way:

Shapes

Restful: Circles and curved shapes are comforting. Repetition of shapes creates order. Triangles resting on a base are stable.

Dynamic: Angular shapes are active. Weird, abstract shapes can be disturbing (even if created accidentally by the way your darks end up in a scrap quilt). Too many different shapes can be chaotic. Triangles resting on point might be upsetting.

Again, a wall hanging might have a different mood turned upside down.

An appliqué of a rooster weathervane would be restful because it represents something traditional. Turned upside down and seen as abstract (unrelated shapes, sharp angles, and diagonal lines), it would be unsettling.

Borders

Restful: Wide borders (or several borders) separate the quilt from background distractions and are restful.

Dynamic: No borders or pieced borders made up of many colors might tend to be visually unsettling (but that can be offset by our feeling that it's a traditional, honest scrap quilt effect).

Find your own balance between design forces: Use many colors, but not all in equal amounts. Use a few warm colors here and there to liven up your cool quilt. Use a few cool colors to make your warm design more rich and pleasing. Have low contrast in most of the quilt, but a high contrast suprise somewhere. You get the idea.

Keep in mind who'll use the quilt. A baby? (You might enjoy soft pastels around your baby, but psychologists say babies like strong colors.) A teenager who likes wild effects? A stressed-out adult who wants to relax? An invalid who needs cheering up?

Remember, what's pleasing to one person may drive another person crazy. I once saw a "Twilight Zone" episode about a punk rocker who didn't mind living a wicked life. He was looking forward to going to hell when he died because of all the excitement there. Instead, he was sent to spend eternity with people showing quiet, restful slides of their vacation trips. While it might be someone else's idea of heaven, it was punishment to him.

Personally, I have enough excitement in everyday life and I want my quilts to be relaxing. I find some contemporary quilts very disconcerting. Of course, they are planned to be that way by artists who break rules in an imaginative way, express their personality, or make a social comment. If your purpose is to please the viewer rather than jangle her nerves, use more of the "restful" suggestions.

How strip piecing affects your design

When you're working with strips, you don't have the control over the design that you do when you build it up piece by piece. Try to get pleasing colors while sewing your first strips together, then add more of a certain color in a later stage if you find you need it. If you have a project that is crying out for a little green, you can pick out some seams and add a few pieces here and there. A design of blues and grays can spring to life when you add an occasional red. Sometimes the border color can do it. Sometimes you need to sprinkle it throughout your quilt.

Arranging blocks into a quilt top

Most quilts in this book are overall designs. You don't see separate blocks when the top is finished. You might look at the entire quilt in the same way you looked at one single block before. But the design is always assembled from smaller units, and you usually have some choice about how to arrange these units. There is no substitute for laying out your blocks or chains on the floor or bed and rearranging them to get a nice effect.

Things you might check for:

1. Are accent colors distributed evenly? It might bother you later if you find all the red is on the left side of the quilt.

2. Are there some "heavy" spots? If a mass of dark colors comes together, does that bother you or is that the effect you wanted?

3. Is a fabric placed next to the same fabric in the next block? Does that bother you? I try to avoid it, but I don't get fanatical. For example, my Garden Path quilt in the color section has two squares of the same fabrics touching, but I don't notice them unless I look for them.

4. Do blocks line up? Your blocks might not all be the same size. If you can't easily correct them, try to use all the largest blocks at one end of the quilt and gradually get to the smaller blocks at the other end.

Keeping your arrangement intact

Once you have an arrangement you like, keep the parts in that order long enough to sew them together.

If you can leave the arrangement laid out on the floor next to your sewing machine, you can pick up two blocks or sections and sew them together, return them to the arrangement, and pick up two more pieces. But most of us don't have room to spread out a big quilt and leave it for hours. Besides, it's annoying to get up from the machine each time you sew a seam. And after you bring the two pieces to the sewing machine, you might accidentally run your seam along the top edges instead of the right side, totally disrupting your scheme.

So, even if my arrangement is laid out by the machine, I usually pin the pieces together into horizontal rows. I pick up one row and sew blocks together, then return it to its place in the arrangement and pick up another row and sew it together.

If I can't sew in the same room where I plan the layout, or can't sew all blocks together in one session, I pin a tag with a number to the first block on the left. I fold up each row's blocks (safety-pinned to each other) into a separate pile. I sew all blocks into rows, then spread out the project again, using tags to tell which row goes where. Then I pin the rows together and take them back to the machine to sew the final seams.

(If you have separate blocks set together with sashing or plain blocks, see pages 10 and 11 in *Fast Patch: A Treasury of Strip Quilt Projects*. That information is not repeated in this book.)

Borders or not?

There are two schools of thought when it comes to borders for scrap quilts:

1. Use wide ones to separate the busy effect of all those colors and shapes from the background. Borders tie everything together and enhance the design. And they are an easy way to extend the size of the quilt.

2. Don't use borders. True scrap quilts often had no borders simply because there wasn't enough of any one fabric to make one.

I noticed that my first scrap quilts tended to have wide borders; my later ones had no border, just a narrow binding of a dark color.

What kind of borders?

As always, use your own judgment and imagination. Here are some ideas to get you started.

1. Borders don't have to be identical. With quilts like Flying Geese, sashing and inner borders often match. But since these are scrap quilts, you can use slightly different fabrics for the sashing strips. Your top border might not match the bottom one (have wider borders at the bottom, if there's a difference). Keep both side borders identical, however.

2. Consider a pieced border. Instructions for string-pieced borders are given in Chapter 3 and sawtooth borders in Chapter 8. Fancy borders or "frames" can be made of any two-tone block, as mentioned in Chapter 4. (Also see Diane Leighton's quilt in the color section.)

3. Have the outer borders wider than inner borders. That's just a general rule. Narrow accent borders can be used anywhere.

4. Contrasting squares can be used in the corners. This is a way to use your chosen border fabric if you don't have quite enough. It can also help avoid some awkward design effects or add a color you need. Sometimes you can use blocks from an abandoned project in those corners (even four different ones).

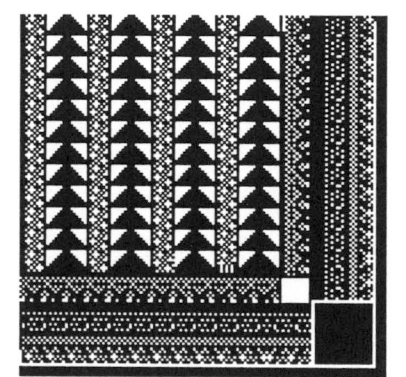

5. Printed border fabrics might give an elegant look. But is an elegant look consistent with your scrappy look? I don't use as many border prints for scrap quilts as I do for those with limited colors, but they are wonderful with Flying Geese. If you don't want to miter the borders, use squares in the corners.

6. The binding is one of the borders. Plan its color as carefully as the others.

   In the Appendix is a page of art you can duplicate to try different border effects (see page 175).

Craftsmanship tips:

1. Cut borders with the lengthwise grain if you have a choice. Fabric doesn't have as much give in that direction.

2. Avoid ruffled edges that may result if the inner part of the quilt is bunched up from quilting but the borders aren't. Cut the final borders a bit small and ease the quilt to fit them if you think this might be a problem.

3. You may be able to tear rather than cut borders if you're making an everyday quilt from 100% cotton. Allow a wider seam if you do.

4. Quilt a design in a wide border.

Backings

Backing yardage for projects in this book. Extra-wide muslin is a favorite with hand quilters. You could also use a muslin bed sheet, but don't use a tightly woven polyester blend if you'll be hand quilting. If you're machine quilting the project, you'll appreciate dark fabric with a random print and you'll probably use regular yardage. Here are some common quilt sizes and yardage needed if 44-45" fabric is used. Remove the selvage, then cut and seam as shown in the diagrams. You might use the remnant to help make your quilt top.

Type of quilt	Size (approx.)	Remnant (approx.)	Yardage
1. Twin throw	up to 54" x 72"	15" x 50"	3 yds.
2. Twin spread, double throw	up to 72" x 87"	none	4 yds.
3. Queen throw, double coverlet	76" x 90"	12" x 90"	5 yds.
4. Queen coverlet, king throw	87" x 90"	none	5 yds.
5. Waterbed, double spread	88" x 108"	none	6 yds.
6. Queen spread	99" x 108"	23" x 99"	8 1/3 yds.
7. King spread	108" sq.	23" x 108"	9 yds.

Pieced backings

It's perfectly respectable to have more than one fabric on the back of the quilt, perhaps in a simple design which repeats a motif on the front. With a little imagination you can use what you have on hand and avoid a trip to the store. See the color plates for two examples. (Pieced backings are a whole new subject which I plan to cover more thoroughly in a future book. I'd love to share your ideas and projects.)

Quilting your project

Although having scraps assembled into a quilt top is a big improvement over having them stuffed into boxes, having the project quilted and on someone's bed is the real goal.

To prepare for quilting:

1. Press quilt top and backing fabric.

2. Trim backing, making it about two inches larger than the quilt each direction.

3. Spread out backing wrong side up on a table, floor, bed, or quilting frame.

4. Spread out batting over the backing, being careful not to stretch it. Trim so it's slightly smaller than the backing fabric but larger than the quilt top.

5. Spread out quilt top, right side up.

6. Baste or pin thoroughly with safety pins (unless using a frame which doesn't require basting).

Hand quilt wall hangings and masterpieces. The stitching pattern complements the patchwork and adds another design element. It's time-consuming, but very relaxing.

Do machine quilting for speed and durability. Quilting can be attractive if done skillfully, but you'll need lots of practice, especially for large projects. For more information, consult Robbie and Tony Fanning's *The Complete Book of Machine Quilting*. See Recommended Reading. Here are some brief directions:

1. Do plenty or basting or pinning with safety pins.

2. Plan straight lines or gentle curves; avoid lots of direction changing.

3. If you will be stitching through many colors of fabric, use soft, fine transparent thread, such as Wonder Thread. Avoid stiff, heavy nylon thread.

4. Roll or fold the project to fit it under the machine.

5. Use a walking foot, if you have one.

6. Test on samples of fabric and batting so you can adjust the tension and the height of the presser foot to get the neatest stitch.

Have a large project commercially quilted. The charge is quite reasonable. The quilting doesn't follow the design, but that doesn't bother me as much with scrap quilts as with other quilts. Consider this solution when you can't design an easy quilting pattern which complements the design (with Log Cabin, for example).

Tie quilts for everyday use. Tying is especially well suited to scrap quilts, in my opinion, and it's ideal for involving children in the project. It's the easiest method, especially with thick batting, but it doesn't complement the patchwork design as much. Make knots every three to five inches with white yarn. Between knots, yarn can go on front or back of project and be cut, tied, and trimmed to about an inch. (Alternate method: Use a long needle and run the yarn through the inside, surfacing every few inches to tie a simple knot or make a lazy daisy stitch; don't clip the yarn and make a tuft.) Tying can also be done with No. 5 pearl cotton or narrow ribbon.

Do fake tying. If you find pulling the yarn through the quilt is too hard, do this: Lay two pieces of yarn along the seam line. Use a stationary zigzag stitch on your sewing machine to tack the yarn down at regular intervals. Remove the quilt from the machine, clip the yarn, tie knots, and trim ends. You can also tack on lengths of ribbon, which you later tie into bows.

For basting, tying, or hand quilting, several beautiful hardwood frames with nice features are available. Although quilting frames usually take a lot of space, some are ingeniously designed to be portable or store work in progress in quite a small place.

One-step quilting

When your final piecing involves a lot of parallel seams, you can machine quilt with a technique called one-step quilting, or quilt-as-you-go. You stitch along the inside seams to quilt the design to the backing and batting at the same time you sew the pieces to each other. It often looks better than regular machine quilting because stitching doesn't show on the front. The idea is quite simple, but it's fairly difficult to do on large quilts. Even on small projects, it takes practice. Once you master the technique, it's fast and durable.

The **String place mats** in Chapter 3 would be an easy project to practice on. The **Border Quilt**, also in Chapter 3, works well, as do several projects in

Chapter 8: **Sawtooth place mats, Sawtooth Flying Geese** (the project shown in the following artwork), **Hundreds of Triangles,** and **Thousands of Triangles.** Also try **Flying Geese** in Chapter 9.

The **Nifty Nine-Patch** block in Chapter 7 can be adapted, but I don't have room to explain it. Write to me, or figure it out yourself. (Hint: it works only with certain layouts, and instead of making individual blocks, you assemble chains which go across the quilt.) Two quilts in the color section were made this way.

Blocks such as **Stacks of Strips**, **Log Cabin**, and **Woodpile** can be done on single-block level. See Robbie and Tony Fanning's *Complete Book of Machine Quilting* or Georgia Bonsteel's lap quilting books for instructions on joining the quilted blocks.

As I said, try the string-pieced place mats in Chapter 3 first. Then come back to this section. Skill at one-step quilting comes only from practice.

One-step quilting with pieced chains

For more complex designs, it's better to machine baste all chains together first, then sew over each seam again, this time doing the quilting. Here is a general guide to get you started. Pay attention; my technique is somewhat different than you may be used to.

1. Choose the right type of backing fabric: This must be stiffer than usual. Starch it heavily if necessary.

2. Machine-baste the final chains together. That's much easier than trying to align seams, protect points of triangles, etc., while wrestling with yards of batting and backing. If your quilt is large, or if it is medium-sized but the final chains go **across** the quilt, one-step quilting is easier if you make the quilt top in two sections. Machine-baste each half, but don't sew them together. Press the project and make any necessary corrections.

3. Measure the quilt top, estimate how much you will need for borders, and cut the backing and batting (a little larger than you think you will need). If you are quilting in two sections, have the batting and backing in two sections also and do each half as if it were a small quilt. Step 14 tells how to combine the halves.

4. Lay out the backing, wrong side up, and spread out the batting on top. If batting is bonded or glazed, have the smoother side up.

5. Baste batting and backing together thoroughly. This holds layers together and is a guide to quilting. Safety pins won't do.

(a) Baste lines across the batting/backing, marking the top and bottom of the quilt. (Lay the quilt top out on the batting temporarily to determine exact length.) Keep this line parallel to the top and bottom edge too.

(b) On a large quilt, find the center vertically. Make sure it is parallel to the edges of the quilt, and baste a line there using a special color of thread.

(c) Baste parallel lines in the direction you'll be quilting. These lines don't need to be an equal distance apart, but they do need to be exactly parallel. You need them to keep the quilting going straight.

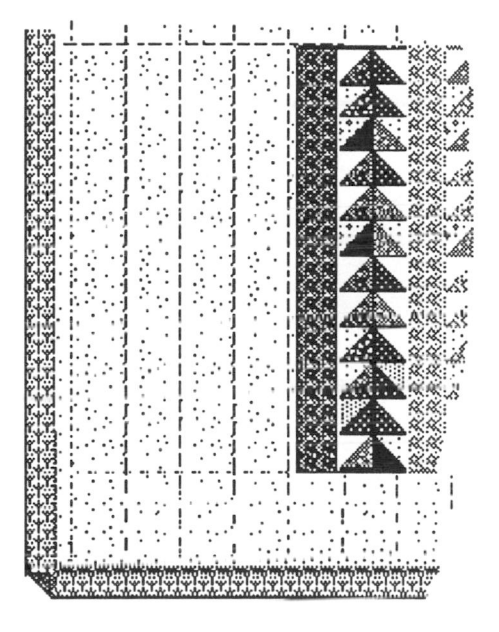

6. Spread the quilt top over the backing/batting again, centering it in both directions. (If you are doing only half the quilt now, have the quilt top come to within an inch of the edge where the other half will be added.)

7. Cover the exposed batting. To keep your presser foot and needle from snagging on the batting as you move the work in and out, fold the edges of the backing over the front to cover it and pin with safety pins.

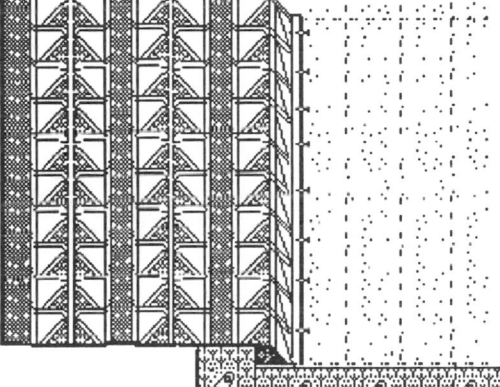

8. Fold part of the quilt top back on itself. Baste or pin the first seam allowance in place.

Large project: Start with the center strip. Pin the seam allowance to the center basted line.

Small project: Pin through the seam that joins the first two strips on the left.

9. Quilt over the first seam.

   (a) Roll up the batting/backing enough to get it under the head of the machine.

   (b) Transfer the work to the sewing machine and start quilting. Sew through the basted seams, the backing, and the batting, using about eight stitches to the inch and a looser setting than normal on the presser foot. Seal off the stitching with tiny stitches at the beginning and end of the row.

(c) Use a "walking" (or "even feed") foot, if you have one. A roller foot or zipper foot could be used instead—both help avoid snagging the batting (so does a piece of light cardboard, which you slide along next to the seam as you sew).

10. Remove the work from the machine and inspect it. Do this after each row! Check both front and back for crooked stitching, tucks, wrinkles, and uneven puffiness. You have to make corrections immediately; you can't do it later. Don't get discouraged; it gets better with practice. I sometimes have to remove much of the first row and do it over. It's important to get that one right.

11. Get ready for the next row of stitching.

(a) Finger-press the design flat at the last seam (or press it with a cool iron).

(b) Fold over at the next seam. Again, pin the seam allowance to the batting and backing, tugging gently as you do to make sure fabric is straight and there's no slack on the front or the back. Resist the tendency the top fabric has to migrate down. Use the basting lines on the batting to keep things squared up.

(c) After pinning, look at the front and back again to make sure both are smooth and straight.

(d) Quilt over that seam.

12. Continue quilting. Inspect the work after each row of stitching. If you started quilting at the middle, go back to the center and work out the other direction. Again, take special care to resist the tendency of the fabric to creep down. If you're doing a large project and the weight of the quilt pulls the work sideways as you get toward the edges, put another table by your machine to support the quilt.

13. Add borders. Sew on borders, quilting them in place as before. You don't need to baste them on ahead of time since there are no seams to line up. Do continue to carefully check your work after each seam. Don't try to miter corners, just lap them (using a corner square as mentioned on page 12, if you wish). Go ahead and add borders to half-quilts too if the seams joining the parts won't be too conspicuous and you are very careful to have borders on both halves exactly the same width. I would probably add dark borders before joining halves, but if borders were light I'd add them after joining.

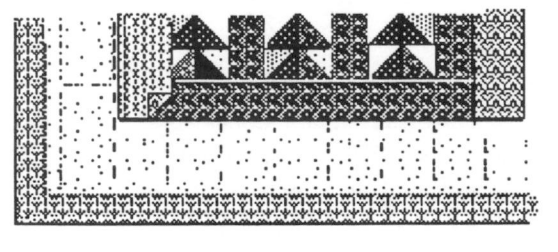

14. If doing the project in two parts: Quilt the other half, making sure the designs on the two halves will fit together. When finished, remove safety pins around edges of both sections. There are several ways to join the halves. Use your own method, or do it like this:

(a) Trim the edges that will be joined.

Left half of project: Machine-baste through quilt top, batting, and backing, then trim the edges evenly (or serge the layers together—trimming as you go).

Right half of the project: Trim the batting flush with the design or a bit smaller. Leave the backing at least an inch larger. Don't baste these layers to each other.

(b) Pin the two parts to each other, through both quilt tops and half of the batting and backing. Fold the unattached batting and backing back out of the way. (The diagram shows borders added before parts are joined.)

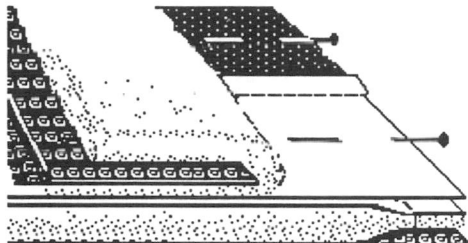

(c) Machine-baste layers together. Check for accuracy. You'll probably need to make corrections since wrestling those big quilt parts makes it hard to sew straight.

(d) Sew over the basting lines, and check again.

(e) Adjust the unattached backing to cover the seam neatly. Hand stitch in place.

(f) Sew on additional borders, if desired.

15. Bind project as usual.

Binding your project

I suggest that you bind scrap quilts with more durable material since they are more likely to get some real use and edges will wear out first.

1. After quilting the project, use your rotary cutter to trim the three layers flush with each other. Slide your cutting mat along under the project as you go. The wide ruler helps you measure the outer border and keep it perfectly even as you cut. Round corners slightly.

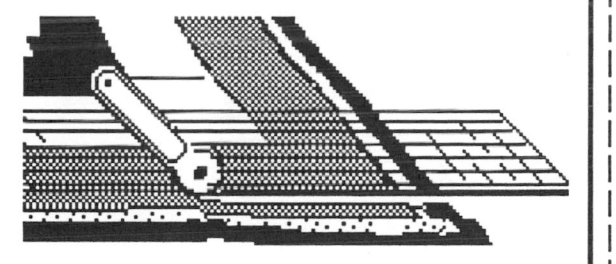

2. Measure to find the distance around the project. Cut 2-1/2" binding strips and piece them together to total that length plus ten or twelve extra inches. Press seams open and press over 1/2" on one end for neatness.

Craftsmanship tip: *To reinforce the edge and make it easier to ease the binding to fit in Step 6, stitch the full length of the binding 1/4" from one edge.*

3. Starting with the folded end, pin several feet of binding (the unstitched edge) in place on quilt. Don't start at a corner. Stretch the binding and ease the quilt slightly if the edges flare because of the quilting.

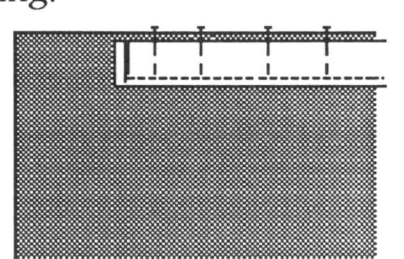

4. Stitch through all layers 1/2" from the edge of the quilt (1/4" from the edge of the binding strip). Stop 1/2" from the corner.

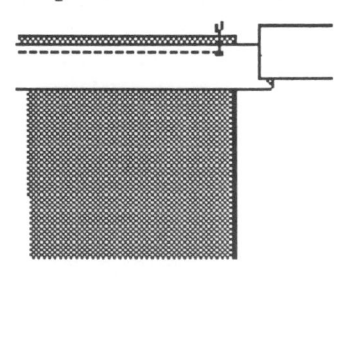

5. Create a mitered corner like this:

(a) Fold the binding up away from the quilt.

(b) Fold it back so the edge is even with the edge of the quilt. Determine where your next stitching will start (next to the diagonal fold of fabric where the other stitching ended) and insert a pin.

(c) Start stitching again right next to last stitch.

Stitch a few inches, then remove the work from the machine and see if a nice miter will be created. If not, try it again with a slightly larger or smaller fold. It might take a little experimenting. It's better to have the corners rounded a bit because there wasn't enough fabric in the fold than dog-eared because there was too much.

Continue around the quilt until you get back to the beginning. Overlap ends an inch or so.

6. Bring binding around to the other side. Fold the edge under at the stitching line and pin thoroughly. Blind stitch by hand, or machine-stitch carefully in the ditch with a zigzag or blind stitch setting.

Length of binding strips

How many yards of strips do you need for binding your project? Look at the quilt sizes in the chart on page 13 and use the chart below:

Quilt size	Binding
1	7-1/2 yds.
2	9-1/2 yds.
3	10 yds.
4	10-1/2 yds.
5	11-1/2 yds.
6	12 yds.
7	12-1/2 yds.

Quick-turn method for finishing small quilts

If you don't like to apply bindings, use this shortcut for finishing baby quilts or small everyday quilts.

1. Cut backing fabric. Spread out quilt top and backing (right sides together). Trim backing to match quilt top, rounding corners slightly and clipping them. Pin edges together.

2. Trim batting to fit. Be careful not to stretch it.

3. Sew around the project. Sew 1/2" from edge, leaving an opening for stuffing (1/4 to 1/3 of the narrow end). You could also leave openings near the other corners wide enough to insert your hand.

4. Turn right side out.

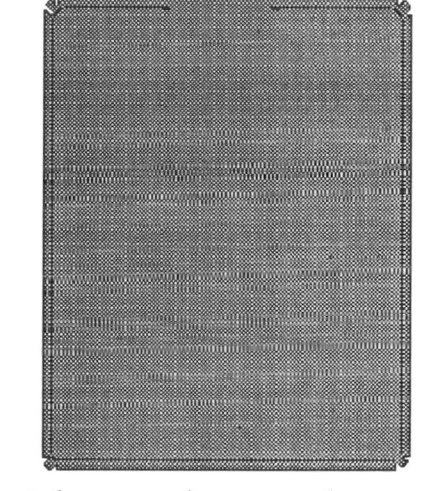

Straighten and press edges; your hand inside helps with this.

5. Roll up batting and stuff it in. Smooth it out carefully.

6. Quilt or tie the project.

7. Close openings by hand stitching.

2. Making the Best Use of Your Fabrics

I can't help thinking of women in other times and places who have desperately needed to make a quilt. Maybe an exhausted mother had to sit and rest but was so overwhelmed by all the work still to be done that she couldn't relax unless her fingers were still working. Maybe someone was cold and needed more bedding, or a daughter was getting married. Or maybe a homesteader or someone living through the depression needed an emotional escape from hard times or isolation. She needed to make something lasting and beautiful but had to use whatever materials were on hand.

Cloth was the one essential thing. (The need to create sometimes died before the batting was needed, just as it does now.) Cloth often meant scraps left from making new clothes and from parts of old clothes. I have an antique scrap quilt that says it all. It has tiny triangles, 1-1/4" on the longest edge. And some of those triangles are pieced together from two smaller scraps! Can you imagine the maker throwing out 1/8-yard pieces of calico?

Most people now have access to an abundant supply of beautiful new fabric, and though cloth gradually gets more expensive, it's still a bargain. Even so, quilt-making is more practical if you can make use of scraps of one quilt to make another.

Managing your scraps can be challenging, but fortunately, it's pleasant—another opportunity for a meaningful relationship with your pretty cloth.

This chapter has many ideas to help you accumulate the best fabric for speed quilting, thin down the surplus, and keep fabrics organized.

The best fabric for projects in this book

100% cotton

Like traditional patchwork, speed-pieced quilts work best with firmly woven cotton fabric of light/medium weight. It is easier to work with and more satisfying, especially when triangles are involved. By all means, buy 100% cotton for any fabric you purchase.

What if you have fabric on hand that you aren't sure of? You can probably tell by careful examination. Polyester blends are usually thinner, smoother, and more slippery and they don't tear well; cotton is usually thicker and rougher and tears well. You can also burn a small piece. Cotton smells like paper burning, has a yellow flame, and leaves a feathery ash. Polyester burns with black smoke and curls into beads. If you think it might be a blend but it looks and acts like cotton, it probably can be treated as cotton in your quilt.

Poor quality fabrics

It's false economy to put poor quality cloth into a project you've invested a lot of time in. A few bad fabrics can ruin your favorite quilt within a couple of years, or require you to remove and replace pieces, which isn't easy. It's safest to buy fabric with a respected brand name, but if you have already got something you aren't sure of, examine it. Squeeze it, check the back, hold it up to the light (along with a good quality piece for comparison, both prewashed).

You will need to find your own balance between serviceability and feel. I know that muslin, being made with shorter fibers,

won't last as long as percale, but I like the feel of muslin and the homey, honest appearance when it's used in scrap quilts. I became more careful in buying muslin, however, after using a piece unwashed. When the project was washed, it had wrinkles that absolutely could not be removed.

Prints and solids

This book features speed quilts made by strip-piecing. You'll have an easier time using random prints or solid fabrics instead of large prints and directional fabrics. Stripes, checks, plaids, one-way designs, or designs with dots or flowers arranged in lines are not recommended for most projects. Use the ones you already have on hand for backings, borders, and a few projects indicated on the chart at the end of the chapter.

What's wrong with directional prints? You can cut only one layer at a time because you have to watch the alignment of the design as you go. You might not like the direction the design takes in the final blocks. To add to your troubles, directional designs aren't always printed straight with the

---

Good quality fabrics
Dyes penetrate to the back.
Threads are long and fine.
Weave is uniform and close.
Reasonably wrinkle-free.
You still love it after prewashing.

Poor quality fabrics
Color on front only.
Threads are short and weak.
Weave is loose or uneven.
Wrinkled when squeezed.
Fabric had a lot of sizing and feels terrible after sizing is washed out.

weave of the fabric. You often have to choose between cutting to match the design or cutting along the grain of the fabric, because you can't do both. Even if you cut carefully, the pieces might look as though you were sloppy.

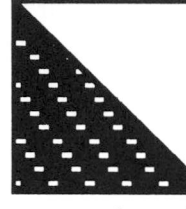

In summary, when buying new fabrics for the blocks:

Look for:
1. Good quality fabric, tightly woven, 100% cotton.
2. Solid colors or small random prints.

Avoid:
1. Polyester or other synthetics.
2. Very large prints.
3. Stripes and diagonal prints.

Prewashing

Prewash fabric to guard against shrinking and bleeding of colors. Before washing, fold all four corners together and clip corners off to help prevent fraying and to signal that the fabric has been prewashed. Add vinegar to the water to set the dyes if you find fabric bleeding. If you prefer the extra body of fabric that hasn't been washed, use spray starch or fabric finish when pressing.

Organizing your fabrics

If you already have lots of fabric, especially scraps and pieces under a yard, you will have to do some organizing—if you haven't already. Otherwise you'll waste too much time pawing through boxes looking for the right colors, unfolding and looking at the same pieces many times to see if they're the right size. How you organize depends on your personality, how upset you get at clutter, and the amount of money, space, and time you have available.

You can spend a lot of time organizing your fabric, which is perfectly fine if you enjoy the process. Maybe you can enjoy your fabrics as much "raw" as you can made into something—just as you enjoy flowers in the garden as much as flowers arranged in a vase.

You're also justified in spending time organizing your fabric if you don't especially enjoy it but do enjoy saving money. More than money is involved. That piece of fabric is here and you don't have to go to the store to get it. Even if you go to the store, you might not find that particular print again.

Treat your prettiest scraps with respect. They have a place waiting for them in a quilt some day. Keep them where you can enjoy them and where you can find them when their day of destiny arrives.

Guilt box

If fabric costs $6.00 a yard …
- Throwing away a 2" strip or a 9" x 10" scrap is throwing away $.33.
- Throwing away a 3" strip or a 10" x 14" scrap is throwing away $.50.
- Throwing away a 4" strip or an 8" x 22" piece is throwing away $.75.

What's more if you need one more $.33 black strip for your border, here's what it might really cost:
- Drive to the store: $2.00 (maybe more if the quilt shop is in the next town) plus 30 minutes of time (maybe more if you have to bundle up baby, strap him or her in the car seat, unstrap, strap, unstrap, and unbundle).
- Buy 1/4 yard of black for $1.25 (then buy $19.35 of other fabrics you spotted and couldn't resist).
- Pre-wash that black piece and the other fabrics before you can use them or put them on your shelf.
So in a way, that 3" strip might cost $22.60 and an hour or two of time. In fact, your opportunity (or desire) to sew might be gone for another day.
Does that make you feel guilty enough?

Goals when organizing fabrics

1. Have the color of every fabric visible.

2. Have some idea of the size of each piece without having to unfold it. You can **see** what color folded fabric is, so organize fabrics by **size** rather than by colors.

3. Let fabric breathe without having it in bright light. Don't store in plastic bags or in direct light.

4. Don't make sorting and organizing too time-consuming. Make it easy to return something to its spot after using it.

5. Have shelves and boxes attractive and durable.

6. Have everything pre-washed.

7. Have non-quilting fabric in a totally different area. You don't want to get the idea you have plenty of red fabric, only to find out that it's actually corduroy or jersey.

One way to organize fabrics

First, you need shelves of some sort. If you don't already have shelves, do some preliminary organizing before you rush out and buy some. Make temporary shelves of sturdy cardboard boxes turned on their sides and stacked. For free shelves for the smaller pieces, check at stores for cardboard displays with neat cubby holes 4" to 10" wide. (Stores throw them out all the time because manufacturers are always sending them more.) You won't need the bulky floor stands, just the compartments. They're quite durable; I have used one for about five years and it's still in good shape.

If fabric is stored in different locations, gather all quilting fabric into one spot, close to your shelves. Use card tables, a bed, or a sheet spread on the floor. If possible, have a place you can leave it for several hours or days because organizing will take time. Move all non-quilting fabric, craft supplies, etc., to a totally different location if you need to free up space.

Supplies needed:

1. A yardstick, tape measure, or your 24" ruler. A tape measure fastened permanently to one of the shelves would be handy.

2. An iron and ironing board

3. A labeling kit. Leave this kit on your shelves to use when you add fabric to your collection or re-file fabric after a big project. Suggested supplies:

> **(a)** Circular key tags or other tags or labels.
>
> **(b)** Safety pins.
>
> **(c)** A pencil or pen.
>
> **(d)** Large rubber bands.

4. Paper bags for pre-sorting.

5. Plastic bags for temporary storage.

6. A filing system if you plan to expand your scrap collection. Supplies for that will be listed later.

The first stage in sorting

1. Remove really small pieces. Toss them into the waste basket or into their own bag or box. I use a couple of wide-mouth peanut butter jars without lids; they are transparent so I can see most of the fabric inside. I use these scraps for "thread grabbers" or "switchers."

2. Decide whether to keep multiple pieces of the same fabric together. How are you likely to use this fabric? If the pieces will be used for different quilts, divide them and file them separately. If they'll be used in the same quilt, keep them together, but still visible so you can use a strip of them for another project. You might put them in short, heavy plastic bags, top open, so the fabric can breathe. (I hang such bags on a special strip with nails high on my workroom wall. I try to do the same thing with abandoned projects, not to feel guilty but to keep the fabric pieces and blocks in plain sight so I can work them into other projects.)

3. Set aside anything under 1/2 yard and lengthwise strips. You'll organize these pieces later; just toss them in grocery bags for now.

4. Get rid of anything you know you'll never use. If you've had a piece of fabric five years and you are turned off every time you see it, put it in a bag for Goodwill and take the bag out of the house at first opportunity. You need the room.

5. Stack pieces 1/2 yard or more on shelves.

(a) Press or smooth out fabric if necessary, but don't take a lot of time fussing because you have a lot of work ahead. (Who am I to tell you what to do? If you enjoy fussing with your fabric, take all the time you want.)

(b) Fold neatly, using a uniform method so fabric fits your shelf size and isn't hidden by over-hanging pieces. Since you'll often cut full-length strips, fold yardage so that it's easy to spread out a doubled piece (22" wide, selvages together) for cutting.

(c) Stack pieces by size, the smallest pieces at one end of the collection, gradually progressing toward the largest pieces at the other end. Measure pieces or develop a good eye for size and just estimate it. (You know, hold a piece of fabric up and measure a yard by the distance from your nose to your thumb.) Measure a folded piece and estimate the total size rather than unfolding.

(d) Label shelves. Consider using temporary labels so you can move stacks and labels as your fabric supply changes.

(e) As you get into the larger lengths such as backing fabrics, there will be a great difference in the sizes. Labels on the shelves won't be practical, so attach tags to the yardage with safety pins and have the tags hang down in front, or put a rubber band around each piece along with a slip of paper giving the yardage.

(f) Pin tags on pieces less than 44" wide and irregular-sized pieces.

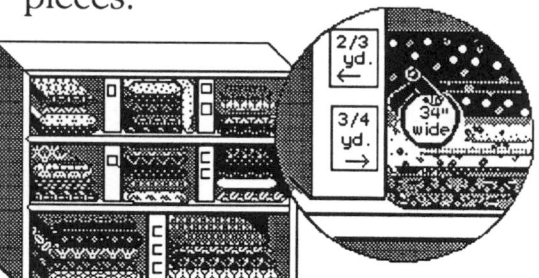

This sketch shows fabric sorted on a recycled cardboard display. Notice the labels and tag pinned to a piece which isn't full width.

Study your shelves

When you finish your preliminary sorting, study your shelves. Will they be adequate for permanent storage? Some things to consider:

(a) Will you decrease the fabric supply by making some quilts right away, then keep the inventory low?

(b) Will you increase your fabric supply? Did organizing all that fabric inspire you to buy more? You'll probably want plenty of white or neutral fabric and black fabric when working with scraps—will you buy it ahead or get it as you need it? Will you stock up on backing fabrics and batting, or buy it as you need it?

(c) Where will you put the scraps you set aside? If you'll sort them with the accordion file system I'll show you next, allow several feet of shelf space for those boxes.

If you found your shelves weren't adequate, start planning for the shelves you need.

Sorting your scraps

Now back to the bags of scraps you set aside earlier. Think some more about which direction you'll be going. This may be just the **opposite** direction from what you decided on for your yardage collection.

Will you be **thinning down** your scraps? Do you plan to use up scraps to free space for new fabrics, then keep scraps at a minimum? See below for ideas.

Will you be **expanding** your scraps? Do you have lots of fabric that you plan to use for quilts? That might reduce your yardage but generate more scraps. Or do you love the look of scrap quilts and want to keep as wide a variety of scraps on hand as possible all the time? See page 30 for ideas.

Thinning your scrap collection

Look over the charts on page 38 and 39, and thumb through the book. Pick four easy projects, each using one of these four main color/fabric types:

(a) Warm colors: maroons, purples, browns, black, beiges, warm greens.

(b) Cool colors: blues, greens, purples, black, grays.

(c) Bright colors: oranges, yellows, bright reds, blues, and greens that don't fit the more subtle shades in the first two categories.

(d) Hard-to-use: heavier fabrics, stripes, plaids, odd-shaped pieces, etc.

Have a box for each project, labeled with the quilt you plan to make, then color/fabric type, then sizes of scraps that can be used. For example, these four projects might absorb all the scraps you want to dispose of: (See chart on page 38.)

(a) "Log Cabin," page 74, for our bed.
Warm colors, 2" strips, any length.

(b) "Border Quilt," page 41, wall hanging for hallway.
Cool colors, 2" strips, any length.

(c) "Garden Path," page 129, for Mary's baby if small quilt, Chris if big quilt

Bright solids and random prints (no stripes).
4" strips and 2-1/2" strips, any length.

(d) "Goodwill Quilt," page 63, for Johnny's clubhouse.
Plaids, stripes, etc., all colors.
Triangles, odd pieces, etc., 6" min.

As you pick up a piece of fabric, toss it into one of the boxes. Add larger pieces of the right color too, because they can be trimmed down or might be used for borders, etc. If a piece seems to fit more than one project, cut strips now and put some in both boxes. If you run into an odd-shaped piece, cut strips as long as possible from it for one of the first three projects, then put the rest into the odd pieces box. Get rid of any pieces that don't fit any of these projects.

Obviously you can change your mind. You might find the second box overflowing and decide to make a large quilt instead of the wall hanging, or you might find you don't have enough pieces in one category to bother with. It's hard to look at a pile of scraps and determine what size of quilt it will make, so stay open-minded about that. Plan on just making as many blocks as you can, then arranging them into some sort of quilt. Or plan a new project if you find you use only half the fabric in the box.

Just making these four projects won't eliminate your scraps, but it might thin them down enough that you'll be able to keep the remaining scraps in one box or give them away without feeling too guilty.

Expanding your scrap collection

A different approach will be used if your scrap collection is a valuable asset you want to maintain or expand. If you truly love scrap quilts and want to make many more of them in the years ahead, have an attractive system that gives you a good feeling whenever you open the door—a system that makes it easy to find just the right pieces for each project.

Temporary sorting aid

If you're in the mood to get your smaller pieces sorted but can't make a filing system right away (maybe because you don't know what type of system you want), sort fabrics temporarily with a collection of small and medium paper bags, opened up, tops folded down, taped or stapled together. For labels to use, read ahead.

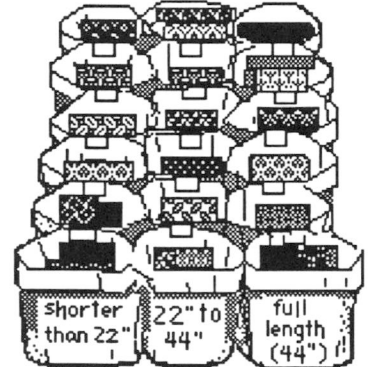

Once you decide how many categories to use, work up a permanent storage system. I give very detailed categories. Part of the purpose of this preliminary sorting is to see whether you want to use all of those categories. Remember the system is to benefit you and not to please anyone else.

The accordion file system

A handy way to keep everything from 2" strips to 1/2-yard pieces is in shallow accordion files. The pockets expand and contract to adjust to the number of scraps in each category, and pieces can't slip down and get lost. It's easy to fold pieces and

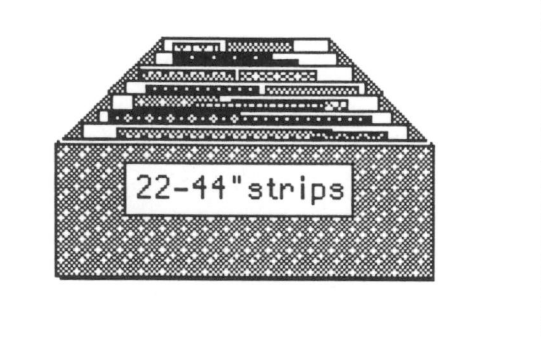

slip them in and easy to flip through the files looking for a piece of purple big enough to cut a 4" x 22" strip. It's also easy to move individual boxes over to your work area and have access to your scraps as you cut and sew.

What **isn't** easy is finding ready-made accordion files the right size. I suggest you make your own. Here's how:

Supplies Needed:

1. Boxes and cardboard

2. A paper cutter (trim board) is wonderful; borrow one if you can

3. A box cutter and straight edge (your sewing ruler will do)

4. Contact paper to decorate the boxes, or a leftover roll of wallpaper

5. Stickers, such as file folder labels

6. Scotch tape

7. A pack of 3 x 5 cards to stiffen the folded fabric so it doesn't flop over (optional)

You'll need five or six sturdy boxes about 5" deep, 7" wide, and 11" long—and three or four larger ones. Cut the lids off and cut to uniform height if you wish.

Buy ten pieces of 22" x 28" poster board, 6 ply or heavier, white so it doesn't distract from the colors of your scraps. (Or get five pieces of larger poster board, 28" x 44".) Paper products get more expensive every year; there are ideas below for using things you might already have on hand.

Measure boxes in either direction and cut cardboard that width. My system is based on eight pockets per box, although you can modify this.

For smaller boxes: Allow 8" per pocket. You can get by with 7 peaks (7 x 8 = 56), which is what you get with two 28" lengths of poster board taped together. Working both directions from the taped part, measure off every 4" using your 4" x 6" transparent ruler.

Draw heavy lines with a ball-point pen to score the cardboard and fold back and forth in accordion style. Tape each length of folded cardboard into a box, forming seven peaks.

For larger boxes: Allow 11" per pocket. An 88" strip of cardboard, made by taping together four 22" lengths (or two 44" lengths) would be needed for each box. This time mark off 5", then 1", then 5", 5", 1", 5", 5", 1", and so on. Fold like this

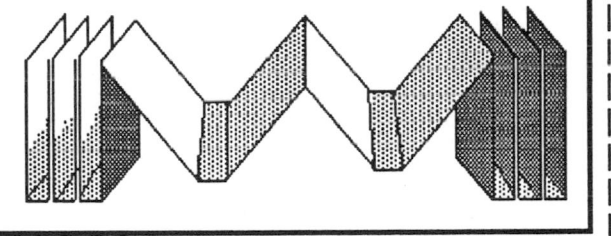

to make eight pockets with wide bottoms to hold more pieces.

Fit inside the box and tape or glue the ends firmly to the ends of the box.

Make as many boxes as needed. Cover with Contact paper for an attractive set. Label boxes and dividers (easiest if you write on stickers, then apply the stickers). Fold the fabric and file it in **front** of the labels. Use 3 x 5 cards (or longer pieces of scrap cardboard) inside the folded fabric if you feel it flops over too much; I don't bother.

Here are my three categories. (Remember, I'm a scrap fanatic, plus I'm making a lot of samples as I write this book. You can simplify the categories if you don't want to save scraps this small or sort them this thoroughly.)

1. Strips, three boxes. Label boxes by length only:

Strips less than 22" long
Strips over 22" long
Full-length strips (44")

Label pockets inside each box: **under 2", 2", 2-1/2", 3", 4", 5", 6",** and **7".** (If you have only seven pockets, omit 2-1/2".)

Another way to arrange boxes: Have **2" and 3" wide strips** in the first box, **4" and 5" wide strips** in the second box, and **6" and 7" wide strips** in the third box. Label pockets by length: **2" strips less than 22" long, 2" strips longer than 22", full-length 2" strips,** and so on. Only

six pockets will be needed in each box.

When you file your fabrics in these three boxes, don't include border prints—they are filed separately.

2. Pieces, four or five boxes. Label these boxes:

Triangles and irregular pieces. (No labels on pockets—file smaller ones at the front, larger as they go back.)

Wide strips, less than 22". (Label pockets **8"-9", 10"-11", etc.,** up to 18".)

Wide strips, 22" or more. (Label pockets **8"-9", 10"-11", etc.,** up to 17".)

Wide strips, full length. (Label pockets **8"-9", 10"-11", etc.,** up to 17".)

Fat Quarters, etc. It's handy to keep together pieces 18" x 22", plus pieces which are larger but can also be used in fat quarter projects. This box should have fewer, but larger pockets. (If you have lots of fat quarters, you might prefer to stack them on shelves or cubby holes or roll up pieces and store them in pretty baskets arranged by color.) Label pockets **Fat quarters, Longer than fat quarters, Wider than fat quarters, Fat halves** (22" x 36"—some stores are offering these precut now, just as they do fat quarters).

3. Longer pieces, one or more boxes. Store narrow pieces longer than 44" in these boxes, as well as border prints that have already been cut apart some what. If two boxes are used, label both, **Long strips & borders.**

Have one box an accordion file for pieces that can be easily folded. Sort by length rather than width since you can **see** the width. You might stack larger pieces of long fabric on top of the box if they won't fit in but you think they might get lost on the shelf with the yardage. That's fine; it's your system.

Some long pieces are stored more easily if rolled up standing on end, so store things that way in the other box. Fold or roll multiple pieces of the same border fabric separately but hold each set together with a heavy rubber band.

Accordion folders from recycled materials

If you like the idea of accordion folders, but the cost of poster board turns you off, look around for free substitutes. It's in the spirit of scrap quilts to recycle cardboard, paper, and other materials too.

File folders

Trim used file folders to the width of your boxes, fold over the sides, and use them for the accordion folds. One stiff folder can be used for two peaks. Folders that are too limp can be overlapped and taped as shown.

Corrugated cardboard supports

If you make dividers from lightweight recycled advertising posters, include supports from corrugated cardboard pieces. In fact, you might include two pieces of cardboard, taped to the two sides so they can separate. Also experiment with rolls of vinyl wallpaper, freezer paper, or whatever you have on hand. You might not want to tackle this unless you have access to a paper cutter (trim board), since it's hard work to cut all that cardboard by hand.

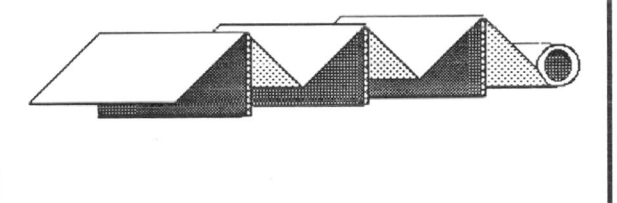

Deluxe accordion files

Very sturdy and attractive boxes can be made by using Contact paper with recycled cardboard (corrugated cardboard plus old file folders). A regular roll of Contact paper is 18" x 9' and will make files for three boxes, 9" wide or less, or two boxes if you cover the outsides too. It's probably cheaper than the basic method using new poster board, but a lot more work unless you have access to a paper cutter to cut your cardboard. Use neutral colored Contact paper or something with a small print which won't distract from your fabrics.

To make each box:

1. Cut 6' (72") of Contact paper, the width of your box.

2. Cut 14 pieces of cardboard that same box width: seven corrugated, 4-1/2" wide, and seven lightweight, 5-1/4" wide (score and fold over 3/4" to make the bottom of the pockets).

3. Attach cardboard to half of Contact paper. You'll need three or four feet of table space for this operation.

(a) Find the center of the Contact paper. With the design side down, carefully cut the lining paper only and start peeling it back in one direction.

(b) Place cardboard as shown, alternating heavy cardboard and light cardboard. After placing seven pieces of cardboard (four thick, three thin), stop. Cut the

lining paper, leaving a few inches of Contact paper still covered temporarily.

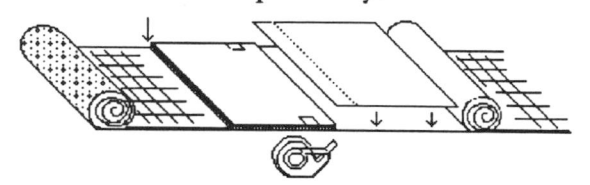

(c) To secure the arrangement, press each piece of cardboard down firmly and tape the edges in a couple of places.

(d) Fold up these sections, if necessary, to free up table space.

4. Attach cardboard to the other half of the Contact paper. Repeat Step 3, working in the other direction, this time starting with the lightweight cardboard and ending with heavy cardboard.

5. Fit inside the box. Peel lining paper off and stick Contact paper to ends as shown in the diagram.

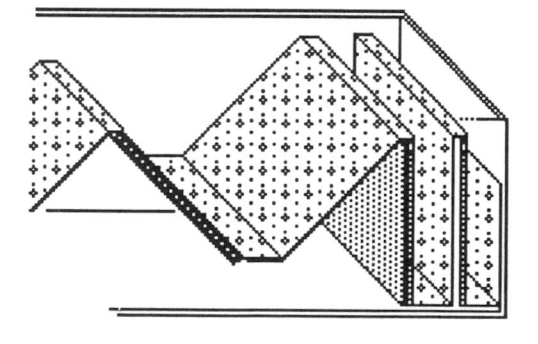

6. Cover outside of box. Bring paper down on the inside of the box to overlap the paper on the ends. Beautiful!

Does it seem like a lot of work to make these deluxe dividers? You aren't sure you'll continue to maintain a supply of scrap fabrics after you use up what you have? Don't worry. These folders are great for storing many other things—recipe clippings, computer disks, letters, bills, cancelled checks, sewing notions—but don't start making dividers for them yet; stick with organizing your fabrics.

Overflow

However you store your scraps, you will find from time to time certain categories have your system bulging. Put them in a bag labeled "3" strip overflow" (or whatever) and plan a project to use that size of strips.

Stick with a system that works for you

However you arrange your fabrics, stick to your system. If you take out a 2-yard piece and cut four 6" strips, immediately put it in the 1-1/3 yard pile, and you won't have to unfold it and measure it again later.

I know, in real life it doesn't work that way. You might have a couple of dozen fabrics pulled out, testing different color combinations. No way can you remember what size they were so you can put them back. When you absolutely have to clear off the table, it's because you absolutely have to do something else. If you can't re-file them promptly, shove them into a bag—but keep it out in plain sight until you have time to sort the pieces again or you'll have some of your most valuable fabrics stuck away in a corner, forgotten.

Making the best use of your fabrics

When making scrap quilts, you spend more time selecting fabric and cutting it than you do with other quilts. I designed this system with the idea of making dozens of scrap quilts over the years. I wanted the fabric selection to be as quick and pleasant as possible. Still there are a lot of decisions to make:

Do you use the fabric you have on hand even if it's not ideal? Or do you go buy a perfect fabric to fill in? Of course, that depends on whether your goal is to use your scraps or to make the most attractive quilt possible. Using whatever you have on hand is more "authentic," but the quilts might not be color-coordinated.

Do you try to use up all of a particular fabric, taking pleasure in getting it off the shelves and "into a good home," or do you try to save some of each fabric for later projects so you'll have a great variety on hand? With the former approach, your collection of scraps will go down. With the latter approach, your collection of scraps will go up and scraps will become smaller and smaller.

Is a particular fabric too "good" to go into a scrap quilt? If you use it up, will you be sorry that you don't have it available any more?

Only you can answer these questions, but remember that you sew quilts for fun and make decisions to please yourself. You aren't accountable to anyone else in this case.

Cutting fabric

When cutting 44" strips, you might cut through only one fabric, doubled over. (Square up the fabric carefully so there's not a bend at the fold line when you open up the strip.)

When cutting shorter strips, you might stack several fabrics to cut at a time. Stack the fabrics with the largest pieces on the bottom, the smaller pieces as you go up. If you are using stripes or directional prints, have them on the top layer so cuts can follow the design.

Do it carefully to prevent waste, but don't fret too much. If you aren't 100% efficient, the scraps you have left can still be used in other projects. It's just that the larger the leftovers, the more efficiently you can use them.

About those boxfuls of non-quilting fabrics

Did you find when organizing your fabrics that you had boxes full of non-quilting fabrics? Are they sitting on the back porch labeled "Donate to Goodwill," but you just can't quite bring yourself to get rid of them? You remember how in 1973 you heard there would be a shortage of polyester double knits because of the oil crisis, so you bought a lifetime supply? You just know there has to be a use for those blue jeans with holes in the knees?

I haven't yet experimented with silk, tafetta, and velveteen, so I haven't included anything about them. If you have a lot of fancy fabrics, look for Ann Boyce and Sandra Hatch's new book, *Putting on the Glitz* (see page 177). I do make quilts occasionally from heavy fabrics.

Using heavier fabrics

Before making a quilt from heavy fabrics, make some solemn promises:

(a) You won't combine radically different types of fabrics.

(b) You'll use the quilts only for camping and picnics.

(c) You won't enter projects in

quilt shows and say you got the idea from my book (unless they turn out gorgeous).

Polyester double knits

You might be drummed out of the quilt guild if people hear you're using double knits for quilts, so don't tell anyone. Light-colored polyester stains badly, so have your contrast between dark and bright colors instead. (Cut up those brown polyester pants that will never wear out and use them with pieces of red or purple polyester from garage sales.)

Recycled jeans

One summer my 10-year-old son and I made a Rail Fence quilt for the coach's wife and baby to sit on at the baseball games. The idea was to have boys on the team donate their old blue jeans. We hoped for a wide variety of denim colors honestly faded to different degrees, depending on how soon the knees wore out compared to the rest of the pants. We got some of that type, but in 1989 jeans with holes in the knees were hot items and boys wouldn't part with their favorite ones. So we got a lot of perfectly good wide-legged 1984 designer jeans that the players' mothers and sisters would no longer wear. I couldn't bring myself to cut them up, so I donated most of them to Goodwill instead. We still had plenty! Let people know you're recycling jeans, and you'll probably be overwhelmed by donations.

It's hard to sew through many layers of denim. Try these tips:

1. Cut points off and make as little bulk as possible where many seams come together.

2. Use a sharp-pointed needle or a Schmetz Jeans/Denim needle (size 100).

3. Rub the stitching line with soap before you stitch, or use a needle lubricant.

4. If your needle still can't penetrate six-layer seams, pound the seams with a hammer to soften up the fibers.

Flannel

Flannelette is cozy for baby quilts. I would use it for lining a quilt, or I would make all the patchwork from flannel. I wouldn't combine flannel and other fabric in the quilt top.

Special fabrics like sailcloth, trigger cloth, wool, corduroy, velveteen

You're breaking rules to even make a quilt from these fabrics, so let your conscience be your guide as to how much mixing of fabric types you do. More than appearance is involved. Combine only fabrics that can take the same needle and thread, are equally stretchy, and have the same washing instructions. Consult a book such as Claire Shaeffer's encyclopedic *Fabric Sewing Guide* (see page 177) if you don't know how to work with a fabric you have.

Which projects for which scraps?

Use this chart to help choose projects which make the best use of fabric on hand.

Chapter	Project	Strings (narrower than 2")	2"-3" strips	4"-5" strips	6"-8" strips	Fat quarters
3	Border quilt	••	•••	•	••	••
3	Stack of Strips	••	•••			•
3	Roman Stripes	•	•••			
3	Rail Fence	•	•••			
3	String-pieced place mats	•••	•••			
3	Checkerboard quilt		•••	•••		••
4	Goodwill quilt				•	•
5	Log Cabin	•	•••			
5	Woodpile		•	•	•	•••
5	Irish Cabin		•	•	•	•••
6	Triangle Connector blocks		••	•••		
6	Roman Stripes with triangles		•••	•••		
6	Nine-Patch with triangles		•••	•••		
7	Nifty Nine-Patch		•••	•••	••	••
7	Masterpiece (simplified)		•••	•••		••
7	Masterpiece (advanced)	•••	•••			••
7	Red Hot Squares		•••	•••	••	••
7	Garden Path		•••	•••	••	••
8	Sawtooth place mats			•••		
8	Sawtooth Flying Geese			•	•••	
8	Hundreds of Triangles				•••	
8	Thousands of Triangles				•••	
8	Sawtooth borders			•••		
9	Flying Geese		•••	•••		
9	Wild Goose Chase		•••	•••		

Fabric categories:
••• = Ideal; quilt is designed to use this type of fabric.
•• = Also work well (or these fabrics make up a minor part of the quilt).
• = Project can be adapted to these fabrics, but directions were't written specifically for them.

Chapter	Project	Triangles and squares	Plaids, stripes, and directional prints	Heavy fabrics	Can turn quilt top on bias	Easy and fast
3	Border quilt		••	•••		◊◊◊
3	Stack of Strips	•••	•	•••	••	◊◊◊
3	Roman Stripes		••		•••	◊◊◊
3	Rail Fence		•	••	•••	◊◊◊
3	String-pieced place mats	•••	••	•••		◊◊
3	Checkerboard quilt	•••	•	•	•••	◊◊
4	Goodwill quilt		•••	•••		◊◊
5	Log Cabin		•	•		◊◊◊
5	Woodpile		•	•	•••	◊◊◊
5	Irish Cabin				•••	◊
6	Triangle Connector blocks					◊◊◊
6	Roman Stripes with triangles					◊◊◊
6	Nine-Patch with triangles					◊◊
7	Nifty Nine-Patch					◊◊
7	Masterpiece (simplified)					◊◊
7	Masterpiece (advanced)					◊
7	Red Hot Squares					◊◊
7	Garden Path					◊◊◊
8	Sawtooth place mats	•••				◊◊
8	Sawtooth Flying Geese					◊
8	Hundreds of Triangles	•••				◊◊
8	Thousands of Triangles					◊
8	Sawtooth borders					◊◊
9	Flying Geese					◊◊
9	Wild Goose Chase	•••				◊◊

Fabric categories:
••• = Ideal; quilt is designed to use this type of fabric.
•• = Also work well (or these fabrics make up a minor part of the quilt).
• = Project can be adapted to these fabrics, but directions weren't written specifically for them.

Easy and Fast:
◊◊◊ = Easiest and fastest
◊◊ = Moderately fast and easy
◊ = More advanced

3. Warming Up and Thinning Down

No, this is not an exercise and dieting book. We're talking about warm-up exercises for folks who haven't had strip-quilting experience, and we're talking about thinning down your supply of scraps to a manageable level, if that's what you need to do. Even if you don't have either problem, read over this chapter because you might want to do some of the projects anyway.

String panels

One of the easiest ways to use scraps is to simply cut them into narrow strips—or "strings"—sew them into panels, and cut cross sections.

You can use odds and ends of different lengths. Sew together long ones first, then shorter and shorter ones. Group them basically in order of length, but use fabrics that look good next to each other. Make panels as large as you want, but no wider than your cutting mat. Avoid having the same fabric as the outside strip in more than one panel. Press the panels, and cut sections the width you want. (Save sections that are too small and combine them to make narrow borders later.)

Lay out the lengths end to end (or do some measuring and calculating) to see if you'll have all the length you need. If you need more, cut some more strips and sew several sections on to each. Cut apart and press.

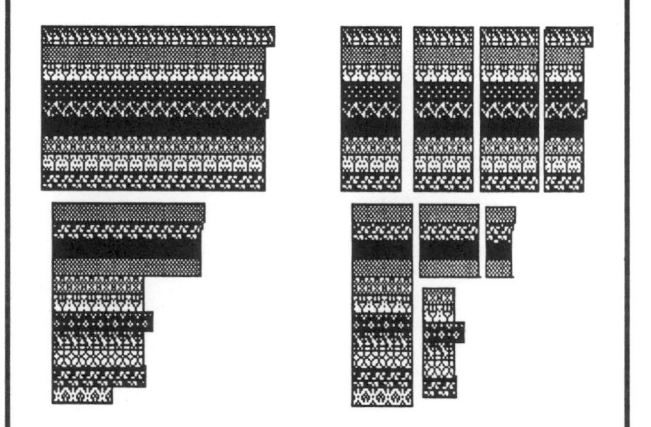

When sewing sections together, mix up the order, reverse sections, and throw in occasional "switchers" (single pieces of new fabric) to make the pattern less predictable.

You can use these strip-pieced panels for borders or binding, the Border Quilt (below and in the color section), or Stack of Strips, later in this chapter.

Border quilt

This project can be made any size, with any width or length of strips. To get you started, here are calculations for a lap robe about 44" x 54".

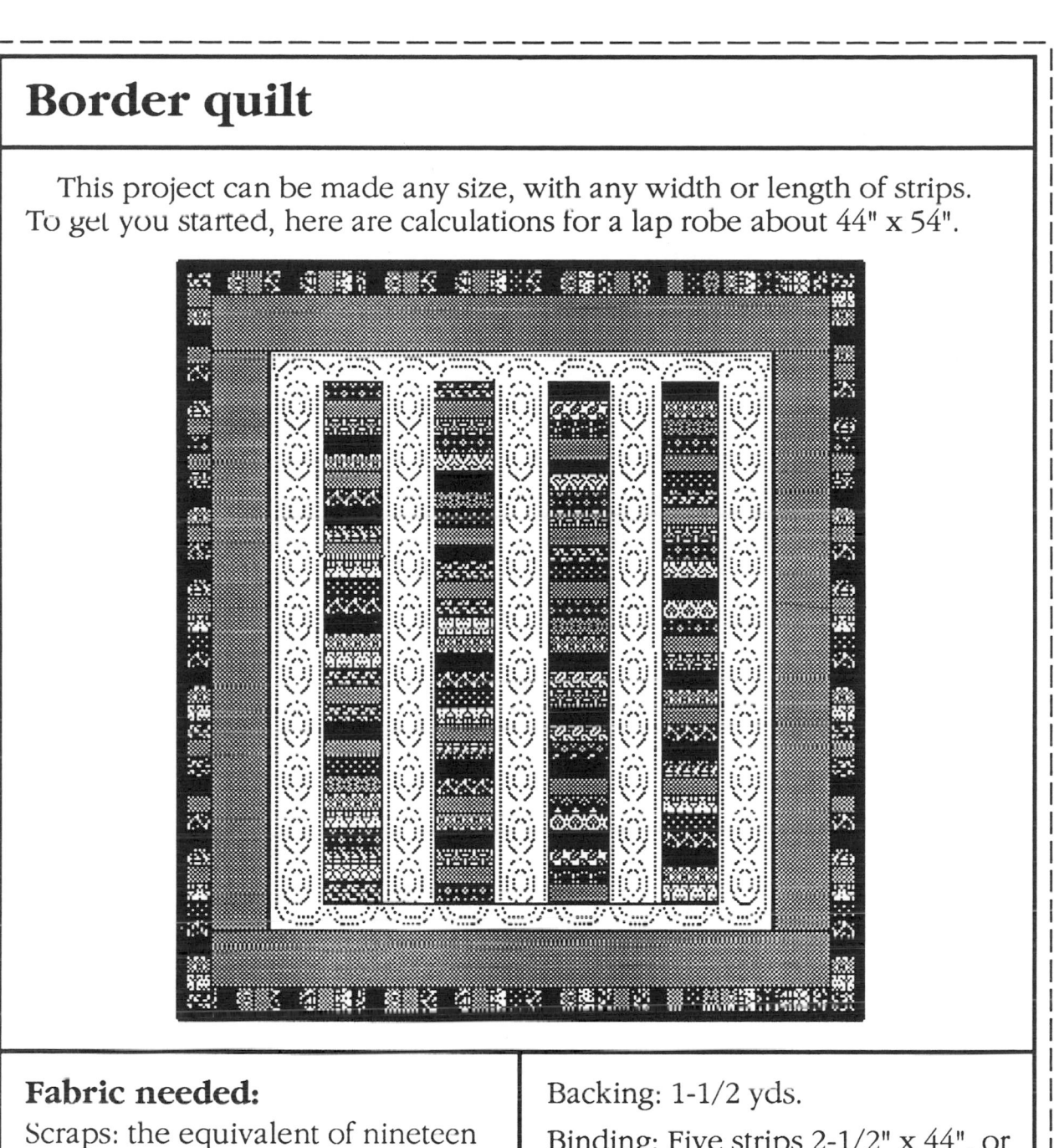

Fabric needed:

Scraps: the equivalent of nineteen strips 2" x 44" (or twelve if outer pieced border isn't used), lights and mediums if sashing is dark, darks and mediums if sashing is light.

Switchers: scraps trimmed to 2" x 4".

Sashing/inner border: 2/3 yd.

Outer border: 1/2 yd.

Backing: 1-1/2 yds.

Binding: Five strips 2-1/2" x 44", or strips totalling 6 yds.

1. Cut strips. Make 2" strips of any length.

2. Make string-pieced panels. Combine eight to ten strips at a time.

3. Cut panels into 4" sections.

4. Combine into four chains, 40" to 44" long. All must have the same number of strips in them and be the same length, so lengthen chains with switchers if needed, or shorten by widening seams or removing strips.

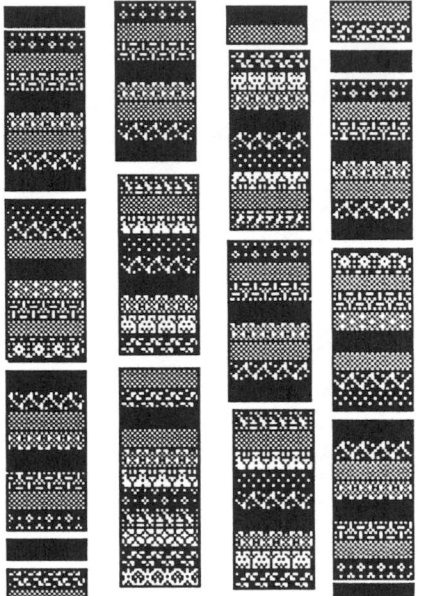

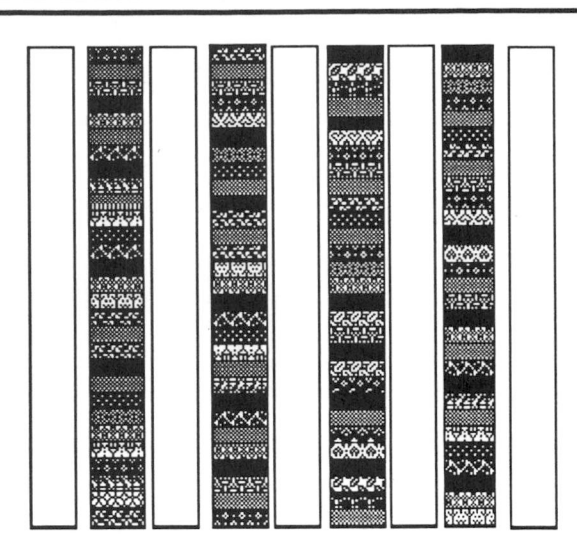

5. Cut fabric for sashing. Cut five 3-1/2" strips the length of the chains in Step 4. You'll also need two strips long enough to go across the top and bottom (about 30"); these can be narrower if fabric is limited.

6. Assemble the inner part of the quilt. Sew pieced chains and sashing, including side borders, together into one panel. Add inner borders.

Note: *If you want to do one-step piecing (pages 15 to 19), stop at this point. Do the quilting before adding top and bottom borders.*

7. Add outer borders. Make them as wide as you wish, but first lay out the project on your backing fabric and check it. There must be an inch or two of backing fabric on all sides after you add all borders.

8. Make pieced border (optional). Cut the rest of the pieced panels into 2" chains. Make more sections if needed and combine all into one chain, about 6 yards long. Stay stitch 1/4" from each edge to keep seams from coming out. Sew to one side of the project, easing project to fit so you end with a complete square, or trimming the end borders a bit to make them come out even. Pick out a seam to free the remaining part of the chain to use on the other sides. Repeat for all sides of quilt.

9. Complete the project. Quilt and bind with your favorite method. See Chapter 1 for more information.

Stack of Strips

Here's another very easy quilt. This one uses blocks cut from strip-pieced panels, this time combined with plain squares.

Select scraps of compatible fabrics and find a color that contrasts with them for the plain squares. For example:

Bright colors, used with muslin squares.

Subtle darks and mediums, used with squares of a pale print fabric.

Pastels, used with dark or medium print squares. (See the nursery scene in the color plates for an example.)

Amish solids or bright prints, used with black squares.

Bright colors, used with squares cut from old blue jeans.

Denim strips, used with squares of red wool or other heavy fabric.

I'm not giving a specific project this time. Just use up all the scraps you want to, then count the blocks and see how big a quilt you can make.

Decide on the width of the strips (from 1-1/2" to 3"), how many strips you want in each block (the chart gives calculations for four or five), and what lengths to use (the chart gives lengths that can be cut into blocks with little waste). Just sew strips together, then cut the panels apart into square blocks.

Suggested strip and block sizes for Stack of Strips

Width of strips	Block size if 4 strips in block*	Good strip lengths	Block size if 5 strips in block*	Good strip lengths
1-1/2"	4-1/2" sq.	10, 15, 19, 24, 28, 33, 37, or 42"	5-1/2" sq.	12, 18, 23, 29, 34, or 40"
1-3/4"	5-1/2" sq.	12, 18, 23, 29, 34, or 40"	6-3/4" sq.	14, 21, 28, 35, or 42"
2"	6-1/2" sq.	14, 21, 27, 34, 40"	8" sq.	17, 25, 33, or 41"
2-1/2"	8-1/2" sq.	9, 18, 27, 35, or 44"	10-1/2" sq.	11, 22, 33, or 43"
3"	10-1/2" sq.	11, 22, 33, or 43"	13" sq.	13, 27, or 40"

This is the approximate block size before final seams, the size of the plain squares. The final block will be 1/2" smaller. Beginners may use seams wider than 1/4", making blocks smaller.

Number of blocks to make

Number of pieced blocks	Number of plain blocks	Total blocks	Arrangements
17	18	35	7 rows of 5 blocks
18	18	36	6 rows of 6 blocks
24	24	48	8 rows of 6 blocks
25	24	49	7 rows of 7 blocks
32	31	63	9 rows of 7 blocks
38	39	77	11 rows of 7 blocks

(You can reverse the numbers for pieced and plain blocks, of course.)

The plain blocks can be new yardage. If you have my book *Fast Patch,* use the chart on page 175 to calculate fabric needed.

How to make Stack of Strips

1. Cut strips. Select the width on the chart on page 44. Stack four fabrics (or five) together and cut all at one time into strips the width you chose and one of the lengths listed for that width. If plaids or stripes are used, have them on top of the stack or cut them individually to keep lines staight. Cut more than one stack from the arrangement if you wish.

2. Sew strips together into panels. If you use the same fabrics in two panels, have them in different order. Press and measure width to find your block size.

3. Cut blocks. Square up ends and cut into blocks. Use your large square grid if blocks are quite large.

4. Cut plain squares, the same size as the blocks in Step 3. You'll need as many squares as you have blocks, or one more or one less.

5. Arrange blocks into quilt top. Alternate the position of the plain squares and the pieced blocks from one row to the next. Pin blocks together in rows, then sew. Pin rows together to make quilt top, then sew. Above are some possible arrangements; there are many others.

6. Add borders, as many as you wish of any width you wish.

7. Complete the project. Press quilt. Layer quilt, batting, and backing together. Quilt and bind with your favorite method. See Chapter 1 for suggestions.

Roman Stripes and Rail Fence quilts

Another very easy strip quilt is made by sewing strips together to make blocks, as in Stack of Strips, then setting blocks next to each other, alternating between vertical and horizontal blocks.

These quilts are sometimes called Roman Stripes, sometimes Rail Fence. In this book I use the name Roman Stripes for blocks with three strips in a dark/light/dark arrangement. Try it first.

Roman Stripes baby quilt

This quilt uses forty-eight blocks about 5-1/4" square. Each 44" panel makes seven blocks. The final measurement is about 38" x 48".

Fabric needed:

Scraps: Fourteen dark strips 2-1/4" x 44", all different if possible

Seven light (or red) strips 2-1/4" x 44" (if all same fabric, get 1/2 yd.)

Borders: 1/3 yd. light for inner borders; 1/2 yd. dark for outer borders

Batting: A piece about 40" x 50"

Backing: 1-5/8 yds.

Binding: Four or five strips 2-1/2" x 44", or other strips totalling 5-1/2 yds.

1. Cut strips. Cut fourteen assorted dark or medium strips and seven light strips, 2-1/4" x 44". (You can substitute shorter strips and more of them, of course.)

2. Sew strips together. Make seven sets of three strips—a dark, a light, and another dark. Press seams toward the darks.

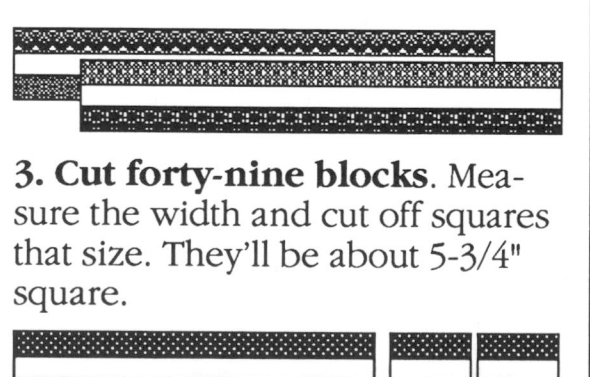

3. Cut forty-nine blocks. Measure the width and cut off squares that size. They'll be about 5-3/4" square.

4. Sew blocks together. Make eight rows of six blocks each, alternating vertical and horizontal directions from block to block and from row to row. Keep a nice color balance.

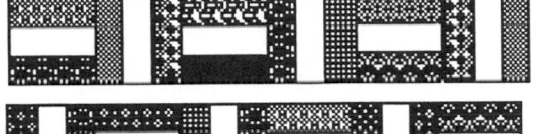

5. Add borders. First cut four strips of light border fabric, again 2-1/2" x 44". Sew borders to the sides first, then to the ends. Cut five strips of darker fabric for the outer borders, piece as needed, and sew in place.

6. Complete the project. Press quilt. Layer quilt, batting, and backing. Quilt and bind with your favorite method. See Chapter 1 for suggestions.

Betsy's variation. If you prefer a more orderly design with limited colors, see the Roman Stripes baby quilt in the color pages. My daughter, Betsy Heath, makes hers like this, with five colors. One of the dark fabrics is repeated in all the panels. Blocks are set together with "7's and L's" (described in the Rail Fence project that follows) and turned on the bias. She makes these pretty quilts on her serger to sell at craft shows.

Note: *Before adding borders, read pages 97 to 99 and decide if you want to turn this quilt top on the bias. It will be about the same size if turned.*

Roman Stripes used a dark/light/dark pattern. If colors are arranged in dark/medium/light order like this, they're usually called "Rail Fence" because you get a strong zigzag effect in the final quilt.

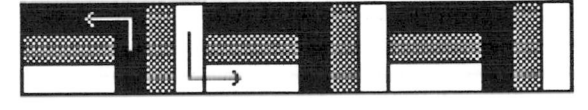

The blocks are just as easy to sew as Roman Stripes, and rows of blocks are as easy to assemble if you remember this simple rule: *The darks make 7's, the lights make L's, or vice versa—be consistent.*

I'll give calculations and projects for using three or four strips in each block. On your own, you can experiment with five or more strips per block and with bright random colors with no dark/light pattern.

Rail Fence twin quilt

This quilt is about 70" x 100". It uses ninety-six blocks 7-1/2" square. See the color section for an example.

Fabric needed:

Scraps (or 44" strips or fat quarters): See Step 1 below

Borders: 2/3 yd. each

Batting: piece about 72" x 104"

Backing: 5-1/2 to 6 yds.

Binding: Cut eight or nine strips 2-1/2" x 44", or use other strips to equal about 10 yds.

Both a ruler (3" x 18" or 6" x 24") and a large square grid are needed for this project.

1. Cut strips. If using scraps:

Cut 3" strips as long as your scraps will allow; 17", 25", 33", and 41" are good lengths with little waste. You will need ninety-six light, ninety-six medium, and ninety-six dark strips when trimmed to 8", but you don't need to cut all of them now. Make some blocks, then cut more strips of colors you need.

If using 3" x 44" strips:

You'll need nineteen strips of light, nineteen of medium, and nineteen of dark fabric (plus a single 3" x 8" scrap of each).

If using fat quarters:

Use seven light, seven medium, and seven dark.

Stack dark, medium, and light pieces together. Cut with the grain (parallel to selvage) making seven 3" x 17" stacks of strips from each fat quarter. Each stack of three fat quarters makes fourteen blocks. Mix the strips up in different combinations in each panel.

2. Sew panels of three strips like this:

3. Cut into blocks. Using your large square grid, measure the width of the panels (should be 8", but if yours are narrower, that's okay). Cut into squares exactly that size.

4. Piece together as shown here, with vertical stripes alternating with horizontal stripes (light colors making an L and darks making a 7). Half the rows start with a vertical block and half start with a horizontal block. When two rows are put together, lights connect up and darks connect up, making a zigzag pattern diagonally. Make twelve rows of eight blocks each.

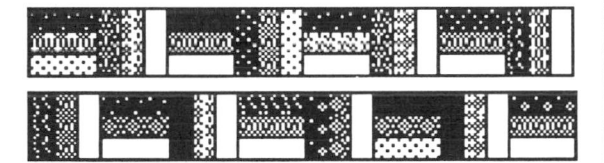

Alternate ways to make this quilt:

(a) Before adding borders, turn the project on the bias as shown on pages 97 to 99. It'll be about the same size when turned.

(b) Make a double bed coverlet (wider and shorter) instead of a long twin quilt. Use eleven rows of nine blocks (make three more blocks). Do not turn on the bias. It will be about 77" x 93" before quilting.

(c) Make a double bed throw turned on the bias. Use fourteen rows of seven blocks (make two more blocks, a total of ninety-eight). The quilt will be about 81" square when turned and borders added.

5. Add borders to fit. Cut border fabric into 3" strips and piece together, or use any fabric and any width you want.

6. Complete the project. Press quilt. Layer quilt, batting and backing (pieced as shown on No. 5 on page 13). Quilt and bind with your favorite method. See Chapter 1 for suggestions.

King-sized Rail Fence quilt

Make one hundred four-strip blocks (10" square) for a quilt about 108" square before quilting.

Fabric needed:

Strips: see Step 1

Borders (3" to 3-1/2" wide): 1 to 1-1/2 yds. each

Batting: piece about 108" square

Backing: 9 yds. (can use remnant to make one of the borders)

Binding: strips to equal about 13 yards

Note: *A large square grid is needed for this project.*

1. Cut strips:

If using 3" x 44" strips:

Cut twenty-five strips of dark fabric, twenty-five strips of medium/dark, twenty-five of medium, and twenty-five strips of light.

If using Fat Quarters:

Get ten dark, ten medium/dark, ten medium, and ten light. Stack four pieces and cut each into five strips 3" x 22" (you may be able to get six strips if you are careful.)

2. Piece together strips in sets of four, progressing from dark to light.

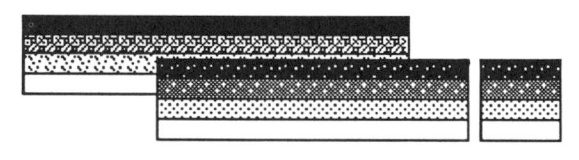

3. Press and measure panels.
They will probably be 10-1/2" wide, but use your measurements.

4. Cut square blocks, using a large grid. You can make four from each panel of 44" strips, two from each panel of fat quarters.

5. Set blocks together. Alternate vertical and horizontal blocks as before, again making L's from the lights and 7's from the darks.

(a) If you will leave blocks in the regular Rail Fence pattern, sew together ten rows of ten blocks each.

(b) If you will turn the quilt on the diagonal (see Chapter 6), sew together fourteen rows of seven blocks each. (Don't worry—it'll be square when turned.) See the color plates for an example.

6. Measure project and cut borders. Cut ten strips, 3" x 44", for inner border. Cut outer border slightly wider, if you wish, and make eleven strips. If you will use remnant from backing fabric for borders, make backing first. Cut surplus into four equal strips, each up to 5" wide.

7. Complete the project. Make backing as shown on page 13, No. 7. Quilt and bind with your favorite method. See Chapter 1 for suggestions.

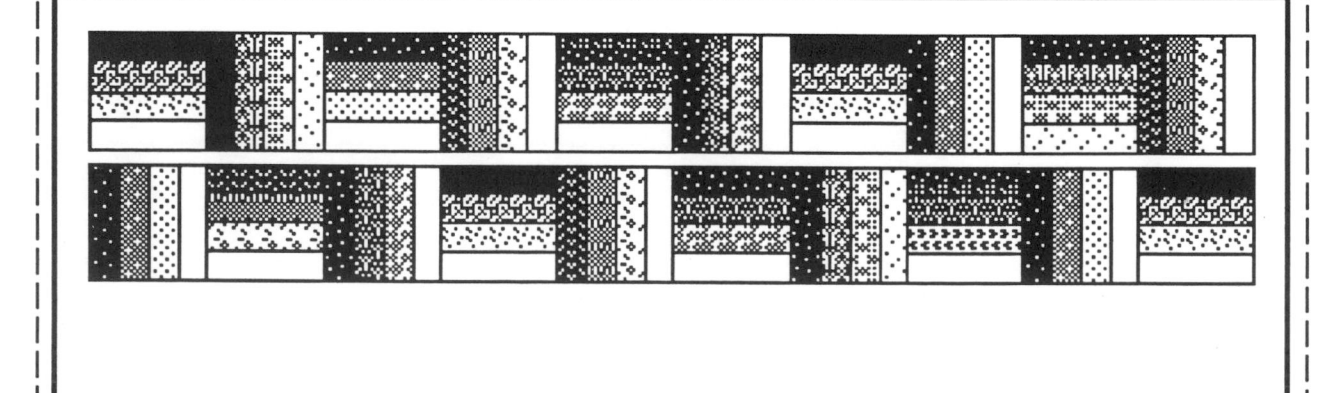

Rail Fence and Roman Stripes charts

Charts for 3-strip projects

(For Roman Stripes blocks, add number of strips for dark and medium; all can be equally dark.)

Small blocks (5-1/4") from 2-1/4" x 44" strips

You can get seven blocks from each set of three strips.

Blocks to make	Dark strips	Medium strips	Light strips
35	5	5	5
42	6	6	6
49	7	7	7
56	8	8	8
63	9	9	9

Large blocks (about 7-1/2") from 3" x 44" strips

You can get five blocks from each set of three strips.

Blocks to make	Dark strips	Medium strips	Light strips
50	10	10	10
60	12	12	12
70	14	14	14
80	16	16	16
90	18	18	18
100	20	20	20

Large blocks (about 7-1/2") from fat quarters

Cut strips 3" x 17". You can get fourteen blocks from each stack of three fat quarters.

Blocks	Dark pieces	Medium pieces	Light pieces
56	4	4	4
70	5	5	5
84	6	6	6
98	7	7	7
112	8	8	8

Charts for 4-strip Rail Fence projects

Large blocks (about 10") from 3" x 44" strips

You can get four blocks from each stack of four strips.

Blocks	Dark strips	Med. dark strips	Med. light strips	Light strips
48	12	12	12	12
60	15	15	15	15
72	18	18	18	18
84	21	21	21	21
96	24	24	24	24
108	27	27	27	27

Large blocks (about 10") from fat quarters

Cut strips 3" x 21". You can get ten blocks from each stack of four fat quarters (may get two extra blocks from some stacks).

Blocks	Dark pieces	Med. dark pieces	Med. light pieces	Light pieces
50	5	5	5	5
60	6	6	6	6
70	7	7	7	7
80	8	8	8	8
90	9	9	9	9
100	10	10	10	10

Checkerboard quilts

This next quilt uses scrap checkerboards. All the projects in Chapters 7 and 8 start with checkerboards much like the ones in this quilt, so try this project as a practice first (or study it thoroughly at least).

Ways to make checkerboards

There are three main approaches for making the checkerboards:

1. You can use "Alpha strips." For projects with triangles, I use this special term for strips four times as long as they are wide, plus an inch for trimming and squaring up the block. Sew the strips together, cut cross sections (the same width as the original strips), and sew the sections together again, turning some so the darks are in the opposite position.

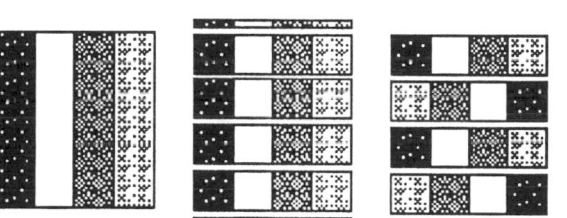

A checkerboard made from only one panel wouldn't have a nice mix of fabrics, so make several panels and take a strip from each for a better variety. Reverse strips so darks and lights alternate.

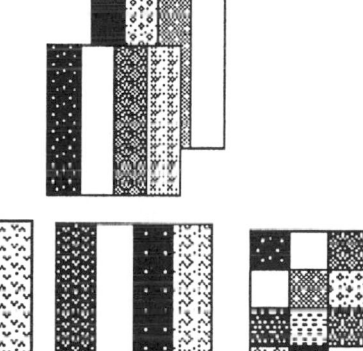

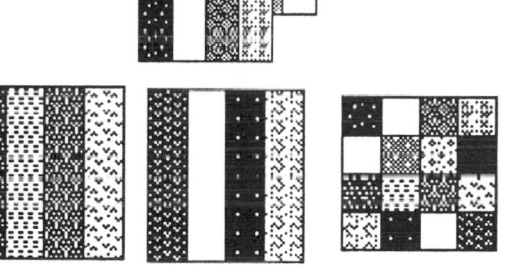

2. You can use 44" strips. Later in the book I'll refer to this as the "Alpha-strip by-pass" method. This is the most efficient approach, especially if you have a lot of yardage but few scraps. Your blocks won't have the random look you want, however, if you are making only a small quilt.

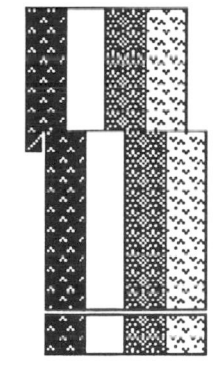

3. You can use all sizes of strips. Just sew together sets of four strips which are about the same length. Cut cross sections and count them.

If you don't have enough, make more panels. When you have all the sections you'll need, start combining them. Try not to make any two blocks alike.

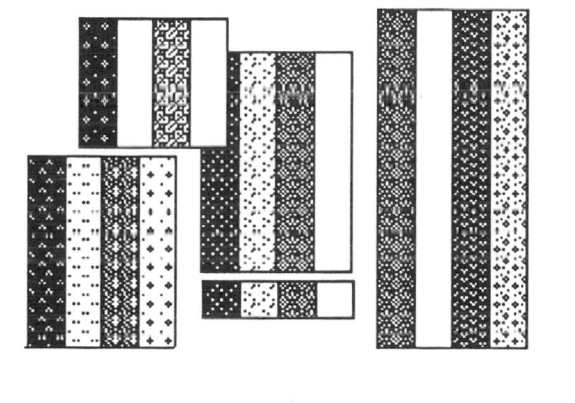

How to make the checkerboard quilt

This quilt has blocks about 10" square made from 3" strips. It is about 62" square. (For a larger version using 4" strips, see my first book, *Fast Patch*, page 20.)

Fabric needed:

Strips: See Step 1

Plain squares: 1 yd. (preferably a color which contrasts with all the other fabrics)

Inner borders (2"): 1/3 yd.

Outer borders (5"): 7/8 yd.

Backing: 3-1/2 yds.

Batting: piece about 64" square

Binding: six strips 2-1/2" x 44", or other strips equal to 7-1/3 yds.

This project needs a ruler 3" x 18" or larger and a grid 12" square or larger.

1. Cut strips. Make eight dark and eight light strips, 3" x 44", all different, including some mediums. Or use Alpha strips (3" x 13"), twenty-six dark and twenty-six light. Or use different lengths of scraps to equal this many.

2. Make panels. Sew together fabrics that look good together into sets of four, alternating lights and darks. Press toward the dark and trim the ends.

3. Cut cross sections, also 3" wide. If using scraps, count to see

if you have fifty-two of them; make more if necessary.

4. Assemble blocks. Make thirteen for a square quilt (twelve for a quilt you will turn on the bias as mentioned in the note at the end of the project). Press them and trim if needed.

5. Cut twelve plain blocks, 11" square or to match the size of the blocks.

6. Sew blocks together. Make five rows; three of one type, two of the other. Join rows into quilt top.

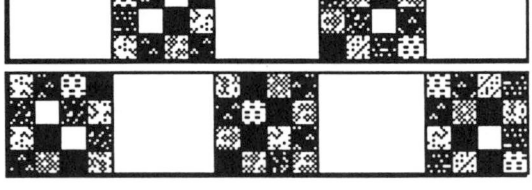

7. Add borders. Cut 2" strips for inner border, or use any width you wish. Piece if needed and sew to project. Cut 5" strips for outer border and sew them on.

8. Make backing as in No. 2 on page 13.

9. Quilt and bind with your favorite method. This is a good project to tie with white yarn. See Chapter 1.

Note: *This project can be turned on the bias as mentioned on pages 97 to 99. Use only twenty-four blocks (twelve pieced and twelve plain) and join them in six rows of four. The project will be about 52" x 66". See the first color page for an example.*

Right

The author's Flying Geese quilt was quilted with the one-step method. Quilting doesn't show from the front, but the solid color backing shows the difficulty of keeping rows of stitching from creeping down and puckering. For your first few tries at this technique, line the project with a print fabric so the problem is not so obvious.

Below, right

This twin quilt from Chapter 5 looks like Log Cabin at first glance, but it's not. It's an easy-to-make fake called simply "Woodpile." Blocks are 9" square and 48 of them are arranged in the Barn Raising pattern. Made by Anita Hallock, it is machine quilted with diagonal lines in the light area, lines outlining the longest dark strips in the dark sections. Photographed at the Lane County Historical Museum.

Overleaf

The old-time logging exhibit at the Lane County Historical Museum made a natural setting for these two Log Cabin quilts made by the author. The large machine-quilted Barn Raising quilt uses 48 Variation A blocks. The child's quilt on the springboard has 24 blocks of Variation B in a Straight Furrows pattern; yarn tufting was done by the author's 10-year-old daughter.

Left
This picnic quilt was made by the author from heavy fabrics, including polyester knits, drill, poplin, and recycled blue jeans. See the border quilt in Chapter 3 for the basic working method. The project was quilted as it was assembled by joining vertical strips of pieced fabrics, batting and backing fabric. The binding was an experiment—would heavy fabrics work for pieced bindings? The answer is no. The binding was sewn in place by machine for the photograph, but it will probably be cut off and replaced because it was impossible to do a neat job sewing through all those layers of thick fabrics at the seams.

Above
"Seven friends and three cats" produced this scrap quilt over a two-year period. They call this one "Irish Cabin" because it's a combination of Irish Chain and Log Cabin. It was designed by the owner, Carolyn Deevy of San Francisco, who got the idea from a painting by Mimi Vang Olson. Each of the seven ladies contributed scrap fabrics so there is a wonderful assortment. This king-sized quilt measures 104" square. If you don't have six friends to help you make your quilt, see the strip-piecing directions in Chapter 5. It's not a beginner project, however, because it does take a lot of skill to line up all those seams. Photographed at the Lane County Historical Museum.

Above

Here's another unusual Nifty Nine-Patch—there seems to be no end to ways these blocks can be arranged! This 48" x 80" quilt was made from 6" Alpha strips by Jane Quinn, of Bozeman, Montana, who teaches at The Patchworks shop. Jane did a beautiful job piecing this quilt, which was then quilted on a commercial quilting machine. Like many projects in this book, it is finished with a simple narrow binding, no borders.

Scrap Quilts

String-pieced place mats

This project would be a good one to learn the one-step quilting technique described in Chapter 2. I'll give calculations for 2" strips, but you can substitute narrower widths or use a variety of widths. Directions are for six place mats about 13" x 17".

Fabric needed:

Scraps: seventy-two strips, 2" x 14" (equal to twenty-four strips 44" long)

Fleece (thin, compressed batting): enough for six pieces 14" x 18"

Backing: 1 yd.

Binding: 10 yds. of wide bias tape

1. Cut backing fabric and fleece. You'll need six pieces of each 14" x 18". (This seems large, but it'll be smaller when quilting is done.)

2. Baste them together. Secure the fleece to the wrong side of the backing fabric with safety pins or by basting.

3. Sew center strip on. Find the center and mark it. (Draw a line lightly with a felt marker, cut notches, use pins, etc.) Pin or baste one strip right side up so that one seam line will be along the center line.

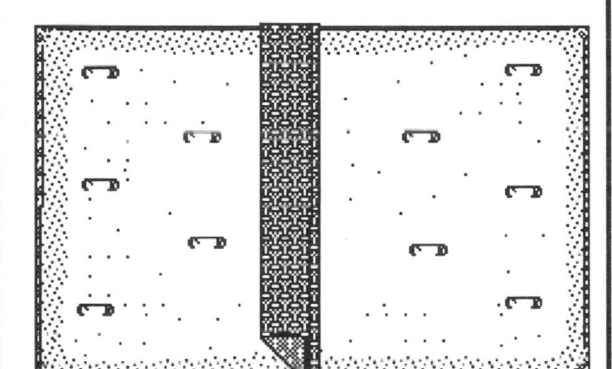

4. Add more strips.

(a) Place the next strip face down over that strip and sew one edge through the new strip, the first strip, the fleece, and the backing.

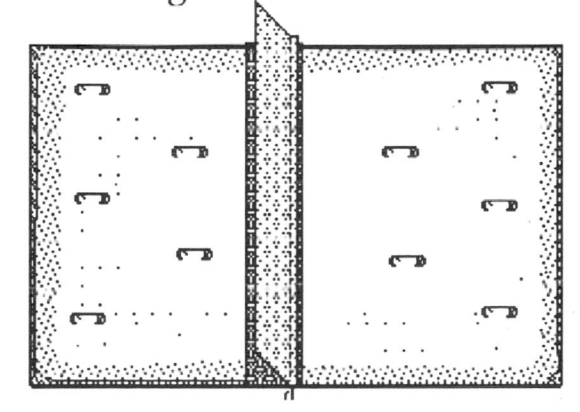

(b) Straighten the second strip out and press it in place with a warm iron.

(c) Line up the third strip in place over the second strip, and sew it in place. Check to see if there are any puckers, in front or back. Press it down.

(d) Continue these steps until you reach the edge.

Important: *If you used safety pins, don't forget to remove them before adding a strip. If you cover them, you won't be able to remove them later.*

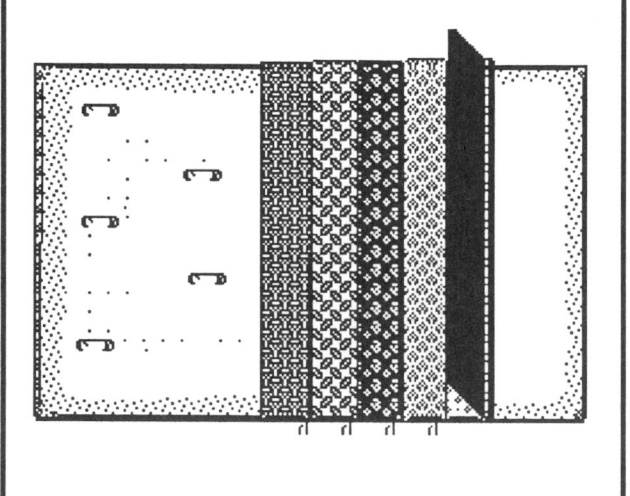

(e) To quilt the other half, turn the place mat upside down, start again at the center, and work out the other direction.

5. Trim edges. The mats can have squared or rounded corners. To round the corners, place a bowl or plate over each corner and cut against it with your rotary cutter.

6. Make remaining place mats.

7. Bind edges. Pin purchased bias binding in place. Sew with zigzag stitch. Or use your own favorite methods for finishing edges.

4. Two-Tone Blocks

Many projects in this book feature blocks which are divided diagonally, dark on one side, light on the other, such as Log Cabin (left) and Nifty Nine-Patch (right). This dark/light division is almost magical. Finished blocks can be turned any direction and put together into many interesting overall designs.

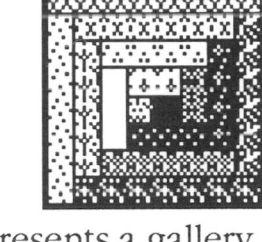

This chapter presents a gallery of block arrangements which you can refer to when doing projects in Chapters 5, 6, and 7.

Three special arrangements

We won't try to show all the ways blocks can be arranged or even assign names to the arrangements we show. But do learn the names for these three special layouts which we'll refer to several times in this book.

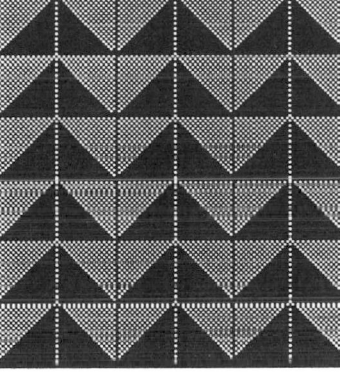 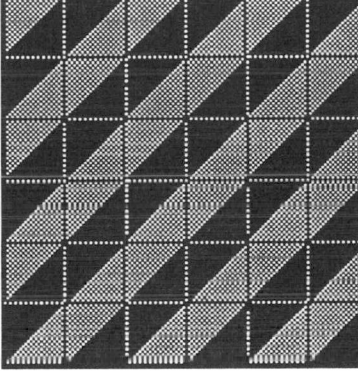

Left: *Barn Raising* *circles the center in a comforting way. It's always a pleasing arrangement, so use it if you don't feel like experimenting. You need an even number of blocks horizontally to be effective for a bed quilt. For a wall quilt, you also need an even number vertically.*

Center: *Flying Geese* *has the relaxing mountain peaks effect when the dark triangles rest on their base. Use an even number of blocks horizontally and any number vertically.*

Right: *Straight Furrows* *can use any number of blocks vertically and horizontally. There is a diagonal movement which isn't as satisfying to me as a symmetrical arrangement, but I often use this arrangement for quilt tops which will be turned on the bias.*

Overall arrangements

First let's look at some overall arrangements that can be adapted to many sizes of quilts.

Even number of blocks both direction

Like most arrangements in this chapter, these need an even number of blocks both directions.

 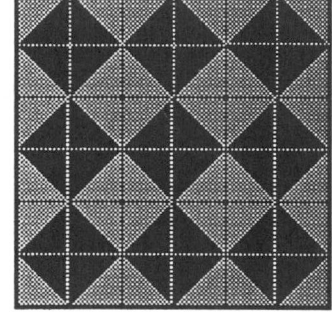 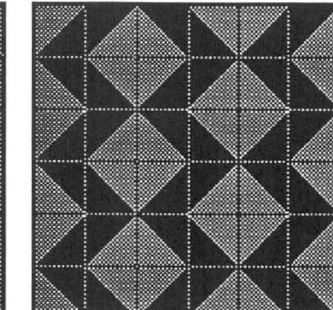

Odd number of blocks in one direction okay

These arrangements need an even number of blocks horizontally, but can be an odd number vertically.

 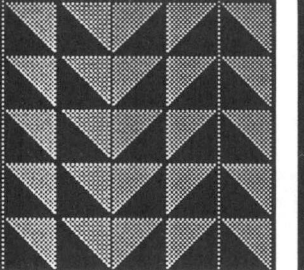  

Odd number of blocks in either direction okay

Here are a couple which can be used for an odd number either direction (one is turned on its side for quite a different effect).

  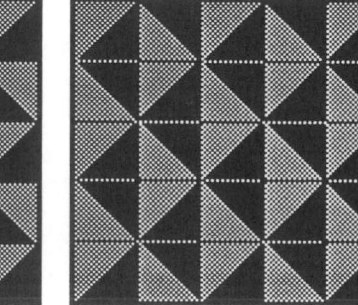

16-block arrangements

For 24-blocks, add a rows of blocks to the top and bottom.

36-block arrangements

64-block arrangements

Four repeats of any 16-block designs make other 64-block arrangements.

100-block arrangements

The larger the quilt, the more combinations you can create. Adapt a 64-block arrangement by adding blocks on each side to make a new 100-block layout. Leave out the middle two rows to make an 80-block layout.

More possibilities

See the color plates for original arrangements. Feel free to make up your own designs, too. You don't usually need to decide ahead of time which arrangement you make. You can just make as many blocks as you have time and fabric for, then spread the blocks out, play with them, and invent your own design. Here are some more ideas.

1. Use sashing between sections, as shown on the cover and in Diane Leighton's quilt in the color pages.

2. Reverse the dark/light pattern in any arrangement given.

3. Let a single block inspire your quilt top. Examples given so far have used Ohio Star, Pinwheel, Sawtooth, Flying Geese, and other designs. For more ideas, look at the blocks in my earlier book, *Fast Patch*, especially Chapters 7 and 8. Many blocks in *The It's Okay If You Sit On My Quilt Book*, by Mary Ellen Hopkins, also can be adapted.

4. Add all-dark or all-light blocks. Can you spot the eight solid dark blocks in this arrangement? These blocks should be built up with the same general technique as the two-tone blocks.

5. Make frames for medallion quilts

You can use two-tone blocks as frames for medallion quilts. Diane Leighton's quilt might also be thought of as an example of a two-tone frame.

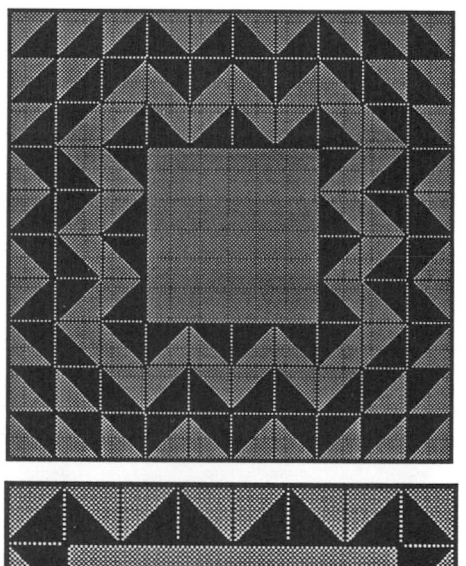

The Goodwill quilt

The simplest two-tone block is just a light triangle sewn to a dark one.

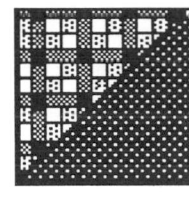

Look at the antique quilt shown in the color plates. In a way that project doesn't fit this book because it isn't made with strips. But it's great for using up short, wide scraps that aren't too useful for strip quilts, or heavy cloth you were getting ready to give to Goodwill to make room for your quilt fabrics. Or you can go to Goodwill and find things there to recycle.

You can get some very different effects depending on the fabrics you use, the size of the triangles, and the arrangement. Give the quilt a fancy name if it turns out beautiful.

How to make the Goodwill quilt

1. Select your scraps. Fabrics you can use:

(a) Plaids, stripes, and directional prints.

(b) Very large prints, where you would want to select only a certain part of the print.

(c) Squarish pieces, triangles, and odd-shaped pieces (including cutting-room scraps from clothing manufacturing).

(d) Heavier fabrics.

2. Cut triangles. Cut apart clothing you will recycle. Press pieces and decide what size of triangle you could cut readily from most of them. The chart has calculations for 5", 6", and 7" finished triangles. (For smaller triangles, use strips; see Chapter 8.)

You'll need an equal number of dark and light (or bright) triangles. So as you cut them, divide triangles into two piles. You might have a medium pile too; add those pieces later to whichever pile needs them.

This chart shows how many triangles you need. The triangle size is the horizontal base of the triangle before seams, the same measurement used for squares cut diagonally into two triangles. The approximate block size (after diagonal seams and seams on each side of the block) is given in parentheses. You might make seams wider than 1/4" with these large triangles, especially if you use heavy or loosely woven fabrics.

Blocks (arrangements in parentheses)	Triangles needed		Quilt sizes before borders		
	Dark	Light	6" triangles (5" blocks)	7" triangles (6" blocks)	8" triangles (7" blocks)
16 (4 x 4)	16	16	20" sq.	24" sq.	28" sq.
24 (4 x 6)	24	24	20" x 30"	24" x 36"	28" x 42"
36 (6 x 6)	36	36	30" sq.	36" sq.	42" sq.
48 (6 x 8)	48	48	30" x 40"	36" x 48"	42" x 56"
64 (8 x 8)	64	64	40" sq.	48" sq.	56" sq.
80 (8 x 10)	80	80	40" x 50"	48" x 60"	56" x 70"
96 (8 x 12)	96	96	40" x 60"	48" x 72"	56" x 84"
100 (10 x 10)	100	100	50" sq.	60" sq.	70" sq.
120 (10 x 12)	120	120	50" x 60"	60" x 72"	70" x 84"
140 (10 x 14)	140	140	50" x 70"	60" x 84"	70" x 98"
144 (12 x 12)	144	144	-60" sq.	72" sq.	84" sq.
168 (12 x 14)	168	168	60" x 70"	72" x 84"	84" x 98"
196 (14 x 14)	196	196	70" sq.	84" sq.	98" sq.
224 (14 x 16)	224	224	70" x 80"	84" x 96"	98" x 112"
256 (16 x 16)	256	256	80" sq.	96" sq.	112" sq.

How to cut triangles: Make templates if you insist, but transparent grids are better because you can see what you are cutting and have a rigid guide to cut against. You can cut through several layers, if you think it's worth the bother of stacking them and lining up edges. Cutting can be done with the regular 6" ruler if you're making 6" triangles, with the large square grid if they are larger.

(a) Put tape on your grid or ruler indicating a 6", 7", or 8" square so you don't have to keep looking for the right marks.

(b) Cut squares if pieces are large enough, keeping the fabric grain lines and design lined up with lines in the ruler. Then cut squares diagonally making two triangles at a time.

(c) Cut single triangles like this: Cover an area that reaches the tape marks each direction and trim two sides.

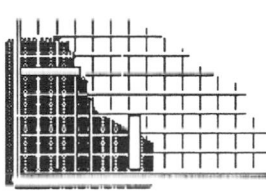

Move the grid over to the opposite corner. Cover the area you want and cut again.

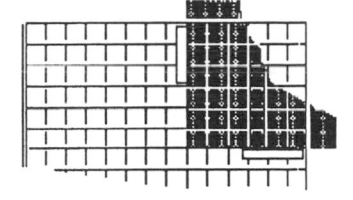

Cut diagonally from corner to corner. You'll automatically make a 45° angle, but you can use the angle line to double-check, if you are using the 6" ruler.

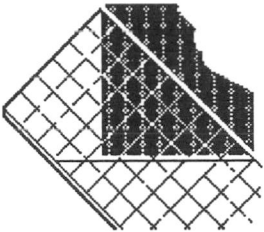

3. Sew triangles together in pairs. Have dark-light contrast and use colors that look good together, of course. Press the blocks.

4. Plan your overall arrangement. Pin rows together and label rows with tags, as mentioned on page 10.

5. Sew blocks together to make quilt top.

6. Add borders, if desired. No border is used on the antique quilt in the color pages.

7. Cut backing. Use diagrams on page 13 for sizes. If you're making a utility quilt of heavy fabrics, you can use a flannel blanket instead of batting. Or use a blanket to serve as backing and batting both.

8. Complete the project. Quilt and bind with your favorite method. See Chapter 1 for suggestions, yards of binding needed, etc.

5. Log Cabin

Chapter 4 showed some of the wonderful arrangements possible with two-tone blocks divided diagonally. This chapter features Log Cabin, the all-time favorite two-tone block.

It's a simple block to make. There's a red center square (the "fire in the hearth") with strips added like logs building up the walls of a cabin—two light strips of the same fabric, two dark ones, two light ones, two dark ones, and so on.

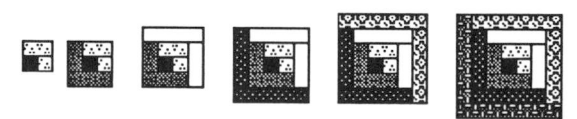

You can vary Log Cabin in several ways:

1. Strips can be as narrow as 1-1/2" or as wide as 2-1/2".

2. You can use a large square in the center, or a center that isn't red.

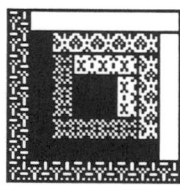

3. You can add more strips for a larger block.

4. You can make all blocks alike (the popular quick-quilt method), but my directions are for scrap quilts.

5. Even in scrap quilts, you can have some color limitations. You can make all lights the same fabric, or have a special color (such as red) always used in the same position in the logs, giving a pleasing overall effect. In this diagram, the second set of dark strips is red.

6. You can have an even more

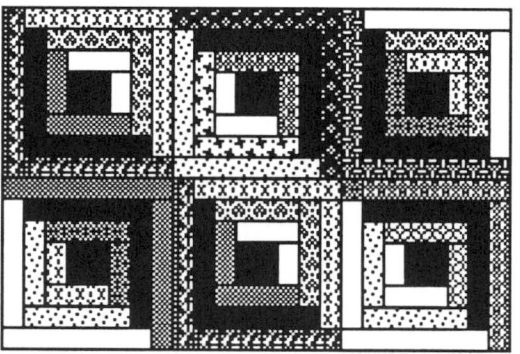

scrappy look by eliminating one of the rules: Instead of fabrics being used in pairs and forming L's, they can be used randomly.

7. And, of course, you can vary

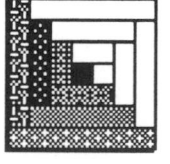

the final arrangement of the quilt, getting ideas from all the different overall arrangements given in Chapter 4 and experimenting with your own.

Some of the ideas I use for

speed-piecing this block were originated by Barbara Johannah in the late 1970's and popularized by Eleanor Burns in *Make A Quilt in a Day*. Those authors and others I've read all seem to use limited colors, but scrap fabrics are much more interesting and authentic. I've worked up some special steps to use scraps but still be as efficient as possible.

I am giving two variations of Log Cabin. To make best use of your scraps and time, make **both** of them.

First, make Variation A with 14" blocks:

(a) Center is red and 3" square.

(b) There are sixteen strips (four on each side of the center).

(c) Strips are added in pairs, forming L's.

(d) Red strips are used in the same position in every block.

You can make this variation entirely from 44" strips for efficiency.

Second, make Variation B with 10" blocks:

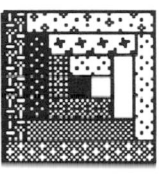

(a) Center is red but only 2" square.

(b) Only twelve strips are added.

(c) Strips are random; no L's are formed.

(d) No red accent strips are used.

You can make this version from leftovers from the first project, supplemented by other scraps and 44" strips.

Getting ready

Although Log Cabin is one of the simplest blocks to sew, it takes careful organizing. If you do only one or two blocks at a time, you're always starting and stopping and progress is slow. If you work on many blocks at once for speed, you can make a big mess with blocks in various stages and stacks of strips in different sizes and colors all over the room. I'll give you ideas to help you minimize the mess, but be as efficient as possible. Though not all are essential, these supplies help:

Supplies needed:
1. A 3" x 18" ruler and a 15" square grid.

2. Scissors, as well as your rotary cutter.

3. Two cutting mats, a large one for cutting your first strips and squaring up the blocks later, a small one within reach of the sewing machine while building up the blocks.

4. A way to sort strips into light and dark and spread them out to see several at a time (two boxes if making a large project; shelves* or table space if making a small project).

5. An iron and ironing surface within reach of your sewing machine.

6. A swivel chair so you can reach all of these things!

* A good investment for this project and others would be "Mr. Cart"—lightweight shelves on wheels, made by Dial Industries.

Log Cabin Variation A: *Using strips*

First, I'll show you how to make Log Cabin a fast way. Then I'll apply those steps to a queen-size quilt. Some special supplies for this variation:

Supplies needed:

1. A shallow box (or designated spot) for partners (explained below)

2. Another large box for the kitty (explained below)

3. Several large pins (T-pins or corsage pins) for "stop pins"

My calculations are for centers 3" square and strips 2" wide. Sixteen strips are added with red used in the #11 and #12 positions. Blocks are about 14" square.

Strip sizes. *This is for reference only. When you build up blocks by adding them to 44" strips, don't worry about the length of strips.*

Centers	*3" square (red)*
#1 Light	*2" x 3"*
#2 Light	*2" x 4-1/2" (same fabric)*
#3 Dark	*2" x 4-1/2"*
#4 Dark	*2" x 6" (same fabric)*
#5 Light	*2" x 6"*
#6 Light	*2" x 7-1/2" (same fabric)*
#7 Dark	*2" x 7-1/2"*
#8 Dark	*2" x 9" (same fabric)*
#9 Light	*2" x 9"*
#10 Light	*2" x 10-1/2" (same fabric)*
#11 Dark	*2" x 10-1/2" (red)*
#12 Dark	*2" x 12" (red)*
#13 Light	*2" x 12"*
#14 Light	*2" x 13-1/2" (same fabric)*
#15 Dark	*2" x 13-1/2"*
#16 Dark	*2" x 15" (same fabric)*

(My numbering system is from Roberta Shroud's Revolutionized Log Cabin Quilt.*)*

Chart for Log Cabin Variation A, 14" blocks

Cut this many 44" strips before you start:

No. of blocks	3" red for centers	2" reds	2" lights	2" darks
16 (lap robe)	1*	8	26 (13 pairs)	20 (10 pairs)
24 (twin coverlet)	2	12	40 (20 pairs)	33 (15 pairs)
36 (double or queen)	3	18	60 (30 pairs)	48 (24 pairs)
48 (queen spread)	4	24	84 (42 pairs)	66 (33 pairs)
64 (king spread)	5	36	110 (55 pairs)	86 (43 pairs)

You'll also need a few single 3" squares of red; they can be different fabrics.

This seems like a lot of strips, but these are large quilts. The 64-block quilt would have 1,088 individual pieces and might be about 115" square after borders. Also, speed-piecing creates leftovers to use for Variation B, so you are really making two quilts at once. If you want a large quilt but don't have enough scraps, make sixteen or twenty-four blocks now and make more blocks later as you accumulate scraps.

General working method

1. Cut strips listed on the chart. Keep these things in mind:

(a) This is just an estimate. Don't waste time re-counting strips. If you need more later, you can add colors you need. If you cut too many, they'll be useful for the second project.

(b) The red accents in the third dark row are optional. If you don't want them, add the number of 2" red strips needed to the dark strips. If you do want them, don't include any **other** reds in your dark fabrics. That would put two reds next to each other—not an attractive effect. Reds can be different fabrics or all the same.

(c) Use two of each fabric or two closely related fabrics. Use as many pairs as you want of each fabric. Keep pairs of strips together.

(d) Use some medium fabrics too. Add dark/mediums to your darks and light/mediums to your lights.

Design tip: *Old-time Log Cabin quilts sometimes had another nice design feature, **medium** instead of **light** strips in the same position in each block, added just before the red strips. If you want to do this, cut about 1/3 of the light strips from medium fabric and set them aside until you get to that part of the block.*

2. Get organized:

(a) Cut the wide red strips into two lengths, a 28" piece and a smaller leftover piece, which you don't need to measure. Set them by your sewing machine since you'll use them first.

(b) Set the 2" red strips aside. You won't need them for quite a while.

(c) Keep light strips together and dark strips together. If you have several pairs of the same fabric, put one pair near the top, one or two near the middle, one near the bottom. If you're making a big quilt, set two boxes on the floor, one for dark strips and one for light strips, and keep several pairs draped over the sides so you can choose the best colors each time.

(d) Create a "partners" pile. Have a box (or special spot) to temporarily hold strips you'll use in a few minutes.

(e) Create a "kitty." This can be a box a little farther away where you toss scraps. You might use some scraps later in this project, but most will be for Variation B.

3. Make center units.

(a) Sew wide red strips to light strips. Use one 28" red strip or two shorter ones each time. Put the matching light strips in the partners pile.

(b) Cut into blocks. Press strips toward the red and cut 3" sets. Toss remnants (including red blocks that are a bit too small) into the kitty for the next project.

(c) Make more if needed. Count the blocks. If you don't have enough, cut a few more 3" squares of red scraps and sew each to one of the discarded light strips in the kitty, putting the rest of that light fabric into the partners pile too. If you have too many red blocks, put the extra in the kitty (or make a spare block or two).

Important: *Keep all blocks using the same light fabric stacked together.*

4. Add the #2 lights.

(a) Sew centers to partners. Pick up a stack of blocks with the same fabrics. Find the matching light fabric from the partners pile. Place the strip in your machine, right side up. Turn the blocks over and sew them to that strip one after another as shown, with the light fabric going into the machine first. Butt the blocks, but don't overlap them. Repeat until all blocks have their matching second strip added.

(b) Cut them apart. Open the blocks, press toward the red, and cut the blocks apart again.

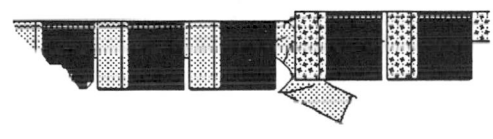

(c) Mix them up. Fabrics must be in random order for the next step.

Craftsmanship tips:

(a) At all stages, when you finish sewing blocks to a strip but still have some strip left, you have two choices: Sew onto a "thread catcher" and cut off the excess strip with your scissors, then feed the next work into the machine. Or just sew off the edge and onto the next strip. Either way, be careful. You may find that you tend to curve toward the edge too soon. Make sure you finish the last block with a straight line before curving off the strip.

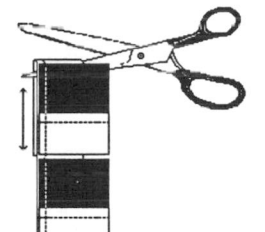

(b) You may prefer to cut the blocks apart with scissors, then press them. (This is handy if your ironing surface is within reach but your cutting mat isn't.) Be careful to keep cuts straight. Have blocks on the outside, strip on the inside. Line up edges of the strip (see arrow*), and hold edges together with one hand while you cut blocks apart with the other hand.*

(c) Check your blocks to see if strips are added correctly. Turn them to different positions and study them. Reading from the inside to the outside, strips go in a counterclockwise pattern at all stages.

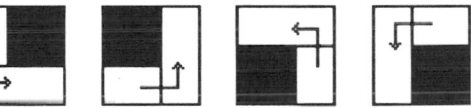

On the back of the block, there is a clockwise progression:

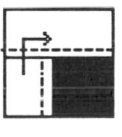

You won't have trouble if you always have the last strip added in Step 3 be the first part of the block to go under the sewing machine needle.

*Remember: **"last added, first in."***

5. Add the #3 darks.

(a) Use "stop pins." Pick up the first pair of dark strips. Put one in the partners box and the other in your sewing machine. Put a pin in it about 3/4 of the way down the strip to remind you not to attach blocks all the way (if you do, you won't have partners for the last two or three blocks).

(b) Sew seven blocks to dark strips. Turn over a stack of mixed-up blocks and sew them to the strip one after the other, with the last strip added in Step 4 going in first.

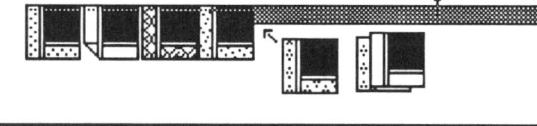

When you reach the "stop" pin, pick up a new pair of dark strips and repeat the process. If you have only one or two blocks left and don't want to start a new strip, start an "add dark strips" pile somewhere.

(c) Cut blocks apart. Toss leftover strips into the kitty. Keep all blocks from each strip stacked together for the next step.

6. Add the #4 darks.
Again, pick up a pile and select its matching strip. Turn the stack over and sew each block on.

Craftsmanship tips:

Change routine if you wish: *You can build up all the blocks at the same rate if you want, but you don't have to. Once you have the method down pat, you can break the routine. If you don't sew enough blocks on to the first strip in a pair and find extra fabric left on both partners, sew another block to the shorter strip, dig the other one out of the kitty while it's still on top of the heap, and complete the block. Go ahead and complete some blocks to get an idea of what your quilt top will look like. Or set some partly made blocks aside if you don't see any strips the right color and want to wait for a prettier fabric.*

*Eventually you'll probably find yourself with three working piles: blocks that need **dark** strips next, those that need **light** strips, and those that need **red** strips.*

*You might find yourself accumulating a fourth pile—one of "**Old Maids**," blocks that are missing their partner. You don't need more piles, so get an Old Maid back in circulation right away. Remove the last strip and start over, or find the right fabric in the kitty (a near-match is okay). Or cut two more strips of the missing fabric, put one in the partners box as usual, sew the Old Maid on to the other, then make it your next working strip.*

You can add blocks at different stages to the same strip, so every once in a while take care of all the blocks in your "add light" pile, etc.

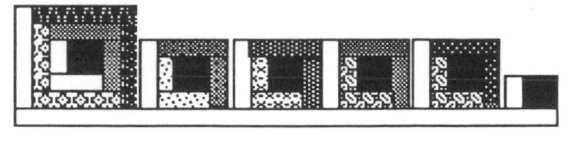

7. Continue to build up the blocks, using a stop pin, sewing blocks partway down a strip, keeping sets together when cut apart, sewing on partners, and mixing blocks up. Eventually you'll find no two blocks alike, and that's the whole idea with scrap quilts.

8. Add red strips. You don't need stop pins when sewing on the first red strips because you have plenty more reds to use for partners.

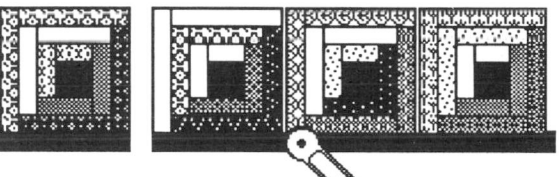

9. Finish the blocks carefully. Before sewing on the #13 lights (the first strips on the outside of the block), you have some special jobs:

(a) Make sure blocks are uniform. Using your grid, measure the blocks and trim them all to the same size. Adjust some seams, if necessary. You'll save yourself a lot of frustration when you put the quilt top together. Not only must blocks be the same size, the last strips you add must line up with each other. By correcting the block

before adding the final strips, you can usually just trim a bit off all sides. You shouldn't have to correct the finished block later. (If you find a block way out of shape or too small, piece together a new one instead of picking out several seams.)

(b) Count your 44" strips. Will you have enough? You will need a pair of lights and a pair of darks for each three blocks. Do you need more variety? When you assemble the blocks to make the quilt, you don't want a block touching another block with the same fabric on the edge (at least, I don't). If you have too many of the same fabrics, toss some into the kitty.

(c) Cut enough strips to complete the blocks. First, lay out the partly completed blocks and study them. Are they crying out for more green? Or do you need more neutrals to tone them down because they are too busy? Do you need more medium colors to break up the extreme light/dark pattern?

Could you raid the kitty to get the strips to finish up the blocks instead of cutting new strips? Probably not. It's hard to find strips long enough for the outer parts of the blocks, let alone two strips of the same fabric. Save leftovers for Variation B.

(d) Complete the blocks.

10. Plan your overall design.
Although I said that you could use any arrangement in Chapter 4, these are quite large blocks, so you might want to avoid blocks where darks are massed together unless the dark is broken up by a lot of mediums. When you find an arrangement you like, pin and tag rows as mentioned on page 10.

11. Assemble quilt top. Add borders if you wish.

12. Complete the quilt. See suggestions in Chapter 1.

Summary of Variation A

There are several advantages to this working method:

(a) You can strip-piece the centers and #1 lights, and the technique for adding blocks can be almost as fast as strip piecing.

(b) You cut strips after they're sewn on the block. Otherwise you'd have to cut seventeen sizes of pieces and have seventeen piles so you could find each type. And you'd often have to trim strips again after sewing because they were a bit too long.

(c) The partners pile makes it easy to keep track of the second strip of each color sequence. You don't want to sew it on right after the first one is added because that would slow you down.

Disadvantages: You use only 44" strips, although you might work in shorter scraps once you understand the process. And you create lots of shorter scraps. As I've said, make Variation B with those.

Queen-size Log Cabin quilt

Now let's apply the general directions to a queen-size quilt, 84" x 112" using forty-eight blocks. You may want to have this quilt machine-quilted commercially since it is so large; it'll be several inches smaller after quilting.

Fabric needed:
Red fabric: 1-3/4 yd.

Light strips: lots of 44" strips, 2" wide, or 1/4 yd. pieces of twenty-one fabrics

Dark strips: lots of 44" strips, 2" wide, or 1/4 yd. pieces of 16 fabrics

(Have some extra fabrics on hand in case you need to cut strips later. Fat quarters don't work with this project.)

Backing: 8-1/2 yds.

Batting: piece about 96" x 114"

Binding: 11 to 12 yds.

1. Cut strips:

(a) Cut red fabric, four strips 3" x 44" and twenty-four strips 2" x 44". If you can't get that many strips from your yardage, cut more 2" strips later from other red fabrics.

(b) Cut light fabric, eighty-four strips 2" x 44" (forty-two pairs), plus one or two shorter scraps.

(c) Cut dark fabric, sixty-six strips 2" x 44" (thirty-three pairs).

2. Get organized. Follow basic instructions on page 70.

3. Sew light strips to the 3" reds to make the centers (one long strip or two short strips in each case). Cut into 3" blocks, stacking like blocks together.

4. Locate partners and sew the second light strips to the blocks. Cut blocks apart, mix them up, and re-stack.

5. Add dark strips (#3 and #4). Choose seven pairs of dark strips. Sew **seven** blocks to first strips in each pair. Sew the leftover block to a dark scrap strip. Cut blocks apart, keeping like blocks together. Sew blocks to dark partners, cut them apart, and mix them up.

6. Sew blocks to light strips (#5 and #6). Choose eight pairs of light strips and sew **six** blocks to first strips in each pair. Cut blocks apart, keeping like blocks together. Sew blocks to light partners, cut them apart, and mix them up.

7. Sew to dark strips (#7 and #8). Choose ten pairs of dark strips and sew **five** blocks to first strips in each pair. Cut blocks apart, keeping like blocks together. Sew blocks to dark partners, cut them apart, and mix them up.

8. Sew blocks to light strips (#9 and #10). Choose 12 pairs of light strips and sew **four** blocks to first strips in each pair. Cut blocks apart, keeping like blocks together. Sew blocks to light partners, cut them apart, and mix them up. You're doing a lot of sewing, but you're making a large quilt and you're about half done now.

9. Sew blocks to red strips (#11 and #12) and cut them apart.

10. Press and measure blocks. Adjust all to same size. Spread blocks out and see if there are any colors you need to add. **Cut more strips**, if necessary, to make sixteen pairs of light and sixteen pairs of dark, as many different fabrics as possible.

11. Sew blocks to light strips (#13 and #14). Sew **three** blocks to first strips in each pair. Cut blocks apart, keeping like blocks together. Sew blocks to light partners, cut them apart, and mix them up.

12. Sew blocks to dark strips (#15 and #16). Sew **three** blocks to first strips in each pair. Cut blocks apart, keeping like blocks together. Sew blocks to dark partners, and you're done.

13. Decide how to arrange blocks. Some ideas: Use Barn Raising or Zigzag, shown below. Use an overall arrangement from Chapter 4 or adapt one of the other arrangements. For example, expand one of the 36-block arrangements by adding rows to the top and bottom, or omit the center two rows in one of the 64-block arrangements and move the sides in.

14. Complete the project. Press quilt. Layer quilt, batting, and backing (pieced as shown on page 13, No. 5). Quilt and bind with your favorite method. See Chapter 1.

Tip: *Standard batting size is only 91" x 108" but you can still use it. Batting might be just a little larger than it says on the package, or your project might be a bit smaller because your seams were wider than 1/4". If the batting is skimpy, center it on the quilt but don't stretch it. Add strips of batting on the ends.*

Barn Raising arrangement

Zigzag arrangement

Log Cabin Variation B: *Using the leftovers*

As mentioned earlier, the rules are different when making a quilt from leftovers. Since pieces are smaller and will take more time to handle, we've simplified the block. Blocks are 10" when finished and look like this:

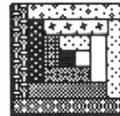

(a) Centers are red but only 2" square.

(b) Only twelve strips are added.

(c) Strips are arranged in dark-light patterns, but otherwise are in random order. No L's are formed.

(d) No red accent strips are used. Random reds may be used in the dark area.

(e) Make logs from leftovers from the first project plus some 44" strips.

Sizes of strips in 10" Log Cabin blocks. Again, this is for reference only. Don't trim strips to this size ahead of time. Strips are shorter than in Variation A because centers are smaller.

#1 Light	2"
#2 Light	2" x 3-1/2"
#3 Dark	2" x 3-1/2"
#4 Dark	2" x 5"
#5 Light	2" x 5"
#6 Light	2" x 6-1/2"
#7 Dark	2" x 6 1/2"
#8 Dark	2" x 8"
#9 Light	2" x 8"
#10 Light	2" x 9-1/2"
#11 Dark	2" x 9-1/2"
#12 Dark	2" x 11"

How to do Variation B

You'll use the same basic technique to build up the blocks as you did the with Variation A, so I won't go into much detail. You won't need the partners pile or kitty this time. Instead use a couple of wide shallow boxes, cookie sheets, etc. (I'll call them "trays" in the instructions.) Have a wastebasket handy for tiny scraps and a box for "Rejects" (small pieces you might keep or discard but don't want to decide about right now).

1. Prepare strips: Do some quick sorting of leftovers from Variation A, along with any other scraps, trimmed to 2". Add some new 44" strips too.

(a) Put dark strips on one tray arranged roughly by size, shortest on one end, longest on the other.

(b) Put light strips on the other tray, sorted the same way.

(c) Put red strips by the sewing machine.

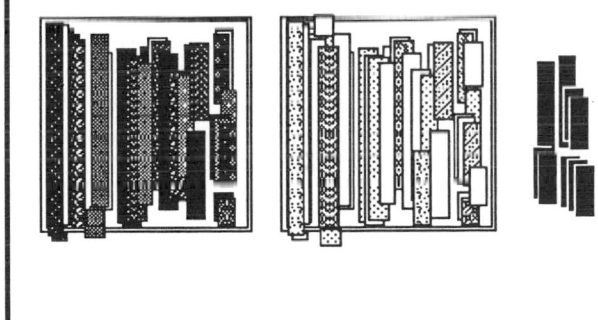

2. Attach #1 light strips and red centers:

(a) Set the tray of light strips so you can reach it as you sew. Start sewing the smallest red strips to the smallest light ones. Just feed them into the machine, one set after another, not taking time to trim lengths to match each other. Press the combinations.

(b) Cut 2" blocks. Count blocks, and make more if you need them (sixteen, twenty-four, or thirty-six would be good numbers to aim for).

(c) Toss other short red strips into the reject box. You won't be able to use anything shorter than 6-1/2".

(d) Add other red strips to the tray of dark strips.

3. Sew blocks to #2 lights. Use short pieces first, then sew the blocks to a 44" strip if you wish. No need to find partners this time. Do continue to follow the rule of "last added, first in," however. Trim and press blocks.

4. Add dark strips. Move the light strips tray out of the way and set the dark strips tray within reach. Sew blocks to #3 dark strips. Again use up some short strips to ease your conscience,

some longer ones for speed. After pressing and trimming, stack the blocks a uniform way (darks on the bottom and right of the pile, for example). Then you can turn the whole stack over and feed blocks onto the next strips without any turning and fussing. Add #4 darks, then move the dark strips tray away and set the light strips tray by the machine.

5. Continue to build up the blocks. Add two light and switch trays. Add two dark and switch trays. Use small strips until you're tired of them or run out, then feed several blocks onto a long strip. You'll probably stop and cut some long strips of colors you need as you go.

If using the top block would make an awful color combination (or put the same fabrics next to each other), set blocks aside and come back to them when a better fabric comes along. (It's fun to see the different color combinations coming together, some you would never have imagined. You'll find some pretty effects you'll want to use for a complete quilt later.) Make two piles of "set aside blocks," those which need dark strips next and those which need light ones.

Remember, you can sew blocks at different stages to the same strips.

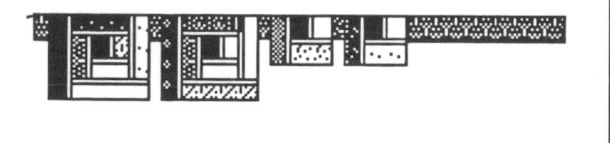

If the project stops being fun: Take a break and come back with a different outlook. Tidy up the work area, if the mess is getting you down. Toss small pieces in the reject box if you're tired of sewing short seams. Cut some long strips of your prettiest fabrics to perk up the blocks. Play some lively music and relax. With this project, you don't have to concentrate much. The only "rules" you need:

(a) Sew lights to light sides, darks to dark sides. (**Caution:** Use some medium fabrics, but don't let them throw you off. You might forget whether a medium strip is supposed to be a "light" or a "dark," and sew the wrong strip on next, so double check.)

(b) "Last added, first in" is just as important as it was in Variation A.

(c) Press and trim the blocks before adding the last set of light strips and last set of dark strips.

Finish up the project as usual. Use wide borders if you want (see the lap robe on the cover), or none at all (see the child's quilt on the color pages).

Variation B in retrospect

I didn't do much manipulating of colors when I made my teaching samples. I thought the casual look made a nice contrast to the more formal projects I usually do.

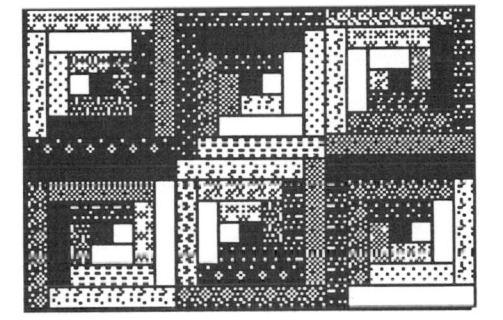

But in thinking it over, I would add this simple rule: Have #5 and #6 the same **value** (darkness). See how much more orderly the sample below looks?

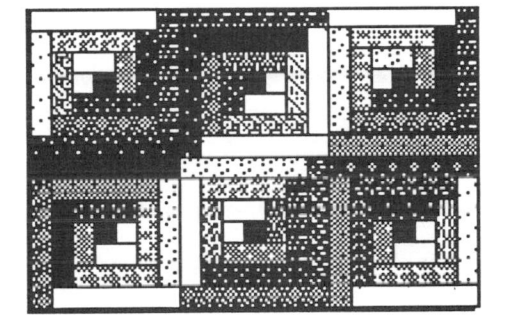

Make up some more rules for yourself, if you want. Spend a little more time coordinating blocks and strips to make this project prettier, but don't expect humble Variation B quilts to be masterpieces. Don't enter them in quilt shows, but do count on them being favorites with the family because they are cheerful and colorful.

The Woodpile block

The rest of this chapter deals with this simple little block. Since it's made of pre-pieced sections, I originally called it "Pre-Fab Log Cabin." But I needed a shorter name, so it became simply "Wood-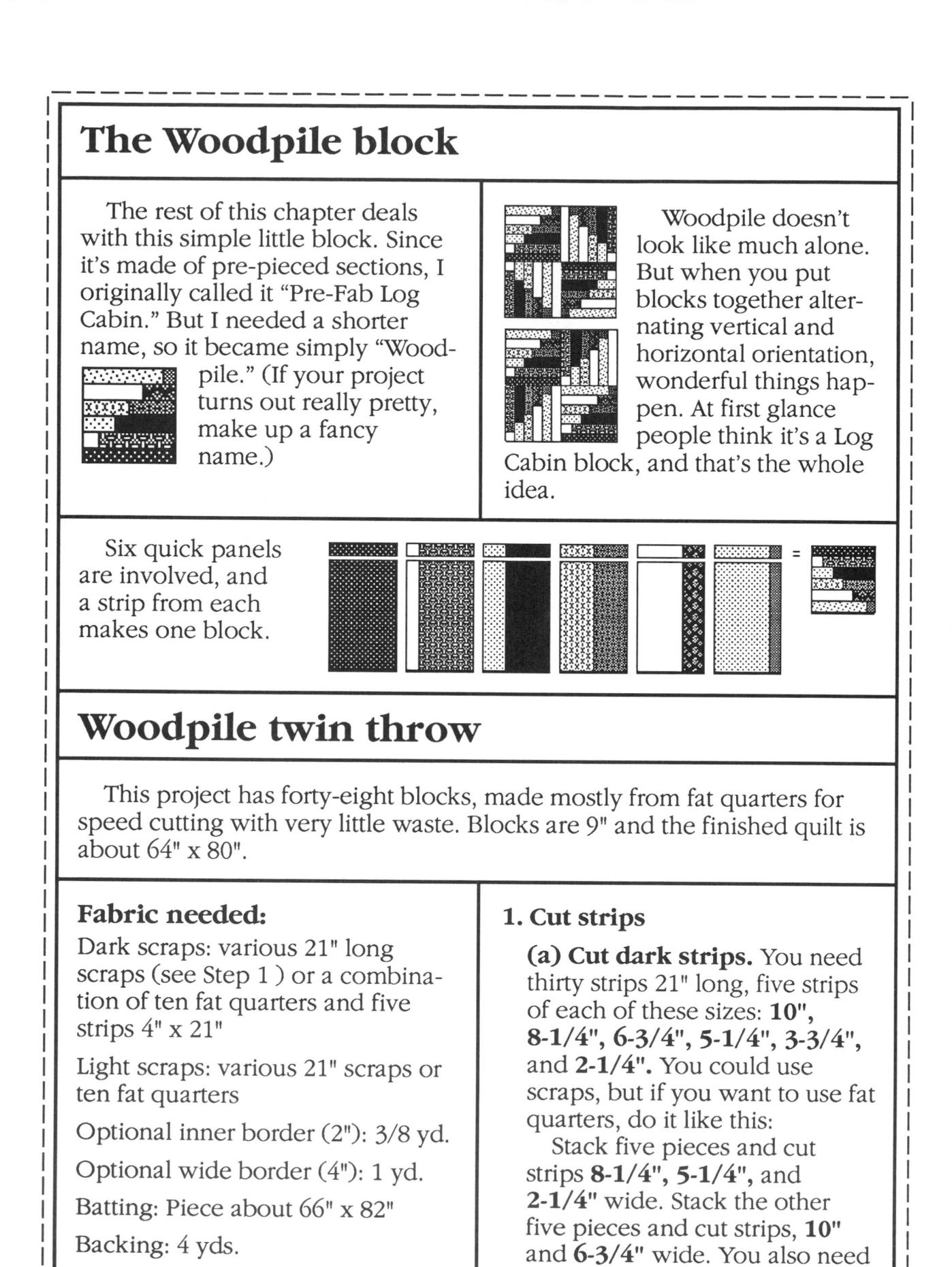pile." (If your project turns out really pretty, make up a fancy name.)

Woodpile doesn't look like much alone. But when you put blocks together alternating vertical and horizontal orientation, wonderful things happen. At first glance people think it's a Log Cabin block, and that's the whole idea.

Six quick panels are involved, and a strip from each makes one block.

Woodpile twin throw

This project has forty-eight blocks, made mostly from fat quarters for speed cutting with very little waste. Blocks are 9" and the finished quilt is about 64" x 80".

Fabric needed:

Dark scraps: various 21" long scraps (see Step 1) or a combination of ten fat quarters and five strips 4" x 21"

Light scraps: various 21" scraps or ten fat quarters

Optional inner border (2"): 3/8 yd.

Optional wide border (4"): 1 yd.

Batting: Piece about 66" x 82"

Backing: 4 yds.

Binding: 8 or 9 yds.

1. Cut strips

(a) Cut dark strips. You need thirty strips 21" long, five strips of each of these sizes: **10", 8-1/4", 6-3/4", 5-1/4", 3-3/4",** and **2-1/4".** You could use scraps, but if you want to use fat quarters, do it like this:

Stack five pieces and cut strips **8-1/4", 5-1/4",** and **2-1/4"** wide. Stack the other five pieces and cut strips, **10"** and **6-3/4"** wide. You also need five strips **3-3/4" x 21"** cut from dark scraps.

(b) Cut light strips*: Cut five each **8-1/4", 6-3/4", 5-1/4", 3-3/4",** and **2-1/4"** wide. Again, you can use scraps. If you want to use ten fat quarters, stack five and cut strips **8-1/4", 5-1/4"** and **2-1/4"**. Stack five more and cut strips **6-3/4"** and **3-3/4"**. (Put away the leftovers immediately so they don't get mixed up with the official strips.)

Another way to make light strips: Have all light strips and wide borders of the same fabric, using 3-1/4 yds. Cut off a piece 28" x 44" and fold it in two (28" x 22"). Tear the large piece in half lengthwise. Set one piece aside for borders. Fold the other into three 28" sections and add them to the other stack, making five layers. Cut one stack of each size strip from that arrangement. (When my daughter Betsy made the sample in the nursery photo on the color pages, she used a light-dominant variation. She used this for cutting the blue strips.)

How I arrived at such weird numbers: Horizontal strips are 2" (1-1/2" after seams). Blocks use six strips, which would be 9-1/2" (9" after outer seams). Vertically there are only two strips, which should also add up to 9-1/2" (9"), shouldn't they? But I found I needed a little extra width to trim the blocks up correctly. So I added 1/4" to the width of each strip and 1/2" to width of the solid piece. It works much better.

2. Make panels. For each set of ten blocks, you need six panels 10" x 21". Five dark pieces are already that size. Sew the other strips together with the widest darks sewn to the narrowest lights and progressing to the opposite combination, widest lights sewn to narrowest darks. (If the total width is 10", you have it right.) Make a total of thirty panels with no two panels having the same color combination.

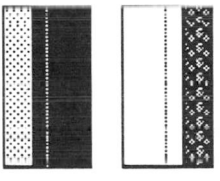

3. Mark the vertical centers. This is an optional step that helps in Step 6. As you press the panels, just fold each panel lengthwise and make a crease. Some panels already have a seam down the center, so they won't need a mark.

4. Cut across all panels into 2" strips. I cut through only one layer at a time so I can constantly keep the seams and edges of the fabric lined up with the markings on the ruler. Try cutting through three or four layers at a time, if you wish.

5. Sort strips, making six stacks. Keep all strips of the same dark-light division together, but mix them up.

6. Piece together blocks. Drawing from all six piles in a random way, assemble blocks. Line up the center creases even if the ends aren't quite even; they can be trimmed later. There are two cautions:

(a) Use exactly 1/4" seams now. Piece together two test blocks. Press, measure, and trim them with your large grid. Are they perfectly square? Try them side by side in different positions. Does the single dark square in the outer row line up with the strip in the adjacent block?

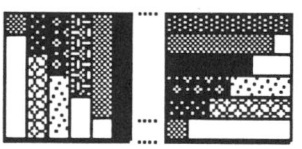

Make your seams a little wider or narrower if necessary. This is a fast, fun block to do if you get your seams right. Seam width is more crucial in this block than any other block in the book.

(b) Have half the blocks slant one way and half the other. The slant of the block is built in; you can't alter it without picking out all the seams.

If panels have the dark strips on the right, and strips are gathered from left to right and assembled in this order (top to bottom), the blocks will slant "downhill." Assemble half the blocks this way.

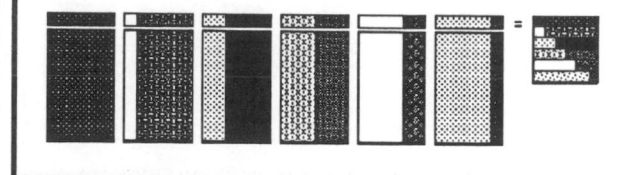

If the cross sections are in the same order, but each is turned around so the dark is on the left side, the slant will go the other way. Assemble half the blocks this way.

7. Square up the blocks. Press and trim them so they're square and a uniform size (about 9-1/2"), and so strips line up with the end squares as mentioned in Step 6.

8. Assemble blocks in the Barn Raising arrangement. Lay the blocks out in rows and experiment to get the best color effects. Pin and tag the rows (see page 10) and sew blocks together.

9. Add borders if you wish. The yardage allowance lets you make borders as shown in the color plate. Or use only a narrow binding as shown below.

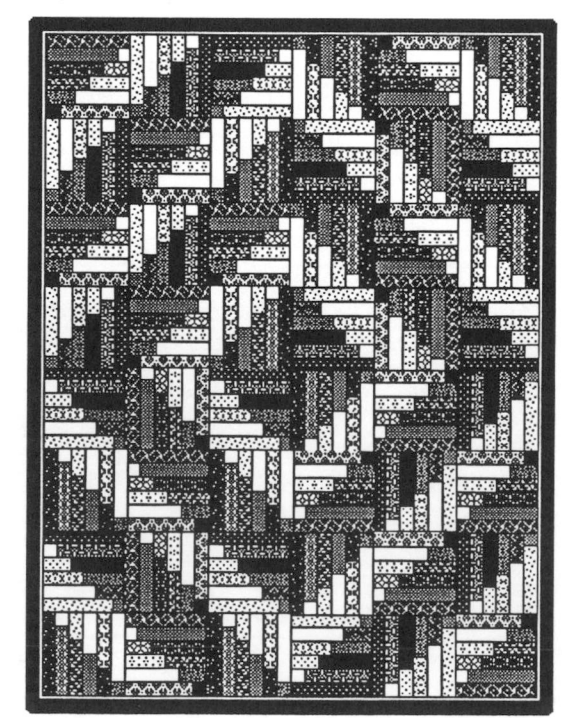

10. Complete the project. Make backing (No. 1 or 2 on page 13). Quilt and bind with your favorite method (See Chapter 1).

Do you always have to make half of the blocks slant each way? No, but it's a good safe rule if you want your quilts to turn out pretty. Don't break it unless you know what you're doing. That combination allows you to make the two most useful arrangements, Barn Raising and Straight Furrows (which we'll revisit in Chapter 6). See the information on pages 84 to 85 to understand this block when you feel ready to experiment with other arrangements.

Chart for planning Woodpile projects

Since fat quarters work so nicely for this block, I'll use it as a basis for calculating yardage. This project is great turned on the bias (see page 99 to 102) so the chart includes information to help you use that option. Project size is before borders and quilting.

Number of blocks	Use like this	Size of project straight	bias	Dark fat quarters	Light fat quarters	4" x 21" scrap (dark or light*)
20	16 blocks (4 x 4)	36" sq.	—	4	4	2
	20 blocks (4 x 5)	36" x 45"	—			
30	24 blocks (4 x 6)	36" x 54"	38" x 51"	6	6	3
	25 blocks (5 x 5)	45" sq.	—			
40	32 blocks (4 x 8)	—	51" sq.	8	8	4
	35 blocks (5 x 7)	45" x 63"	—			
	36 blocks (6 x 6)	54" sq.	—			
50	48 blocks (6 x 8)	54" x 72"	50" x 76"	10	10	5
	50 blocks (5 x 10)	—	63" sq.			
60	56 blocks (7 x 8)	63" x 72"	51" x 89"	12	12	6
	60 blocks (6 x 10)	54" x 90"	63" x 76"			
70	63 blocks (7 x 9)	63" x 81"	—	14	14	7
	64 blocks (8 x 8)	72" sq.	—			
	70 blocks (7 x 10)	63" x 90"	63" x 90"			
80	72 blocks (6 x 12)	—	76" sq.	16	16	8
	80 blocks (8 x 10)	72" x 90"	63" x 101"			
100	100 blocks (10 x 10)	90" sq.	—	20	20	10

If dark is dominant, these 4" strips must be dark. If light is dominant, they must be light. (You might even have half of them light and half dark if you're doing a special variation.)

Advanced information:

Information on these two pages is for advanced use only. Don't worry about it unless you plan to make a lot of Woodpile blocks and get tired of Barn Raising. Here are some of the things I have discovered about the Woodpile:

1. Blocks still slant the same way if they are turned upside down, but the dark/light pattern changes. Both of these slant "downhill."

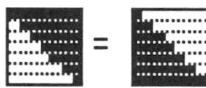

2. Blocks slant the opposite way if they are turned on their sides. When strips are horizontal, this block slants "downhill." When turned on its side (either direction), strips are vertical and the block slants "uphill."

3. A block can be assembled to slant in either direction, then turned to achieve four different looks. Blocks in the first set are not interchangeable with blocks in the second set because they were not assembled the same way originally.

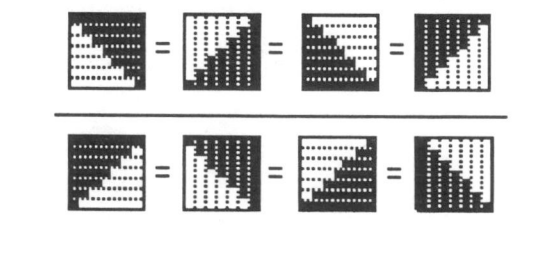

4. To get the Log Cabin effect, blocks that touch each other must be turned different directions (on all sides). So, there are two things to juggle: the diagonal slant and the vertical or horizontal direction of the strips. Even if the diagonal slant is right, a block might not fit in a particular spot because the orientation is vertical when you need horizontal.

5. Arrangements other than Barn Raising can be used if you created blocks which slant the directions you need. But be careful. You can't just count the uphill and downhill blocks in a design and go by that count. There are two safe approaches:

(a) Half the blocks slant one way and half the other. That is what basic directions called for. You can make these arrangements:

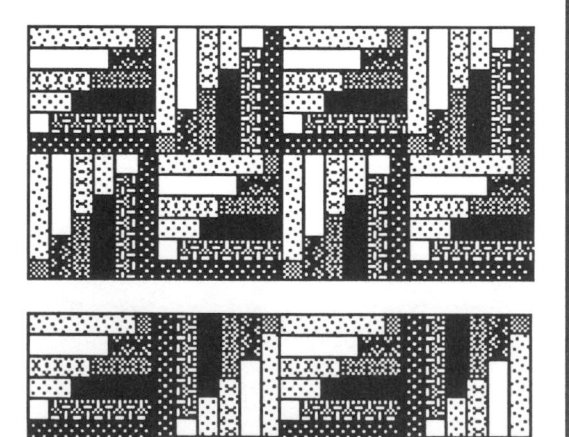

The slant of the blocks

(b) All the blocks have the same slant. Here are a couple of ways they could be used.

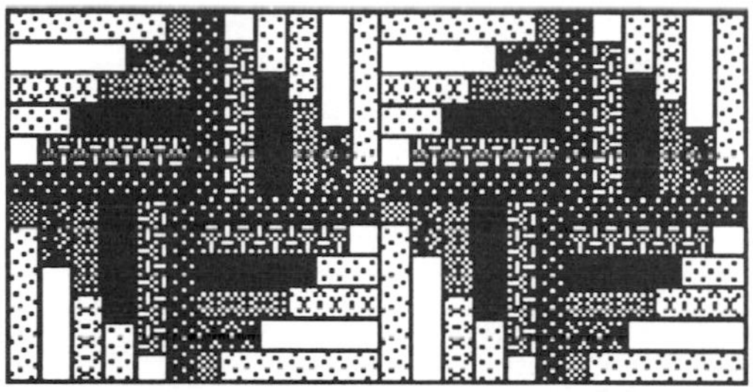

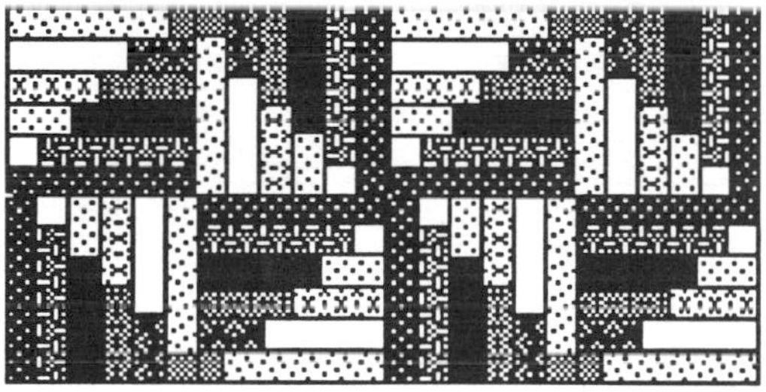

Most arrangements in Chapter 4 can be made with one combination or the other, but not all. Some need 3/4 of the blocks slanting one way, 1/4 the other, or some other arrangement. If you are determined to try a risky design, first sketch it out or photocopy it. Then draw arrows on each block alternating between vertical and horizontal from block to block and row to row. Then check each block against the chart and keep a tally on what you need.

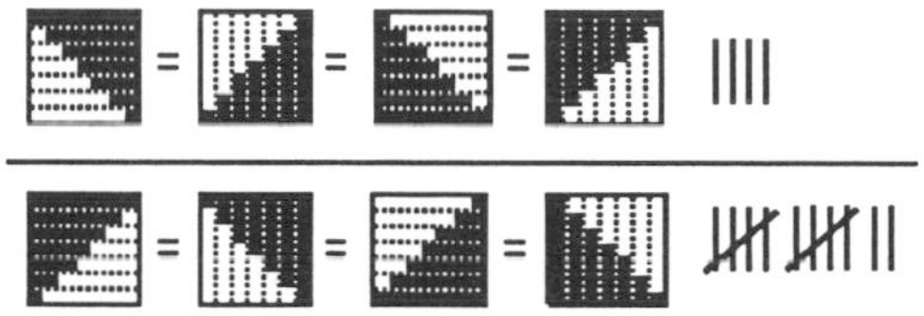

You can also analyze a 4-block or 8-block motif to find what you need, then multiply your score by the number of times that motif is repeated. But be careful.

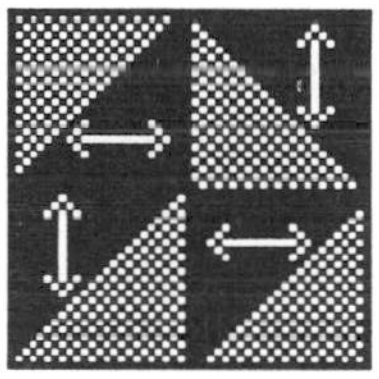

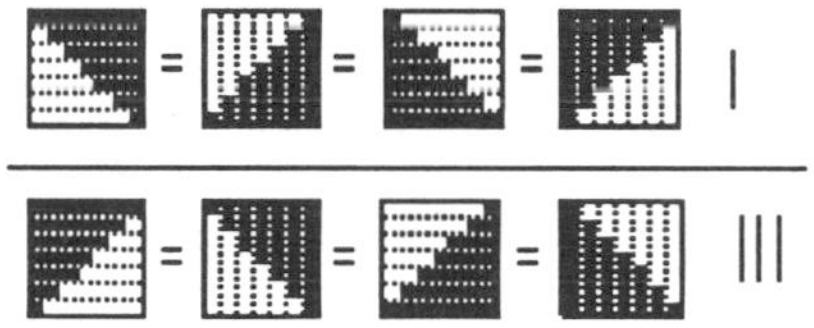

6. Unfortunately, even if the blocks all slant the right way and the strips go the right direction, you might not like the effect. I didn't care for this arrangement, for example.

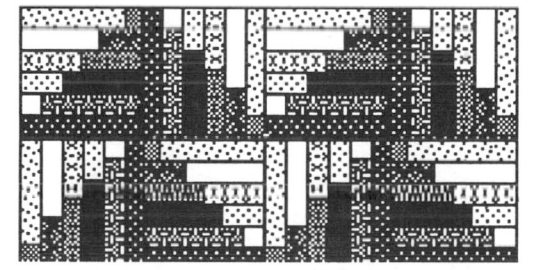

If these two pages have confused you more than they've enlightened you, that's all the more reason to stick with the basic directions and the good, safe Barn Raising arrangement!

Woodpile variations

Woodpile really is a wonderful block. Make a few projects following the basic directions, then try some variations:

1. Build in some color surprises. For example, you can take advantage of the "windmill" effect you get when four blocks come together. Even if a lot of different blocks are used, have the longest strips always the same color. (For this motif, all blocks slant "uphill.")

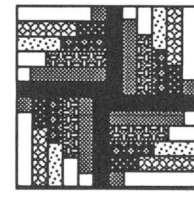

2. Experiment with other arrangements in Chapter 4. Use the information on pages 84 and 85 to make sure you have the right mix of blocks to achieve that arrangement.

3. Have half the blocks made with light strips dominant. Mixing both dark-dominant and light-dominant blocks gives a nicer effect in arrangements like this. (All dark and light blocks must slant the same way.)

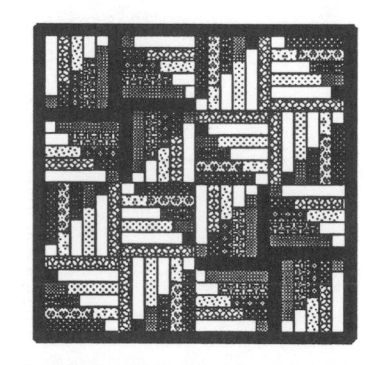

Here's how to make blocks with light dominant:

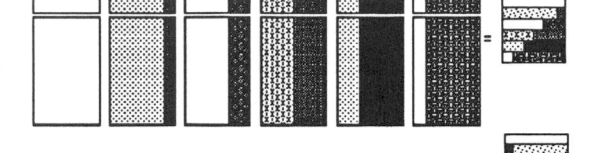

The large blue quilt in the nursery photo in the color pages has light dominant in all blocks.

4. Turn the quilt top on the bias. See Chapter 6. Use Straight Furrows arrangement shown on page 100 through 102.

5. Use the blocks for a frame around a quilt. Having all blocks in a row have the same orientation is a creative solution if you find your blocks are longer one way than the other and just don't work with usual arrangements. This works if half the blocks slant in each direction.

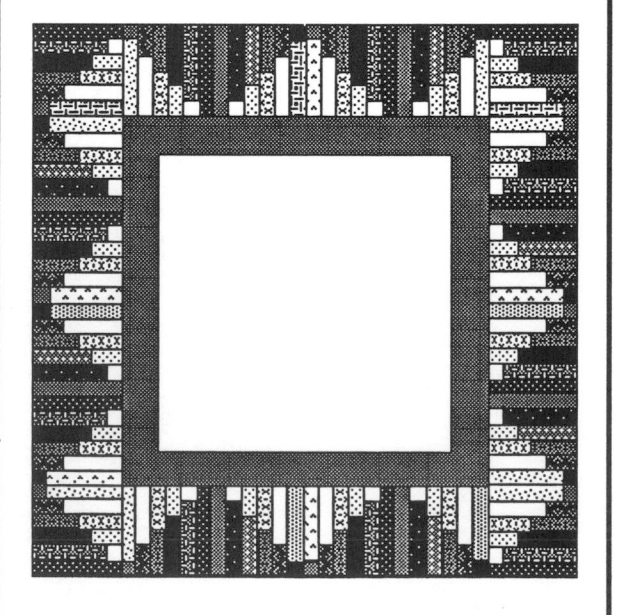

6. Make Irish Cabin. The fanciest variation I've seen is the one which gave me the idea for the Woodpile block in the first place. It was made by friends in the San Francisco Bay Area. Since it's a combination of Irish Chain and Log Cabin, they called it Irish Cabin. See it in the color pages.

They spent two years making the quilt, but could have cut down the piecing time significantly with this method of strip piecing. You'll need blocks going both ways. Dark strips can be the same size as usual. Narrow strips of light colors and red are substituted for the solid light areas; make them each 2" wide and be very accurate so all those seams will line up. This is not a project for beginners.

I don't have room for charts for this version, but you can plan your own. (Or write to me—I'll do some calculations and diagrams on the computer.)

Here's one idea for 12 Irish Cabin blocks. The solid dark strip is omitted from the blocks that meet in the center of each side.

Woodpile blocks to play with

To help you experiment with the wonderful Woodpile block, here are diagrams of two versions of the dark-dominant block, and two of the light-dominant, each with both slants. Make several photocopies, cut out the blocks and try out different arrangements.

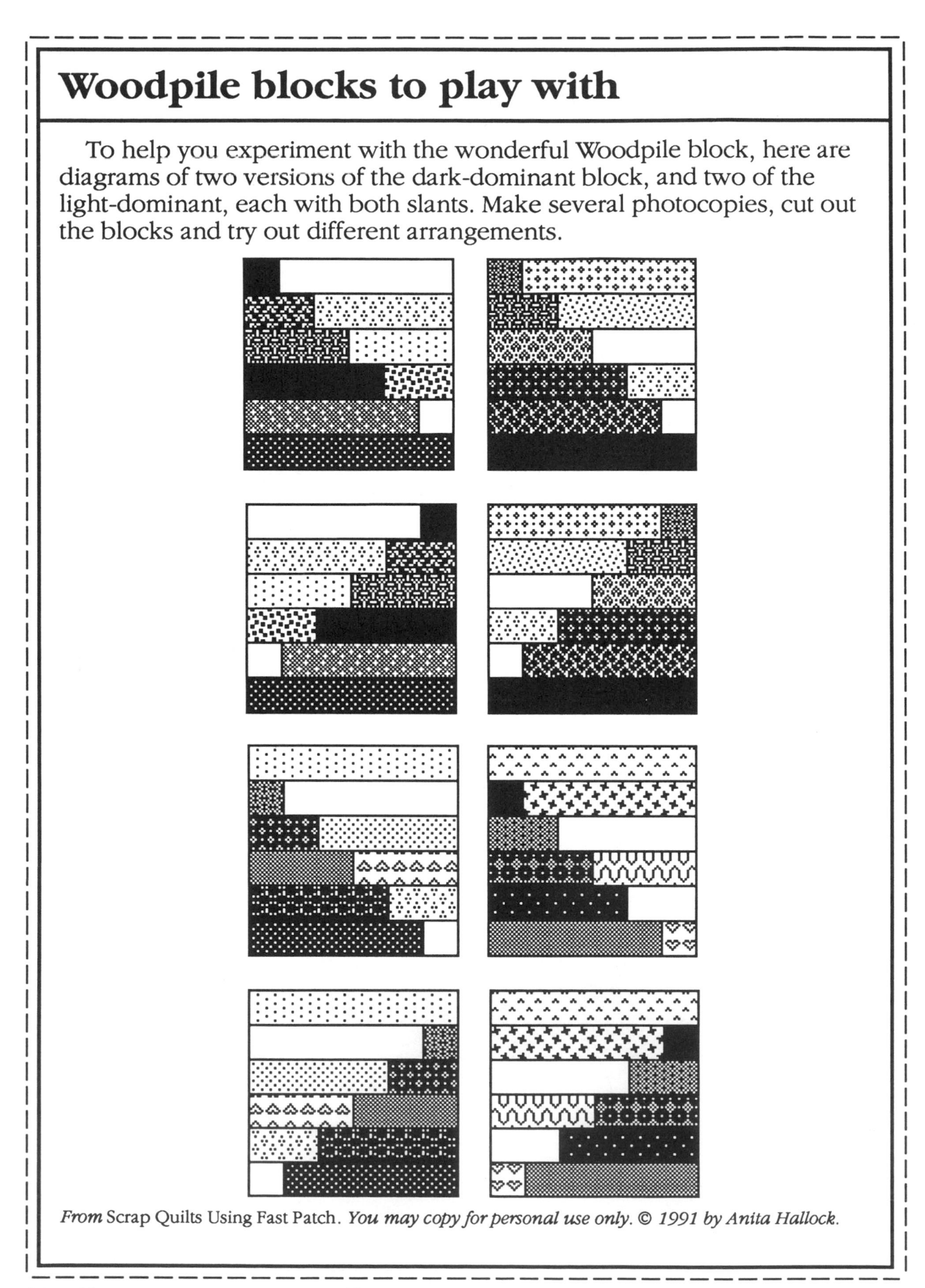

6. A New Twist

In this chapter I will introduce some ideas you might find quite strange unless you've read some of my other books. But they all do one thing—turn something ordinary into something exciting by giving it a diagonal twist. Try a simple 2 x 4 checkerboard first.

Turning a 2 x 4 checkerboard on the bias

Cut one light and one dark strip, 4" x 17". (These are Alpha strips, four times as long as they are wide, plus an inch, as mentioned on page 53.)

Sew them together. Trim ends and cut cross sections, also 4" wide. Reverse them and sew them into a very small checkerboard with two squares one way and four squares the other, a "2 x 4 checkerboard."

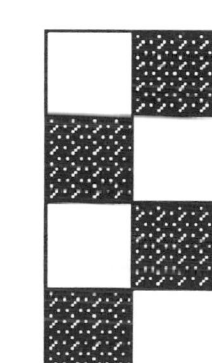

Now I'll show you the easiest way to turn that little checkerboard into triangle blocks like this.

There are four steps:

1. Cut diagonally from one corner. You'll find that a straight cut trims off a bit of the next square (see the circle). That's okay.

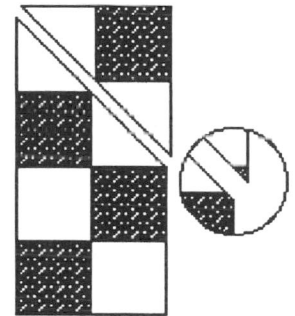

2. Sew the piece you cut off to the other end. The triangles won't seem to fit the squares (see the circles). But that's okay too. There are seam allowances involved.

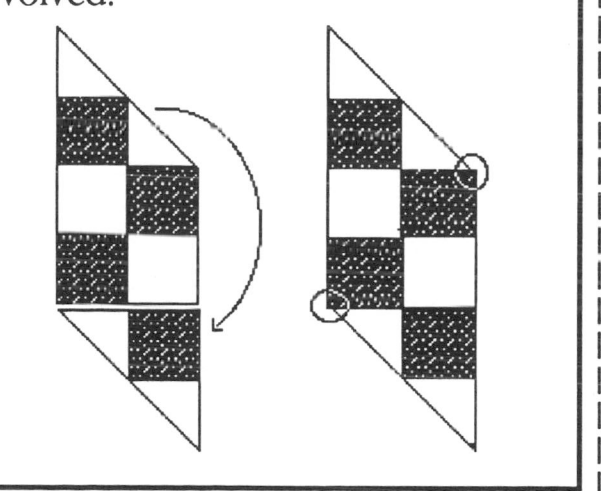

3. Cut in the other direction.

4. Sew pieces together. (Here's where you use that seam allowance.)

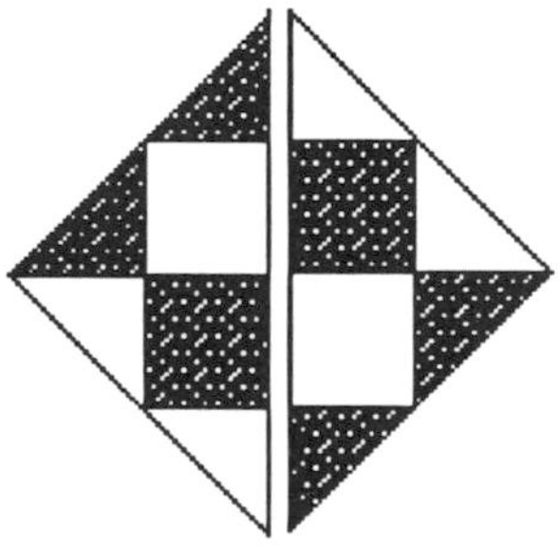

Cut out sets of triangles with no waste, no short seams.

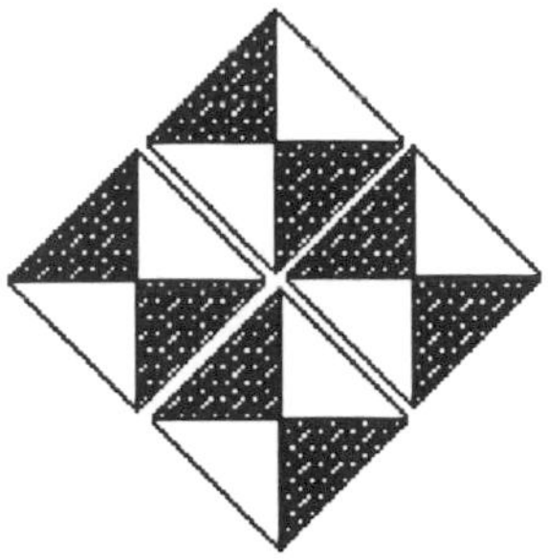

This transformation is almost magical. You can apply these same steps to checkerboards of almost any size. In fact, that's what you'll be doing for the rest of the book.

Although this was a practice exercise, you can put those four triangle sets to good use. Set them aside, and make more from other sizes of checkerboards.

Turning a 4 x 4 checkerboard on the bias

Remember the checkerboards for the quilt on page 52 to 54? Now make one from 4" strips. Use two light strips and two dark strips, 4" x 17", each a different fabric with colors that are compatible with those in the 2 x 4 checkerboard. Sew them together and press toward the dark. Cut cross sections and make a 4 x 4 checkerboard.

erboard.

Again, it takes four steps to turn it on the bias:

1. Cut diagonally from one corner.

2. Move one piece and sew it to the other side. (Remember, the triangles won't seem to fit the squares at the circled places because of the seam allowance.)

3. Cut diagonally again where the direction changes.

4. Sew the pieces together.

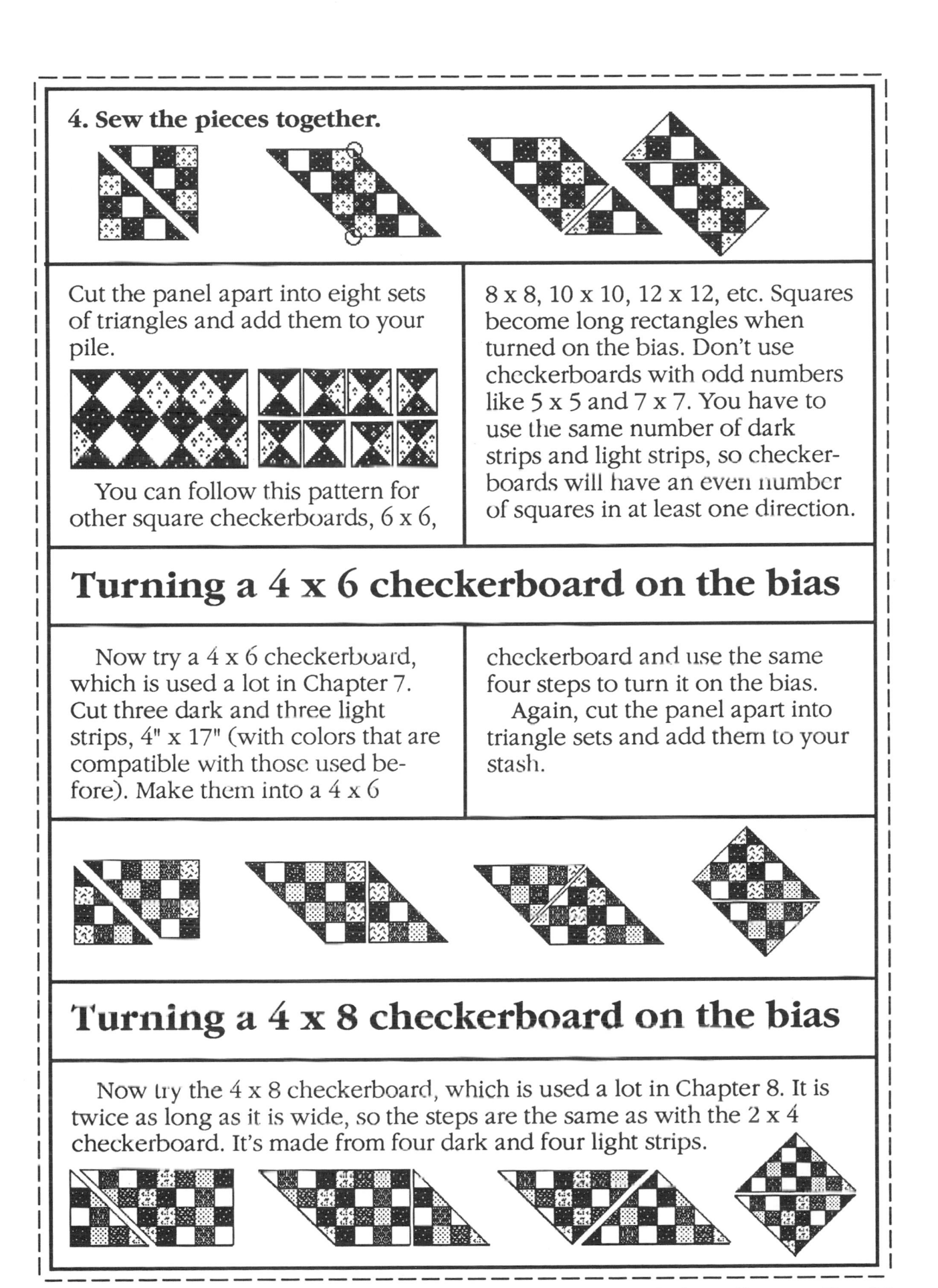

Cut the panel apart into eight sets of triangles and add them to your pile.

You can follow this pattern for other square checkerboards, 6 x 6, 8 x 8, 10 x 10, 12 x 12, etc. Squares become long rectangles when turned on the bias. Don't use checkerboards with odd numbers like 5 x 5 and 7 x 7. You have to use the same number of dark strips and light strips, so checkerboards will have an even number of squares in at least one direction.

Turning a 4 x 6 checkerboard on the bias

Now try a 4 x 6 checkerboard, which is used a lot in Chapter 7. Cut three dark and three light strips, 4" x 17" (with colors that are compatible with those used before). Make them into a 4 x 6 checkerboard and use the same four steps to turn it on the bias.

Again, cut the panel apart into triangle sets and add them to your stash.

Turning a 4 x 8 checkerboard on the bias

Now try the 4 x 8 checkerboard, which is used a lot in Chapter 8. It is twice as long as it is wide, so the steps are the same as with the 2 x 4 checkerboard. It's made from four dark and four light strips.

Again, cut the panel apart into sets of triangles and add it to those you've already got.

Many sizes of checkerboards can be turned on the bias. Here are some general rules:

1. If there are an even number of squares on the longer side, a checkerboard can be turned on the bias. It's okay if there is an odd number of squares on the shorter side. You might sometimes find a 3 x 4 or 5 x 8 checkerboard handy.

2. The shorter side should have at least half as many squares as the longer side.

3. Square checkerboards are turned on the bias as the 4 x 4 checkerboard was. They become **long rectangles**, twice as long one way as the other.

4. Long checkerboards (half as many squares one way as the other) are turned on the bias as the 2 x 4 and 4 x 8 sizes were. They become **squares**.

5. "Fat rectangle" checkerboards are turned on the bias as the 4 x 6 checkerboard was. They become **fat rectangles**, usually a somewhat different size.

Review of ways to make checkerboards

As I said on page 53, there are three basic ways to cut strips and piece the panels. In all cases, you have an even number of dark and light strips and you alternate them. You usually cut cross sections from several panels and mix them up to make several checkerboards.

1. Use "Alpha strips"

The math usually works best if checkerboards have four squares (or double that—eight squares) in one direction. You'll see why in Chapter 7.

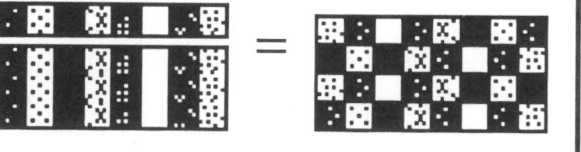

Over the years, I found myself using strips that were four units long, plus an inch to trim. Those became my standard strips and were called **Alpha strips**. Having a standard proportion for strips made it possible to work up charts for any number of blocks from any size of strips; you'll see dozens of such charts in my other books. The Alpha sizes I use most often are 4" x 17", 5" x 21", and 6" x 25".

Another size that's handy is the **double-length Alpha strip**, eight times as long as it is wide, plus an inch.

2. Use 44" strips

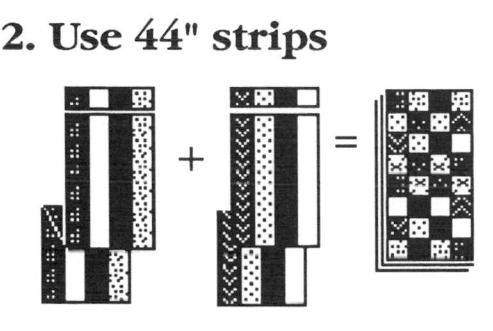

Alpha strips still are great for doing calculations, and great for projects where you remove part of the fabric for borders, then cut dozens of strips of the same fabric at a time. But working with scraps is different. It's more time consuming to find and spread out a wide variety of fabrics and cut single strips from each. It's easier to use strips a full 44" long. Sew strips into long panels, cut cross sections, mix them up, and combine them.

Only two strips left? Just sew them together, cut the pair in half, and re-assemble into a panel of four strips. (Don't do this with the checkerboard quilt on page 52; you wouldn't want only two colors in any cross sections. It works fine for the checkerboards in the rest of the book because that's not the final effect.)

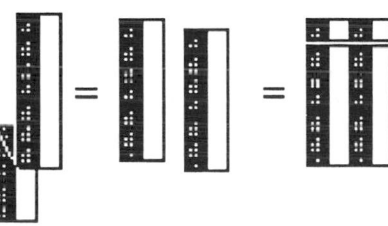

I call this method **Alpha-strip by-pass**. If you want to use blocks from any of my other books for scrap quilts, see page 173 for charts which convert Alpha-strip requirements to full-length strips.

3. Use all sizes of strips

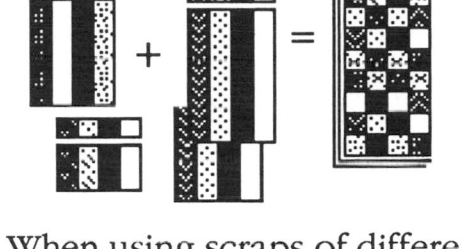

When using scraps of different lengths, be even more flexible. Make several sizes of panels. Cut cross sections, mix them up, and sew them into checkerboards. Cut more strips and make more checkerboards until you get all the cross sections you need.

To summarize:

1. When doing projects from other *Fast Patch* books which were intended for limited colors: Use Alpha strips (four times as long as they are wide, plus an inch) or double-length Alpha strips (eight times as long as they are wide, plus an inch).

2. For fastest cutting and piecing: Use full 44" strips (Alpha-strip by-pass).

3. For best use of scraps and the most variety: Use strips of any length available.

4. With any method: Use an equal number of light and dark strips, have squares alternate between light and dark, and mix up cross sections from different panels to get a random effect.

Triangle Connector blocks

Now, back to those sets of triangles you made when practicing turning different sizes of checkerboards on the bias. Trim them to a uniform size and use them for a wall hanging or baby quilt.

1. Cut plain squares. Count your triangle sets. You should have forty if you've done all your homework. Measure them. They'll be about 4-3/4" or 5" square. Cut that same number of plain blocks—half of dark fabric and half of light fabric, using as many different fabrics as you want.

2. Sew blocks together. Alternate the triangle sets with plain blocks—the light blocks against the dark sides of the triangles, and the dark blocks against the light sides. Triangles must be turned one direction in the first row, and in the other direction in the second row to get this effect.

An uneven number of blocks each way works best because then you can make a symmetrical project with uniform corners. Make a small quilt with nine rows of nine blocks or eleven rows of seven blocks. Make more sets of triangles if you want a larger project.

This is a simple arrangement with all kinds of creative possibilities. Experienced quiltmakers will recognize the **Ohio Stars** linked together. You can emphasize the stars by the way you use the colors.

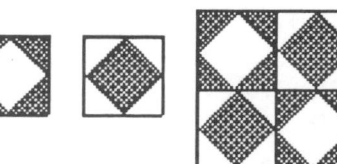

Looking at the quilt on an angle, you see diamonds within squares, or "reversing squares." See the blue and white quilt in the color pages for a superb example of a quilt which you can imitate by making blocks as shown above.

There are several other simple blocks you could link together with Triangle Connectors.

1. Connect Roman Stripe blocks. Make Roman Stripe blocks (page 46) using 2" strips. All blocks must be the same size, so you may need to trim down the triangle blocks (evenly on all sides, so lines still go exactly to the corners) or trim the striped blocks to fit.

Variation A. Use the dark squares as in basic directions, but substitute the Roman Stripe blocks for the light squares.

Variation B. Have half the blocks use two dark strips and one light, and half use two lights and one dark. Assemble them like this. You create "arrows" that can all go the same direction or can alternate as in this example.

2. Connect Nine-Patch blocks. Many different effects are possible.

Variation A. All Nine-Patch blocks have dark corners and are about equally dark. See the quilt in the covered wagon photo in the color pages for an example.

Variation B. Half the blocks use darker fabrics; they are used between dark triangles. Lighter blocks touch the light triangles.

Variation C. Again, half the blocks are darker. This time, use lighter blocks against the dark triangles, and darker blocks against the light triangles (below, altered to show how Ohio Star motifs might emerge).

Nine-Patch blocks are very easy to make with strips. For each set of six blocks start with 2" x 44" strips—a dark and a light. Sew them together. Cut off 13". Join another dark strip to the long piece, and another light strip to the shorter piece. Cut cross sections and put your blocks together.

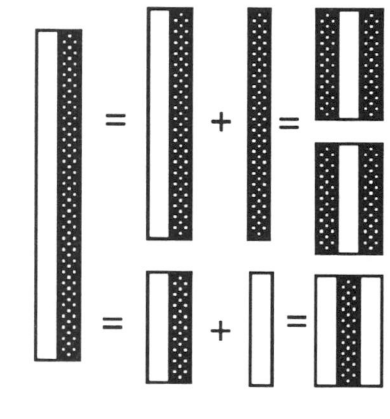

3. Use only triangle blocks. Simply put triangle sets side by side, alternating the directions so dark is against light each time. Build up as large a center panel as you want, then glorify the project with fancy borders, such as a string-pieced border from Chapter 3.

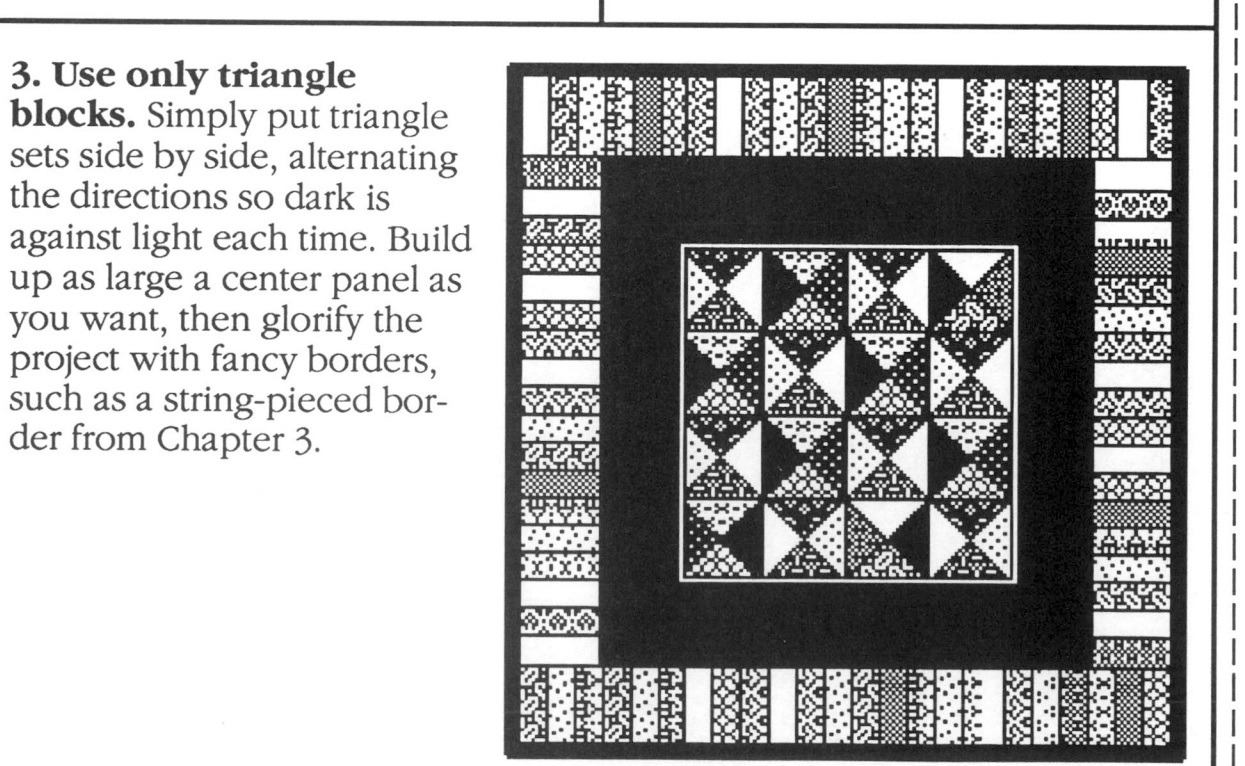

Turning a whole quilt top on the bias

A quilt top that is basically a checkerboard can be turned on the bias (before borders are added, of course). The difference can be quite dramatic. Review what I said about turning checkerboards on the bias on page 92. Here are some more rules that apply:

1. Use a quilt top with simple blocks in an alternating pattern. These can alternate between:

(a) Dark and light blocks.

(b) Pieced and plain squares, as in the Checkerboard quilt on page 52.

(c) Vertical and horizontal blocks, such as Rail Fence in Chapter 3 and Woodpile in Chapter 5.

2. Have a complete sequence of blocks along the longest side.

Generally the rule given earlier in the chapter, "have an even number," covers that because there's usually a sequence of two. But occasionally you have blocks with a sequence of four or more, such as Rail Fence made with limited colors where there are two different blocks, each turned in a different direction. (See the very first color plate in this book.) You must have multiples of four blocks on the longer sides in that case, and an even number of blocks on the ends. This rule probably won't apply to a scrap version of Rail Fence, but if you are counting on a predictable sequence in your colors, it might. Contact me for special information.

3. Your first cut creates the long edge of the quilt. If you want the design to go in a certain direction in your final project, keep that in mind.

4. Draw your cutting line first and stay stitch on both sides to stabilize the bias edges. Make sure your tension is adjusted so this stitching doesn't pucker it up.

Quilts in Chapter 3 which can be turned on the bias are **Stack of Strips**, **Roman Stripes**, **Rail Fence**, and the **Checkerboard** quilt. Quilts in Chapter 5 which work well are **Woodpile** and **Irish Cabin**. The following pages give diagrams for some of them.

Turning Rail Fence or Roman Stripes on the bias

Remember, your first cut creates the long edge of the quilt. The zigzag design is more restful going across the quilt, so cut "across the fence." The second cut can be anywhere in the area marked on the third stage.
Watch where the little circle ends up.

Roman Stripes has a somewhat different effect. As with the Rail Fence example, there are eight rows of six blocks to start with.

Here's what the Checkerboard quilt would look like if you started with six rows of four blocks:

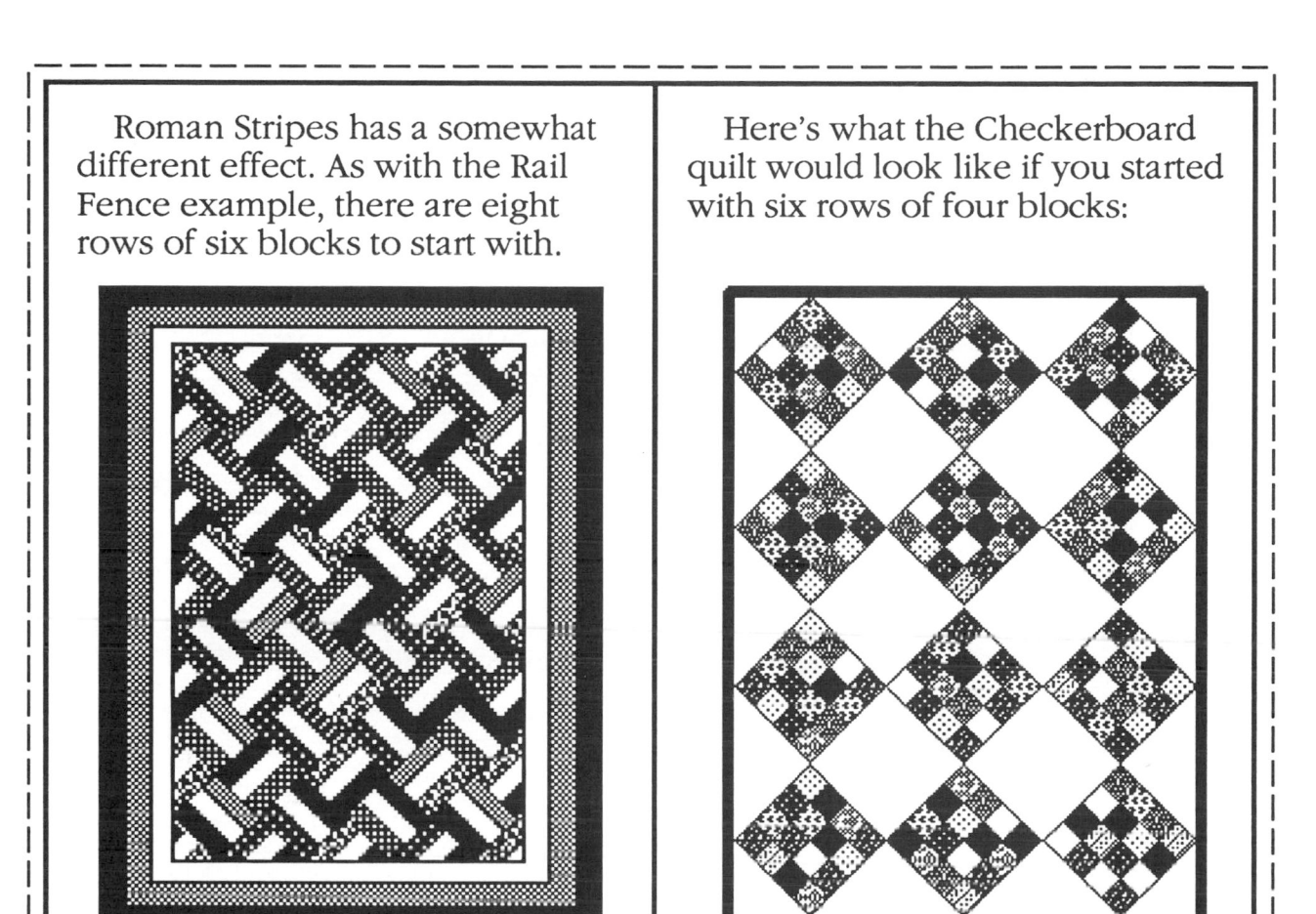

Turning Woodpile or Irish Cabin on the bias

1. Use only the Straight Furrows layout (shown in the diagram on page 100). If you absolutely insist on Barn Raising, see the Two-for-One-Split later in the chapter.

2. Plan ahead. Copy the diagram on page 100, cut off a section the size of your quilt, and try it with scissors and Scotch tape first.

3. One cut will start at a corner, the other in the middle of the block—the dark area on Irish Cabin. The cut you make first

depends on which way you want the design to go, vertically or horizontally.

In the first example, on page 101, the first cut is made through the dark area in the center of the blocks because we want the design to run vertically, with dark along the sides.

In the next example, on page 102, the first cut is made across the line of the design because we want the design to be horizontal.

Woodpile cutapart diagram

Cut off a section to represent the quilt you want to make. Use scissors and scotchtape to turn it on the bias. This can be used for Irish Cabin also.

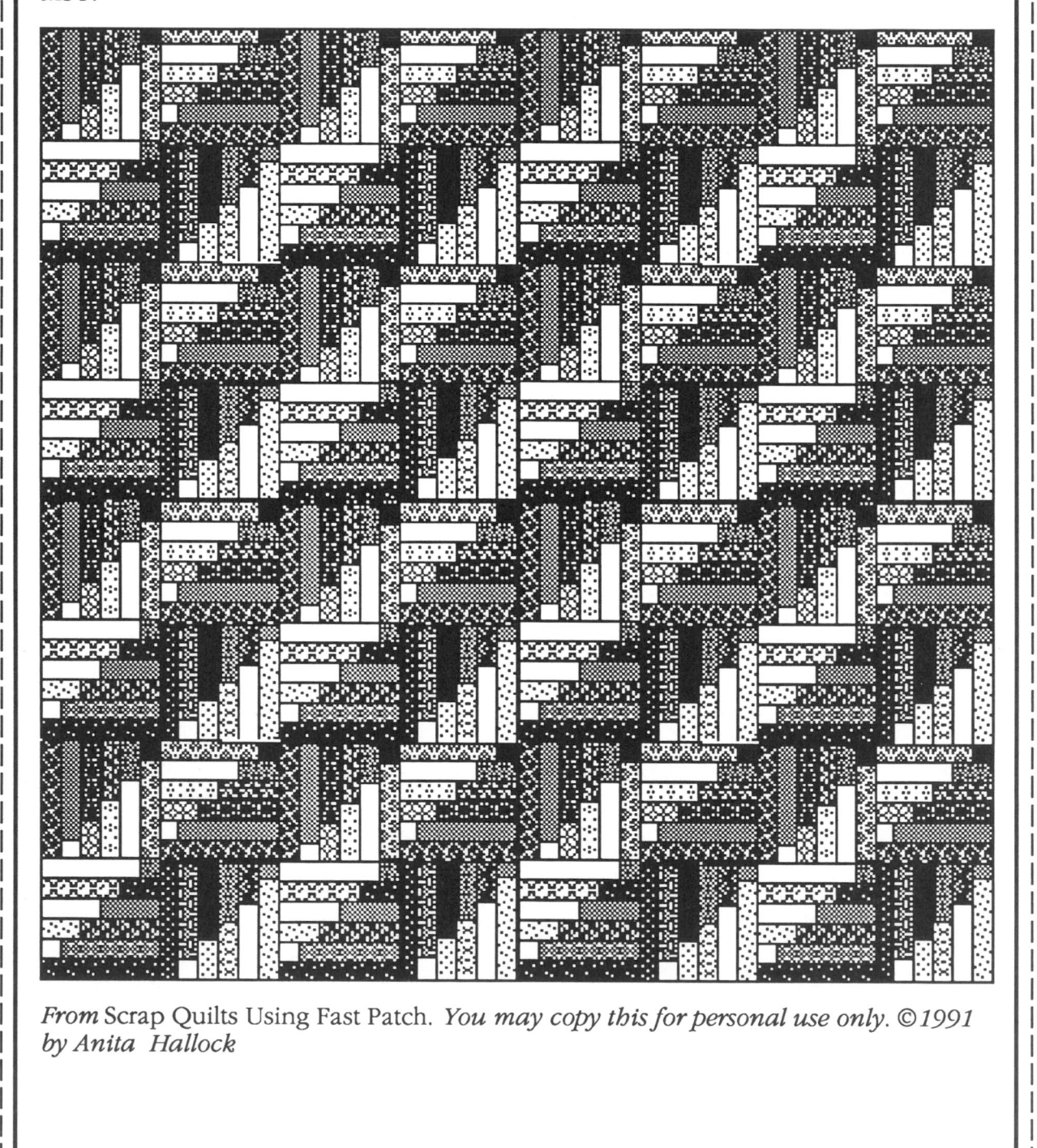

From Scrap Quilts Using Fast Patch. *You may copy this for personal use only. ©1991 by Anita Hallock*

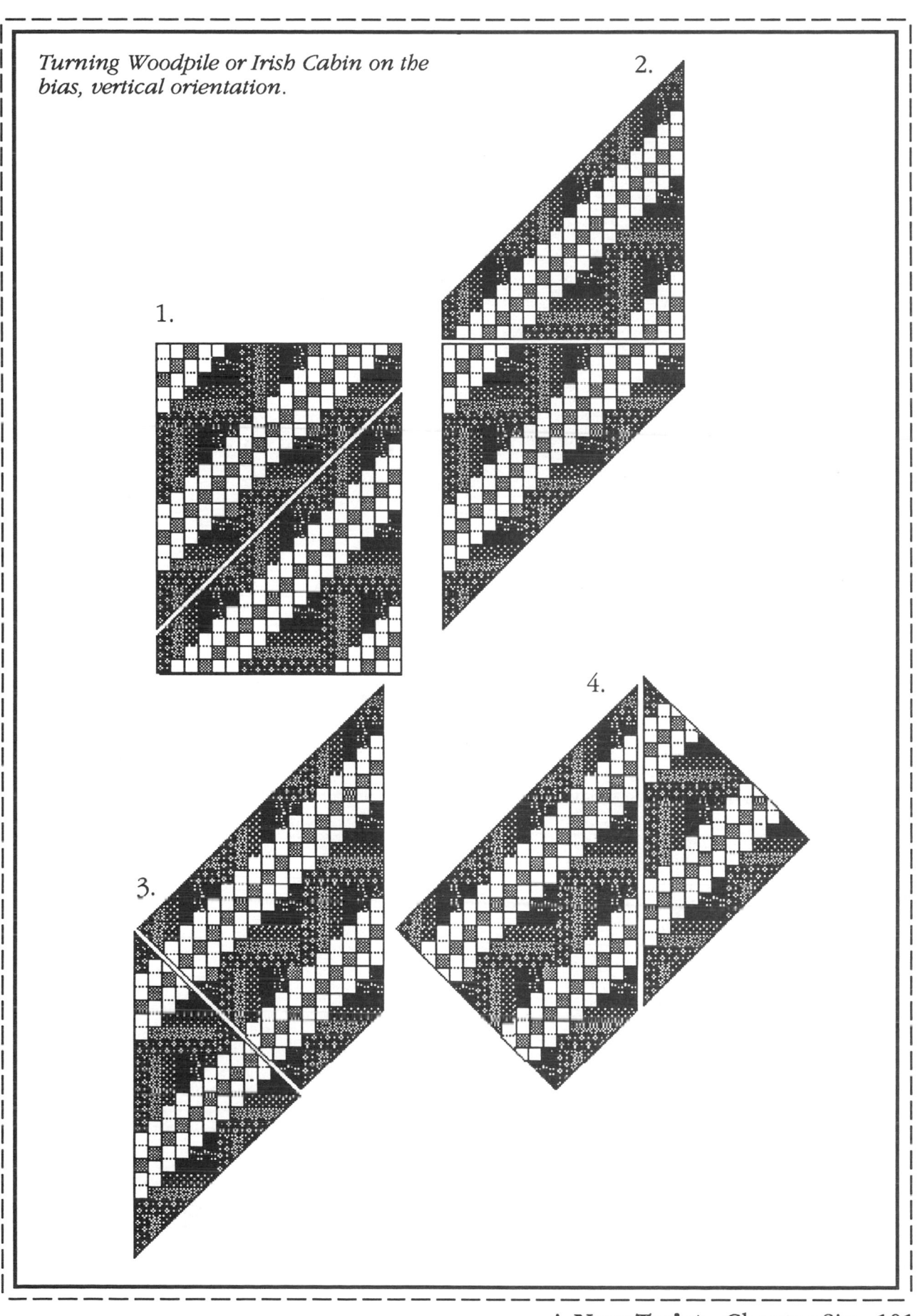

Turning Woodpile or Irish Cabin on the bias, vertical orientation.

1.

2.

3.

4.

Turning Woodpile or Irish Cabin on the bias, horizontal orientation.

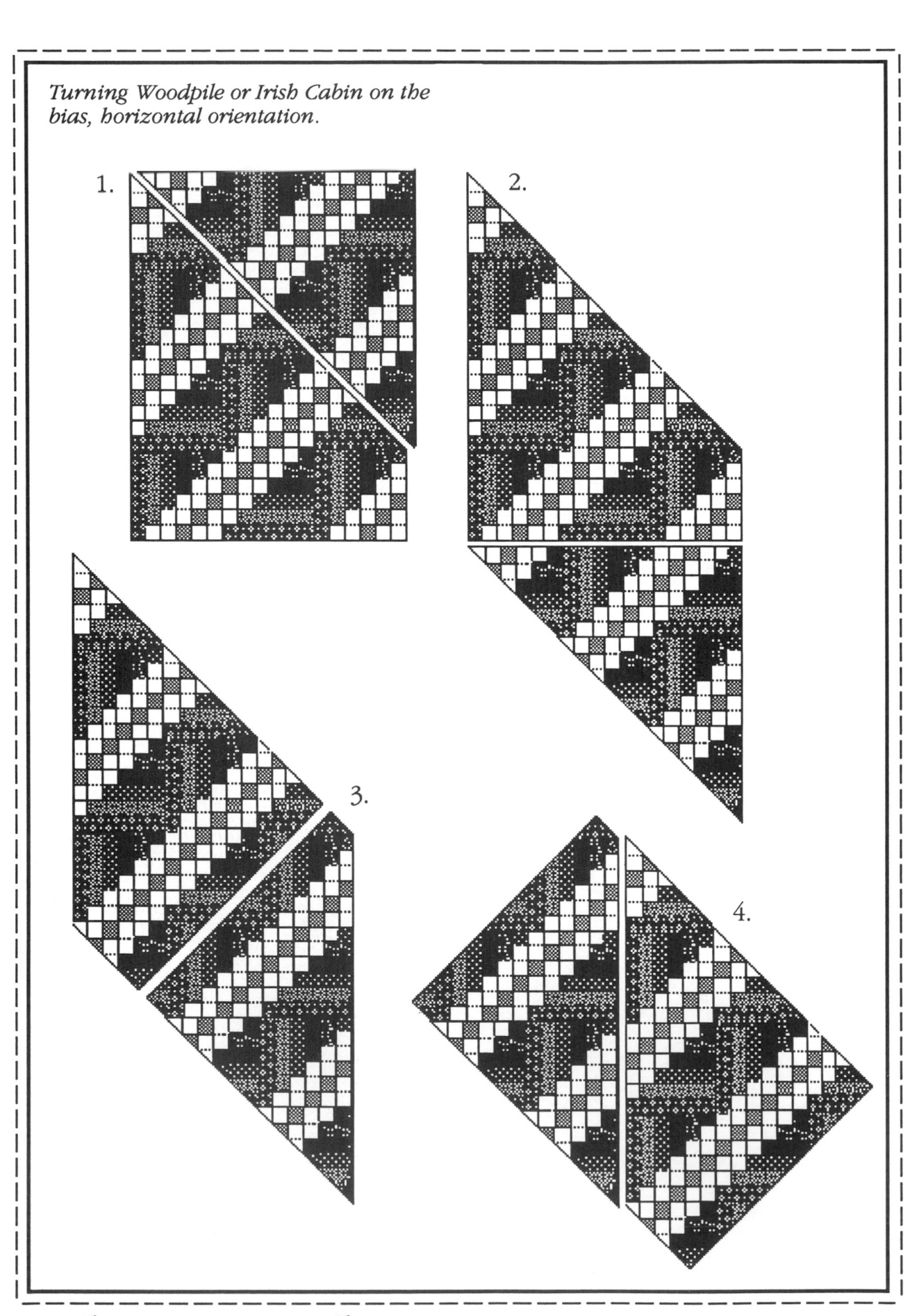

Craftsmanship tips:

1. Draw the cutting lines first. Then stay stitch on each side of the line before cutting.

2. If your cutting mat isn't large enough, slide it along under your work as you cut.

Is it worth the effort? Look in the color pages at the gorgeous Irish Cabin quilt that seven ladies took two years making. If you don't have two years and six helpers, use your imagination, do your homework, and save yourself a lot of time.

Two-for-One-Split

Have you ever made a project for someone, then liked it so much you couldn't part with it? Here's a way to "have your quilt and give it away too." Make two square quilts that are much alike. They're easy to make and look fantastic. (This project will give your brain a rest too, if all those strange ideas in the last few pages are getting you down.)

1. Make 100 Woodpile blocks (or Irish Cabin, in case you're really ambitious). See the chart on page 83 or directions on the Impossible Quilt, page 104 for specifications.

2. Assemble blocks into four 5 x 5 arrangements, twenty-five blocks each.

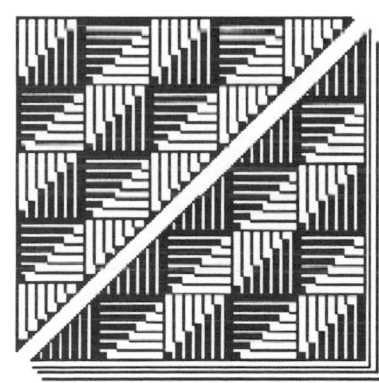

3. Cut each diagonally through the center.

Use the left triangle in each set for one quilt, and the right triangle for the other quilt.

4. Assemble triangle sections like this.

One quilt will have this dark/ light pattern, and the other will have darks and lights in the opposite position. They'll be about 64" square before borders.

Impossible Quilt

Has your brain had a rest? I hope you are ready for some more strange ideas. Here's how you can turn the Two-for-One-Split into just one quilt that is reversible. If you hate binding edges, this is the project for you because there are no edges to bind. Impossible? What if the design just continues around the other side of the quilt? Since it's hard to visualize this, I've given you a paper version of this quilt to practice on. Read through the instructions, then try it with paper, and decide whether you would like to try it with fabric. You will need 100 Woodpile blocks for this quilt.

Fabric needed:

Dark fabric: Twenty fat quarters plus ten strips 4-1/2" x 22"

Light fabric: Twenty fat quarters

Batting: a piece about 66" square.

1. Make 100 blocks.

2. Sew blocks together.
Sew ten rows of ten blocks each in a Barn Raising pattern.

3. Turn the quilt corners back.
Lay the quilt, wrong side up, on the floor. Fold back all four corners. They meet in the center and you have a reversible quilt!

4. Close the project up part way.
Lay the batting inside now and hand stitch up all four seams, but do as much as you can on the sewing machine first.

(a) Sew the two end seams. Fold quilt in half, right sides together, dividing it into two long rectangles. (Try this with your paper diagrams; bring Corner A and Corner D together and tape the end. Bring Corners C and F together and tape that end, too.) Match seams and strips carefully; sew up the ends.

(b) Sew as much as you can on the other two seams. Use your paper diagram to remind yourself where to sew. Start sewing the edges together at Point B and proceed toward the center; leave the final 10" open for turning. Start at Point E and do the same thing.

5. Turn the project and press it flat.
Along the edge, press midway between the dark and the light areas; you'll get a neat scallop effect on each side.

6. Cut batting.
Measure the flattened-out quilt; it will be about 63" square. Cut batting that size. Stuff batting inside and spread it evenly into all corners. Baste or pin thoroughly with safety pins along the edges of all the dark areas. Try to line up the design on the top with that on the bottom.

7. Stitch up the opening.

8. Quilt or tie the project.
If machine quilting, stitch through the dark areas with dark transparent thread (light thread on the bobbin). Then turn the quilt over and stitch the darks, which are in an opposite position there.

Can you try this idea with other sizes of projects? Yes. If you use thirty-six blocks (six rows of six), the final project will be 38" square; sixty-four blocks (eight rows of eight) will make a project 51" square; and 144 blocks (twelve rows of twelve) would make a project 76" square.

To be honest, a quilt is prettier with borders and binding. This project requires enough blocks for two quilts but makes only one; however, it uses a lot of scraps. Also it baffles people, and more importantly, you didn't have to bind the edges.

7. *Squares and Triangles*

In the last chapter you read how ready-made clusters of triangles could be cut from checkerboards turned on the bias. This chapter, like the rest of this book, will also feature triangles, but from now on they'll come in narrow strips. A 4 x 6 checkerboard turned on the bias makes six strips.

They are wonderful because you can sew them to straight strips to mass-produce chains with both squares and triangles. That opens up a whole new world for strip-piecing. You may have already used my earlier book, *Fast Patch:*

A Treasury of Strip Quilt Projects, which shows hundreds of blocks that can be made. (Many of those blocks can be made with scraps, by the way—see suggestions on page 176.)

This is the only chapter in this book with squares and triangles combined. Our feature block is the wonderful two-tone block, the Nifty Nine-Patch, which can be used in all the arrangements shown in Chapter 4.

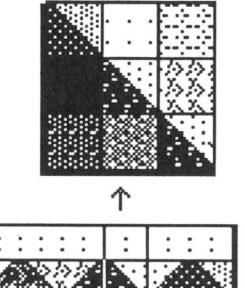

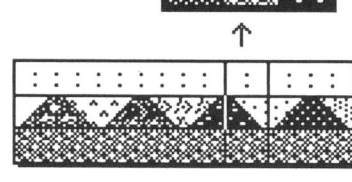

Alpha and Beta strips

When planning blocks with triangles and squares it's handy to have some standard sizes of strips. That way you can readily convert to larger or smaller blocks by substituting strips of a different size but the same proportion. I call these standard strip sizes "Alpha" and "Beta" strips.

Alpha strips become strips of triangles

In Chapter 3 I introduced Alpha strips, rather wide strips that were made into the most useful sizes of checkerboards. They were four times as long as they are wide (plus an inch for trimming). In Chapter 6 you experimented some more with Alpha strips and saw how the checkerboards could be turned on the bias to make triangle sets. Now Alpha strips are transformed into strips of triangles like these.

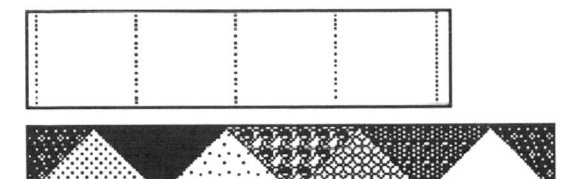

Beta strips become squares

You need a new size of strips to make the squares. They have to be exactly the same size as the strips of triangles—which happens to be eight times as long as they are wide. These are **Beta strips.** (Beta means second, and they are cut in the second cutting session.)

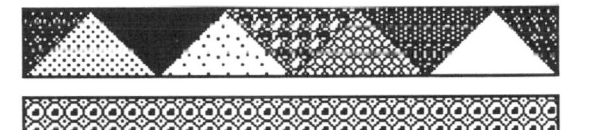

You added an inch for good measure when making Alpha strips, but don't do that with Beta strips. The triangle strips are on the bias and must be sewn to something that is just the right size so they aren't stretched or eased, causing puckers in your final blocks.

Mark the Beta strips for more accuracy

Study the strip of triangles. One side has three dark triangle points, which mark the four divisions of the strip. If careful workmanship is important, mark the Beta strips in fourths too:

(a) Fold once.

(b) Fold a second time (it's more accurate to fold each layer separately).

(c) Press a crease or cut notches along one side.

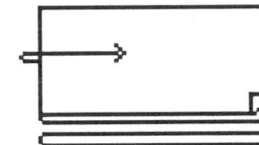

Align these marks with the points of the triangles to ease the bias evenly.

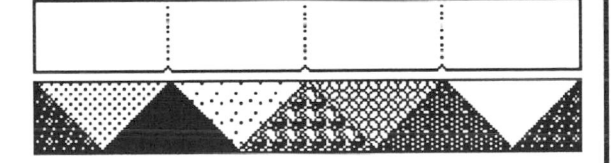

The other side of the strip of triangles has four points of light triangles. A Beta strip sewn to that side would have to be marked off in eighths for those points to line up with a mark. (Or you could mark the centers of the triangles as is done in Chapter 8.)

You'll see what I mean when you try your first project. If you handle strips carefully and pin them in place, you might find that you don't need to mark the Beta strips at all.

By the way, you might find your darks and lights in the opposite position, which is fine.

Clip off the masses of seams

There will be masses of seam allowances built up at the points of some triangles. When possible, clip them off before joining strips of triangles to each other or to Beta strips. Otherwise, your sewing line might be crooked—the machine sews around the mass rather than stitching in a straight line over it. Do some more clipping after cutting the final chains.

The lost points

When you sew strips of triangles to each other or to straight strips, the points are lost. These blunt points are not only inevitable, they're necessary to give a seam allowance for the next cut and seam. You get the points back later, so don't worry. Do keep the points equally blunt, about 5/8" wide.

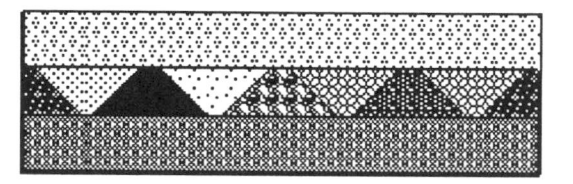

Where there is a blunt point, you will make a cut later. The result will be a chain of ready-made triangles and squares complete with seam allowances.

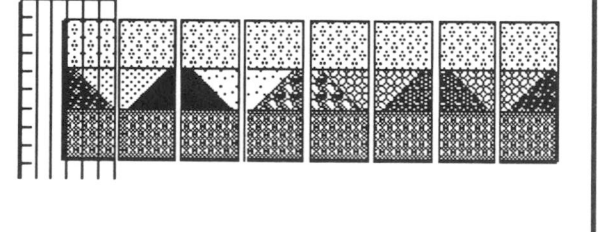

Sizes of Alpha and Beta strips and blocks

I won't give you absolute sizes for Beta strips. Your own personal size depends on whether your seams are really 1/4" or are actually 5/16" or 3/8". I could be hard-nosed and say everyone must make seams exactly 1/4", but we're not engineers, we're sewing for fun. It doesn't matter exactly how large your blocks turn out as long as everything fits together. Don't feel guilty about your strip size; just make sure your Beta strips are the exact same size as your strips of triangles. Some possible sizes are on the following chart.

Alpha strips (4 times as long as wide, plus 1")	Beta strips (8 times as long as wide, match triangle strips)	Finished size of square or triangle set	Size of blocks in this chapter
4" x 17"	**2-1/2" x 20"** or 2-3/8" x 19"* or 2-1/4" x 18"	**2"(scant)** or 1-7/8"* or 1-3/4"	**5-3/4"** 5-5/8"* 5-1/4"
5" x 21"	**3-1/4" x 26"** or 3-1/8" x 25"* or 3" x 24"	**2-3/4"** or 2-5/8"* or 2-3/8	**8-1/4"** 7-3/4"* 7-1/4"
6" x 25" (see note below)	**3-7/8" x 31"** or 3-3/4" x 30"*	**3-3/8"** or 3-1/8"* or 3-5/8" x 29"	**10"** 9-3/8"* or 3" 9"

*The size in **bold print** is the theoretical size. The size with the asterisk (*) is the more common size. The last size given is less common, but if that's your size, that's okay. Remember, if you use a different sewing machine for some of your sewing, the size may change because you might unconsciously line up your seams with the edge of the presser foot.*

Beta width is often used for sashing and borders, by the way; and **Beta-sized squares** might be used as switchers.

"Skimpy six-inch"

When using Alpha strips 6" x 25", there's another Beta strip problem if you work with 44" strips: A Beta strip is about 31" long if you use 1/4" seams, so leftovers are only 13" long, not enough for half strips. So use skimpy strips—Alpha strips 5-3/4" x 24". Mark that width on your ruler with masking tape to speed up your cutting and to remind you to cut cross sections the same width. Beta strips should be 28" or 29" long, and you can cut one full and one half-strip each time. Final blocks should be about 9" square.

Nifty Nine-Patch

You'll see many Nifty Nine-Patch quilts in the color pages because I wrote a small book on this block several years ago and people have generously shared quilts they made. I called the block "Mock Log Cabin" (as Mary Ellen Hopkins did in *The It's Okay If You Sit On My Quilt Book*). People tended to confuse that name with regular Log Cabin, so I made up a new name. "Nifty Nine-Patch" fits because blocks are so easy to make and so versatile.

Here's how the block is made:

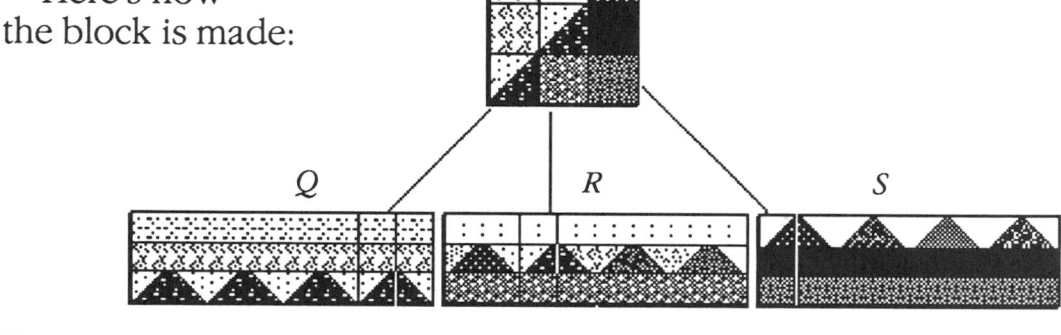

Three panels are used to make each set of eight blocks. Each panel has one strip of triangles and two Beta strips. **Q Panels** have two light Beta strips sewn to the light triangles. **R Panels** have a light strip sewn to the light side and a dark strip sewn to the dark side. **S Panels** have two darks sewn to the dark triangles. As you choose the strips to sew on, take care not to use a fabric that is already used in one of the triangles.

Because strips of triangles are used three at a time, the math works out best with 4 x 6 checkerboards. Each uses three dark and three light Alpha strips and yields six strips of triangles, enough for two sets of blocks.

Remember how a 4 x 6 checkerboard is turned on the bias? (Review Chapter 6 if necessary.)

Caution: *Be sure to cut strips the long way so my calculations will work out right.*

Using only 4 x 6 checkerboards gives multiples of sixteen blocks, but that might not be what you need. You'll also use 4 x 4 or other sizes of checkerboards. See Chapter 6 to review how to turn them on the bias.

Here are some general rules about strips used for Nifty Nine-Patch:

1. Cut half of all strips from dark fabric, and half from light. Keep a strong contrast in the Alpha strips so triangles are sharply defined. Use some medium-dark or medium-light fabrics for the Beta strips.

2. The more fabrics, the better. Use scraps for small projects; for larger projects, you can use fat quarters or other yardage. The same fabrics can be used in the Alpha and Beta strips if you're making lots of blocks. To use only a few fabrics, see the six-color version on page 123.

3. You need twice as many Beta strips as Alpha strips.

4. You can use the "Alpha-strip by-pass." See pages 53 and 93.

5. You can use half-length Beta strips. Your goal is to use up scraps on hand, not create more. If you cut Beta strips from 44" strips you might have leftover pieces that can be used for half-length strips. Use them at the outer position at a place where you will cut later:

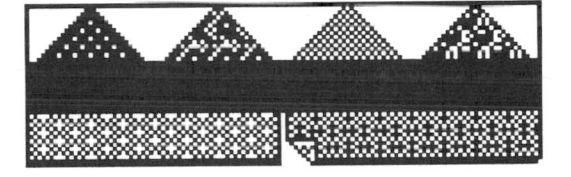

Or cut the strip of triangles in two also, and use short strips in both of the other positions:

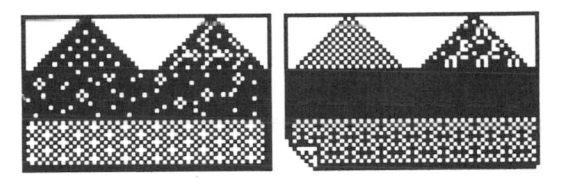

In fact, if you're making only a few blocks, you can make 2 x 4 checkerboards and use **only** half-length Beta strips just to work more fabrics into the project.

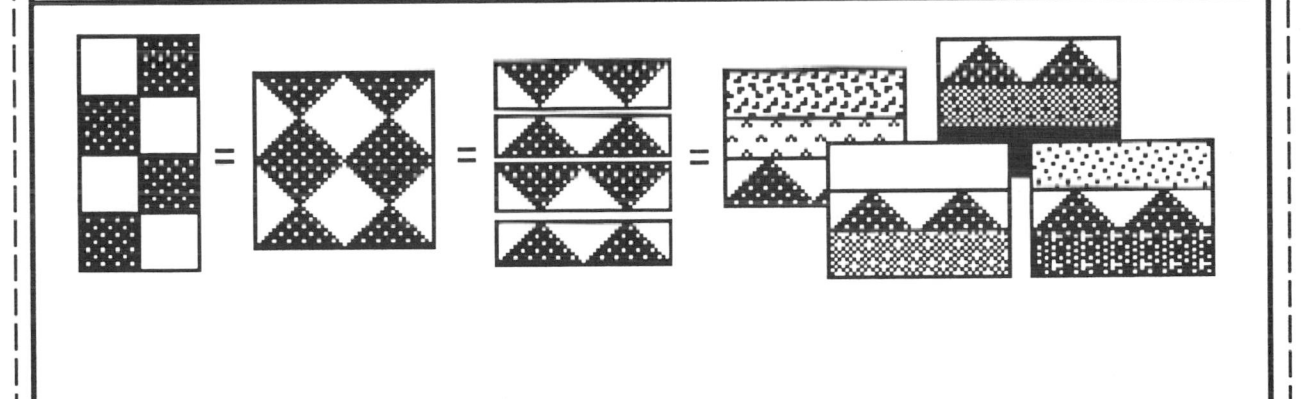

Nifty Nine-Patch wall hanging

This 40" square wall hanging uses sixteen medium blocks (7-1/2" to 8"). It is fairly hard to get a good mix of fabrics with only sixteen blocks, so split some of the Beta strips. Also have switchers handy to substitute during the final assembly.

Fabric needed:

Scraps: See Steps 1 and 4 below

Switchers: Beta-sized squares (3-1/4" sq., or your measurement)

Borders: 1/4 yd. to 2/3 yd.

Batting: 42" sq.

Backing: 1-1/4 yds.

Binding: 5 yds.

1. Cut Alpha strips, three dark and three light strips, 5" x 21", from scraps.

2. Make a 4 x 6 checkerboard.

3. Turn the checkerboard on the bias. Cut six strips of triangles.

4. Cut Beta strips. Measure the triangle strips. (They'll be about 3-1/4" x 26" but use your measurement.) Cut six dark and six light strips. These must all be from different fabrics. Use more scraps and make half strips of some for even more variety.

5. Make six panels, two Q, two R, and two S panels. Clip off masses of seam allowances. Remember, you lose the points of the triangles temporarily but get them back later.

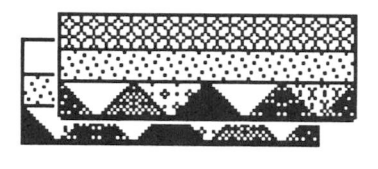

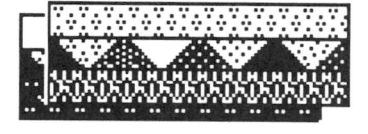

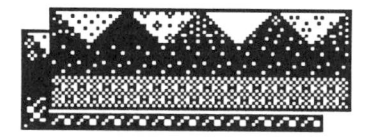

6. Cut cross sections. Mix up colors and fabrics and sort into six stacks, based on the slant of the triangles and the position of lights and darks.

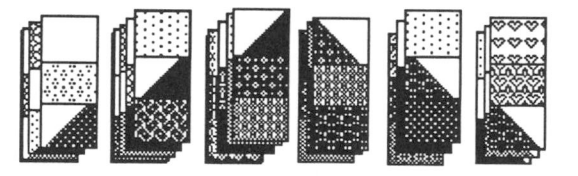

7. Assemble blocks. Take care to line up seams carefully and keep straight diagonal lines.

8. Arrange blocks as shown in artwork or color pages, or use any other 16-block arrangement in Chapter 4. Sew blocks into rows of four, then combine rows to make quilt top.

9. Add borders. Cut four 3" strips and sew in place. (Or use any other borders you prefer.)

10. Complete the project. Cut batting and backing to fit. Arrange layers, quilt or tie, and bind with your favorite methods. See Chapter 1 for ideas.

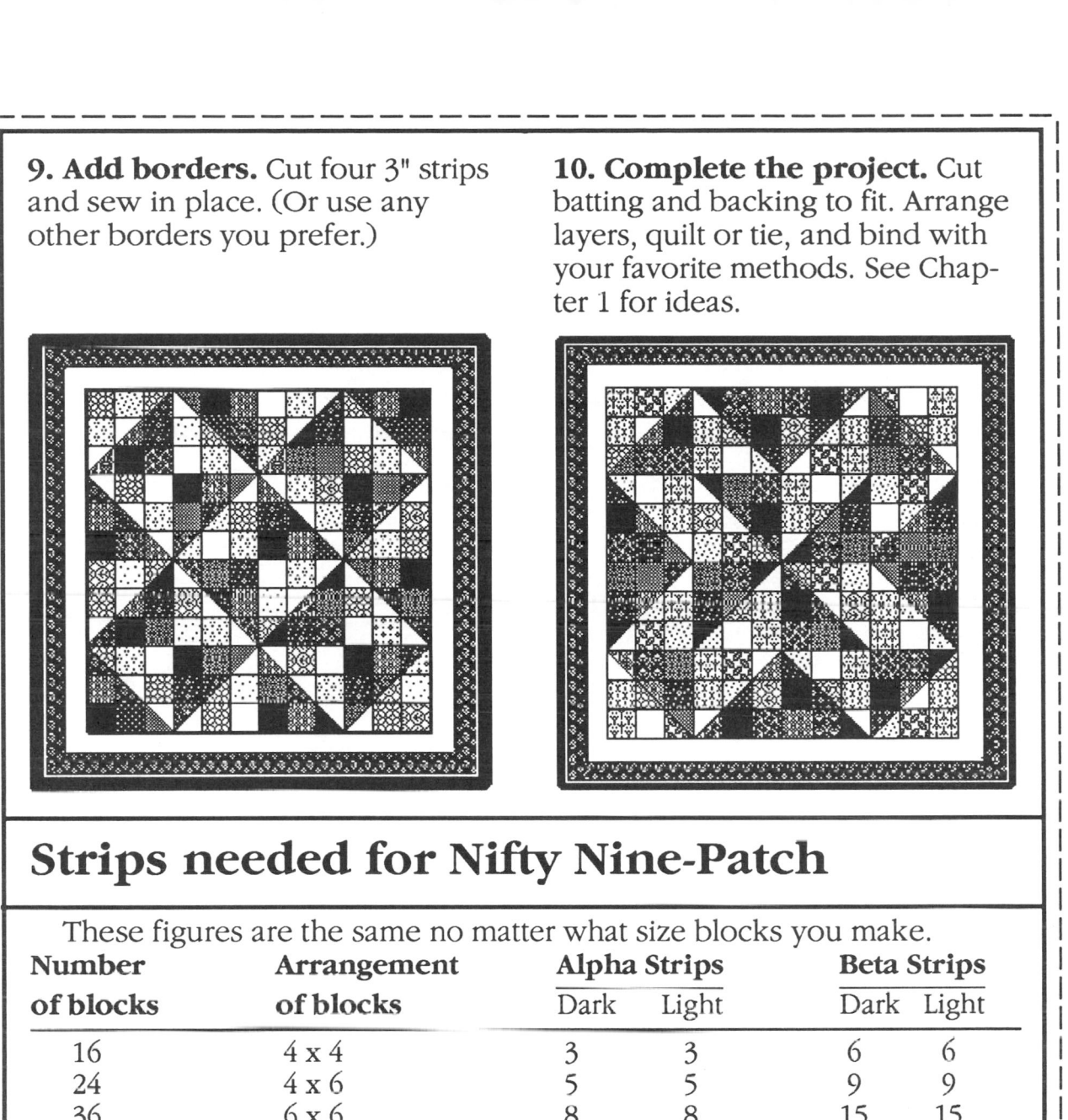

Strips needed for Nifty Nine-Patch

These figures are the same no matter what size blocks you make.

Number of blocks	Arrangement of blocks	Alpha Strips		Beta Strips	
		Dark	Light	Dark	Light
16	4 x 4	3	3	6	6
24	4 x 6	5	5	9	9
36	6 x 6	8	8	15	15
48	6 x 8	9	9	18	18
64	8 x 8	12	12	24	24
80	8 x 10	15	15	30	30
96	8 x 12	18	18	36	36
100	10 x 10	20	20	39	39
120	10 x 12	23	23	45	45
140	10 x 14	27	27	54	54
144	12 x 12	27	27	54	54
168	12 x 14	32	32	63	63
196	14 x 14	38	38	75	75
224	14 x 16	42	42	84	84
256	16 x 16	48	48	96	96

If you will use only scraps and don't care what size the project turns out, this chart may be all you need. To plan yardage, see later charts.

Nifty Nine-Patch double bed quilt

This double-bed quilt, about 80" x 100", uses eighty large blocks.

Fabric needed:

Scraps: See Steps 1 and 4 below

Switchers: Beta-sized squares (3-7/8" sq., or your measurement)

Borders: 3/4 yd. to 1-1/3 yd.

Batting: 86" x 102"

Backing: 6 yds. (8-1/3 yds. if you have very wide borders)

Binding: 11 or 12 yds.

1. Cut Alpha strips. See "Skimpy six-inch" note on page 109.

   If scraps: Cut fifteen dark and fifteen light strips, 5-3/4" x 24".

   If 44" strips: Cut nine dark and nine light, 5-3/4" x 44", all different. Leave them full length and use the Alpha-strip by-pass (page 93).

If buying yardage: 3/8 yd. pieces work best for this size of block. Buy twelve dark fabrics and twelve light fabrics, all different (this gives you enough for your Beta strips too). Cut nine dark and nine light strips 5-3/4" x 44". (Cut two from the same fabrics in most cases to leave large pieces for the Beta strips later.) Leave strips full length and use the Alpha-strip by-pass (page 93).

2. Make checkerboards. Sew strips together into panels of four strips. Cut 5-3/4" cross sections and mix up sections from different panels to get a nice variety. Make five 4 x 6 checkerboards.

3. Turn checkerboards on the bias. Cut strips of triangles and clip off the thick masses of seam allowances you find at some points.

4. Make Beta strips. Measure strips of triangles to find your Beta strip size (will be about 3-1/2" x 28").

If using scraps: Cut **thirty dark** and **thirty light** strips. Some can be medium fabrics.

If you want to use 44" strips: Use twenty light and twenty dark (Beta width). Cut each into one Beta strip and one half strip.

If you purchased 3/8-yard pieces: Cut each into three strips (Beta width). Divide each strip into one Beta strip and one half strip.

5. Make Q, R, and S panels. You'll need thirty altogether, ten of each type. (Some may be half-panels.) Clip off thick masses of seams.

6. Cut cross sections. Mix up chains and sort into six stacks.

7. Make blocks.

8. Assemble quilt top. Use the Barn Raising arrangement shown here, or get ideas from the color pages or from Chapter 4. (You can adapt 100-block projects by leaving off outer blocks, or omitting center blocks and moving sides in.)

9. Add borders. Add whatever combinations of fabrics and border widths you desire. Remember the quilt will be smaller after quilting.

10. Make backing. Measure the project. If piecing backing from 44" fabrics, use No. 5 on page 13 if quilt is less than 86" wide, No. 6 if it is wider.

11. Quilt or tie and bind with your favorite method. See Chapter 1 for ideas.

Nifty Nine-Patch Masterpiece quilt

See the color pages for a beautiful version of the Nifty Nine-Patch made by Jayne Hanich of Missoula, MT. That was an ambitious project since she used tiny blocks and did lots of hand quilting. I'll give directions for that project on pages 118-120. First, I'll give a simplified version.

Simplified version

The wide border has been left off this project, so you'll have no elaborate quilting to do, and the blocks aren't as small. The project will be about 80" square.

Fabric needed:

Scraps (can substitute 44" strips or fat quarters): See Steps 1 and 4 below

Dark borders: 1-1/2 yds. (2-1/4 yds. if you want to avoid piecing and cut some strips for blocks)

Switchers: Beta-sized squares (about 2-2/3" sq.)

Light borders: 1 yd. (2 yds. x 22" if you want to avoid piecing)

Batting: 83" sq.

Backing: 4-2/3 yds.

Binding: 9 to 10 yds.

1. Cut Alpha strips:

If using scraps: Cut **twelve dark strips** and **twelve light**, 4" x 17". Include one strip from each fabric selected for borders if you wish.

If using 44" strips: Cut **five light** and **five dark** strips 4" wide. Leave them full length and use the Alpha-strip by-pass method (page 93).

If using fat quarters: This is the quickest and most convenient. The Small Blocks chart on page 120 says to get six fat quarters of light and six of dark (which gives you enough for the Beta strips too). But buy enough for the scrap borders too while you're at the store—a total of **ten light** and **ten dark**. Stack with lights and darks facing each other and cut one 4" x 22" stack from each arrangement. Use these for the Alpha-strip by-

pass method. Leave the fabric arrangements intact, if possible, for Step 4.

2. Make four 4 x 6 checkerboards. Use any of the techniques on pages 92 or 93 .

3. Turn on the bias. Cut strips of triangles and clip off masses of seam allowances from some points.

4. Cut Beta strips and strips for the string borders. Measure strips of triangles to find your Beta size (about 2-1/2" x 20") and cut **twenty-four dark** and **twenty-four light**. It's efficient to cut strips for the pieced borders at the same time because they can be the same width and and use the same fabrics. You won't need quite as many strips for the borders, and you can make them a bit narrower if that fits your fabric better. (Be careful not to mix the border strips with the Beta strips if they aren't the same size.)

Scraps work nicely and give a big assortment but take more time to cut.

If using 44" strips: Use **twenty-one dark** and **twenty-one light** strips, every strip different, if possible. Cut all Beta width, then cut one Beta-length strip from each fabric, two from some. Use the leftovers for the borders.

If using fat quarters: Remnants from Step 1 should be 13" to 14" wide and 22" long. First cut two stacks of Beta strips from each. Then cut one or two more stacks from each for the string borders, leaving them the full 22" long.

5. Make Q, R, and S panels, eight of each type, a total of twenty-four.

Q   R   S

6. Cut apart chains. Mix up colors, then sort them into six stacks according to dark/light pattern and slant of triangles.

7. Make sixty-four blocks. You will have no leftover chains this time. If you ruin or misplace some, make a 2 x 4 checkerboard and make some spare parts.

8. Arrange blocks into eight rows of eight. Use the arrangement shown, or any 64-block arrangement in Chapter 4. Sew blocks together and press. The project should be about 44" square now.

9. Add plain borders. You can cut borders for Steps 9 and 11 at the same time.

(a) Cut 4" strips lengthwise from dark fabric. Sew to project, lapping corners.

(b) Cut all light border fabric into 2-1/2" strips. Sew in place.

10. Add string borders. See page 40 in Chapter 3. The artwork shows borders about 7" wide, but yours can be a different width to fit the size of your panels better. Sew enough sections together to fit the top and bottom of the quilt. Pin in place, adjusting so strips come out even, and sew. Repeat the process for the sides.

11. Add outer borders, a narrow light one first, then a wide darker one (or vary this to fit your fabric).

12. Finish the project. Make backing (No. 2 or 3 on page 13). Quilt and bind with your favorite method. See Chapter 1.

Masterpiece quilt, Jayne's version

The size of Jayne Hanich's quilt in the color pages is about the same as the simplified version, but blocks are tiny (about 3-3/4") so you'll need to do some precise work to get everything to line up. There is also a wide border for hand quilting. This is an advanced project, so directions will be brief.

Fabric needed:

Scraps (or 44" strips): See Steps 1 and 4 on page 119

Switchers: Beta width squares (about 1-3/4" sq.)

1-3/4" strips for border

Dark borders: 1 yd. (6" of it can be used for Alpha or Beta strips)

Light borders: 3-1/2 yds.

Batting: 85" sq.

Backing: 4-2/3 yds.

Binding: 9 or 10 yds.

Left

The large quilt, "Purple Mountains' Majesty," was made by Lorna Pack of Bloomfield Hills, Michigan, and machine quilted with the one-step method described in Chapter 1. The 80 large Nifty Nine-Patch blocks were made from 6" wide Alpha strips. This attractive quilt measures 83" x 103". The Flying Geese wall hanging project is in Chapter 9. Made by Anita Hallock. Photographed at the Lane County Historical Museum

Below, left

This Nifty Nine-Patch uses 48 blocks. It was machine quilted with the one-step technique in long chains going across the quilt. This was the project which prompted the rule that chains should be machine basted together first to match up seams. This wasn't basted first, and it was hard to keep points accurate and seams lined up while sewing directly to the puffy batting.

Overleaf

Here are triangle connectors used with simple Nine-Patch blocks. The author spotted this beautiful quilt at the Presbyterian Ladies' quilt show in Reedsport, Oregon. Pat Gruenhagen of Reedsport, Oregon, spent months piecing and hand-quilting this beauty, which she calls "Boot Camp." It gave her "lots of prayer time" and took her mind off her anxiety over her firstborn son's leaving for the Marines. If your kids are still home and you don't get much time to sew, you can make the blocks with shortcuts described in Chapter 6 and the pieced borders with techniques in Chapter 3. Photographed at the Lane County Historical Museum. Hanging in the background is a partly made king size Rail Fence quilt, shown turned on the bias in another color plate.

Scrap Quilts

Above

This gorgeous hand-quilted wall hanging has 64 blocks in an imaginative arrangement. Who would have thought of expanding the quilt with sashing? The maker, quilting teacher Diane Leighton of Yuba City, Calif., didn't feel limited by textbook arrangements; she designed her own and so can you. These Nifty-Nine Patch blocks are 6" square and the total size is 51" square. Photographed at the Lane County Historical Museum..

Above
This 48-block wall hanging is made from Garden Path blocks, a variation of the Nifty-Nine Patch. See if you can spot the individual blocks, then turn to page 128 to see if you are correct. Blocks can be arranged much like Drunkard's Path. Pieced by Anita Hallock and hand quilted by Dorsy Hancock.

Scrap Quilts

Before starting, divide the light yardage into lengthwise pieces 22" wide. Remove a piece 22" x 36" to use for strips in Steps 1 and 4. The rest will be used for narrow and wide borders.

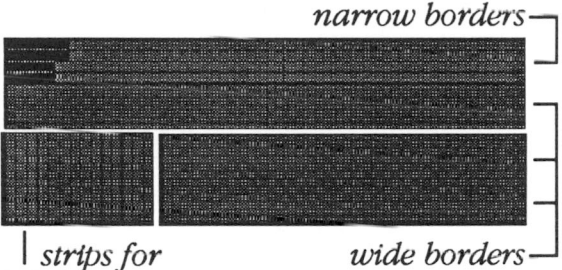

narrow borders

strips for Steps 1 and 4　　　*wide borders*

Light yardage

1. Cut Alpha strips:

If using scraps: Cut **six dark** and **six light**, 3" x 26". (These are double-length strips—easier to work with. You could use twelve dark and twelve light, 3" x 13" for greater variety.) Use a strip from the dark border fabric, and some of the 36" piece of white fabric.

If using 44" strips: Cut **four light** and **four dark** strips 3" wide. (For one strip, substitute two 3" x 22" strips cut from the white yardage.)

2. Make four 4 x 6 checkerboards. Turn on the bias.

3. Cut Beta strips and strips for string borders. Cut **twenty-four dark** and **twenty-four light** Beta strips (will be about 1-3/4" x 14"). Use a strip from the dark border yardage and several from the square of white border yardage.

Cut plenty of strips for string borders while you're at it, the same width and any convenient length.

If using 44" strips: Cut fifteen dark strips and fifteen light strips, Beta width. Cut Beta length strips needed, saving leftovers for the string borders.

4. Follow Steps 5 through 8 in simplified project on page 118. Inner design will be about 32" square.

5. Add first borders. Cut strips for Step 7 while you are at it.

(a) Cut dark yardage into eleven strips 4" wide. Use four of them for borders now. Set the rest aside for Step 7.

(b) Cut four border strips 2-3/4" wide from white yardage, as shown on the cutting layout. Remove enough from each strip to fit the quilt at this stage; set longer pieces aside for Step 7.

6. Make string borders. Piece together strips cut in Step 3, following directions in Chapter 3 and in the simplified project (page 118). Add more strips if needed to make enough border to go around the quilt. Border sections can be 6" or any width that fits your panels and looks good to you.

7. Add outer borders.

(a) Add another narrow white border.

(b) Add another dark border.

(c) Cut the remaining pieces of white yardage into 11" wide sections, as shown in Step 1, or any desired width.

8. Make backing (No. 4 on page 13). Hand quilt and bind as desired.

Nifty Nine-Patch quilt sizes and fabric needed

These charts are for small, medium, and large blocks—each with fabric needed calculated two ways:

A. By 44" strips (Alpha width and Beta width).

B. By yardage (fat quarters or 3/8-yd. pieces).

Use only section A **or** section B—not both! If you prefer smaller scraps, see the general chart on page 113. Of course, you can combine scraps, 44" strips, and yardage, if that suits your needs.

Small blocks

Alpha strips are 4" x 17", Beta strips about 2-1/2" x 20", and blocks are 5-3/4" or smaller.

Blocks	Quilt size approximate, before borders	A. If 44" strips Alpha (4") dark	light	Beta width dark	light	B. If fat quarters dark	light
16 (4 x 4)	22" sq.	(use short strips only)				(not recommended)	
24 (4 x 6)	22" x 33"	(use short strips only)				(not recommended)	
36 (6 x 6)	33" sq."	4	4	8	8	(not recommended)	
48 (6 x 8)	33" x 44"	4	4	9	9	5	5
64 (8 x 8)	44" sq.	5	5	12	12	6	6
80 (8 x10)	44" x 55"	7	7	15	15	7	7
96 (8 x12)	44" x 66"	8	8	18	18	8	8
100 (10 x 10)	55" sq.	8	8	20	20	8	8
120 (10 x 12)	55" x 66"	10	10	23	23	10	10
140 (10 x 14)	55" x 77"	12	12	27	27	12	12
144 (12 x 12)	66" sq.	12	12	27	27	12	12
168 (12 x 14)	66" x 77"	13	13	32	32	13	13
196 (14 x 14)	77" sq.	16	16	38	38	16	16
224 (14 x 16)	77" x 88"	17	17	42	42	17	17
256 (16 x 16)	88" sq.	20	20	48	48	20	20

Cutting instructions:

A. 44" strips: Use Alpha-strip bypass (page 93). Cut two Beta strips from each strip.

B. Fat quarters: You'll probably need more, but buy them later (if that's convenient). Stack layers and cut two 4" Alpha strips from each. Leave stacked to cut four Beta strips. If you can cut only three Beta strips from some pieces, go ahead and make some blocks so you'll know which colors you need more of. Get one more fat quarter for each six Beta strips needed.

Medium blocks

Alpha strips are 5" x 21", Beta strips are about 3-1/4" x 26", and blocks are 8-1/4" or smaller.

Blocks	Quilt Size	A. If 44" strips				B. If yardage			
	approximate,	Alpha (5")		Beta width		fat quarters		+ 3/8 yd.	
	before borders	dark	light	dark	light	dark	light	dark	light
16 (4 x 4)	32" sq.	(use short strips only)				(not recommended)			
24 (4 x 6)	32" x 48"	(use short strips only)				(not recommended)			
36 (6 x 6)	48" sq.	4	4	10	10	(not recommended)			
48 (6 x 8)	48" x 64"	5	5	12	12	4	4	plus 3	3
64 (8 x 8)	64" sq.	6	6	16	16	4	4	plus 4	4
80 (8 x 10)	64" x 80"	8	8	20	20	6	6	plus 5	5
96 (8 x 12)	64" x 96"	9	9	24	24	6	6	plus 6	6
100 (10 x 10)	80" sq.	10	10	26	26	7	7	plus 7	7
120 (10 x 12)	80" x 96"	12	12	30	30	8	8	plus 8	8
140 (10 x 14)	80" x 112"	14	14	36	36	10	10	plus 9	9
144 (12 x 12)	96" sq.	14	14	36	36	10	10	plus 9	9

Cutting instructions:

A. 44" strips: Two Alpha strips fit nicely on each 5" strip. For Beta strips, cut one full-length strip and one half length (about 13") strip from each.

B. Yardage: Use fat quarters for Alpha strips, cutting three from each. Beta strips don't fit fat quarters, so use 3/8 yd. lengths (13-1/2" x 44"). Cut each into four Beta width strips, then trim to make one full strip and one half strip.

Large blocks

Alpha strips are 6" x 25", Beta strips are about 3-7/8" x 31", and blocks are 10" or smaller.

Blocks	Quilt Size approximate, before borders	A. If 44" Strips Alpha (6")		A. If 44" Strips Beta width		B. If yardage 3/8-yd. pieces	
		dark	light	dark	light	dark	light
16 (4 x 4)	36" sq.	(use scraps instead)				(not recommended)	
24 (4 x 6)	36" x 54"	(use scraps instead)				(not recommended)	
36 (6 x 6)	54" sq.	5	5	10	10	6	6
48 (6 x 8)	54" x 72"	6	6	12	12	7	7
64 (8 x 8)	72" sq.	7	7	16	16	9	9
80 (8 x 10)	72" x 90"	9	9	20	20	12	12
96 (8 x 12)	72" x 108"	11	11	24	24	14	14
100 (10 x 10)	90" sq.	12	12	26	26	15	15
120 (10 x 12)	90" x 108"	14	14	30	30	17	17

Cutting instructions:

A. 44" strips. Use the Alpha-strip by-pass. For Beta strips, trim to the exact width needed, then cut each into one full length strip plus a half length (14" or your measurement).

B. 3/8-yd. pieces. Alpha strips: Cut as many 6" x 44" strips as are given in the A section, two from each 3/8 yard piece. Beta strips: Cut each remaining 3/8 yard piece into three Beta width strips. Cut each into one full-length and one half-length strip.

Six-color Nifty Nine-Patch

   If all blocks were identical, you would really be limited in your arrangements. Squares in one block would usually be the same fabric as the squares they touched in the adjoining blocks. You can prevent this simply by making two slightly different blocks. Study the diagrams below and you'll see what I mean.

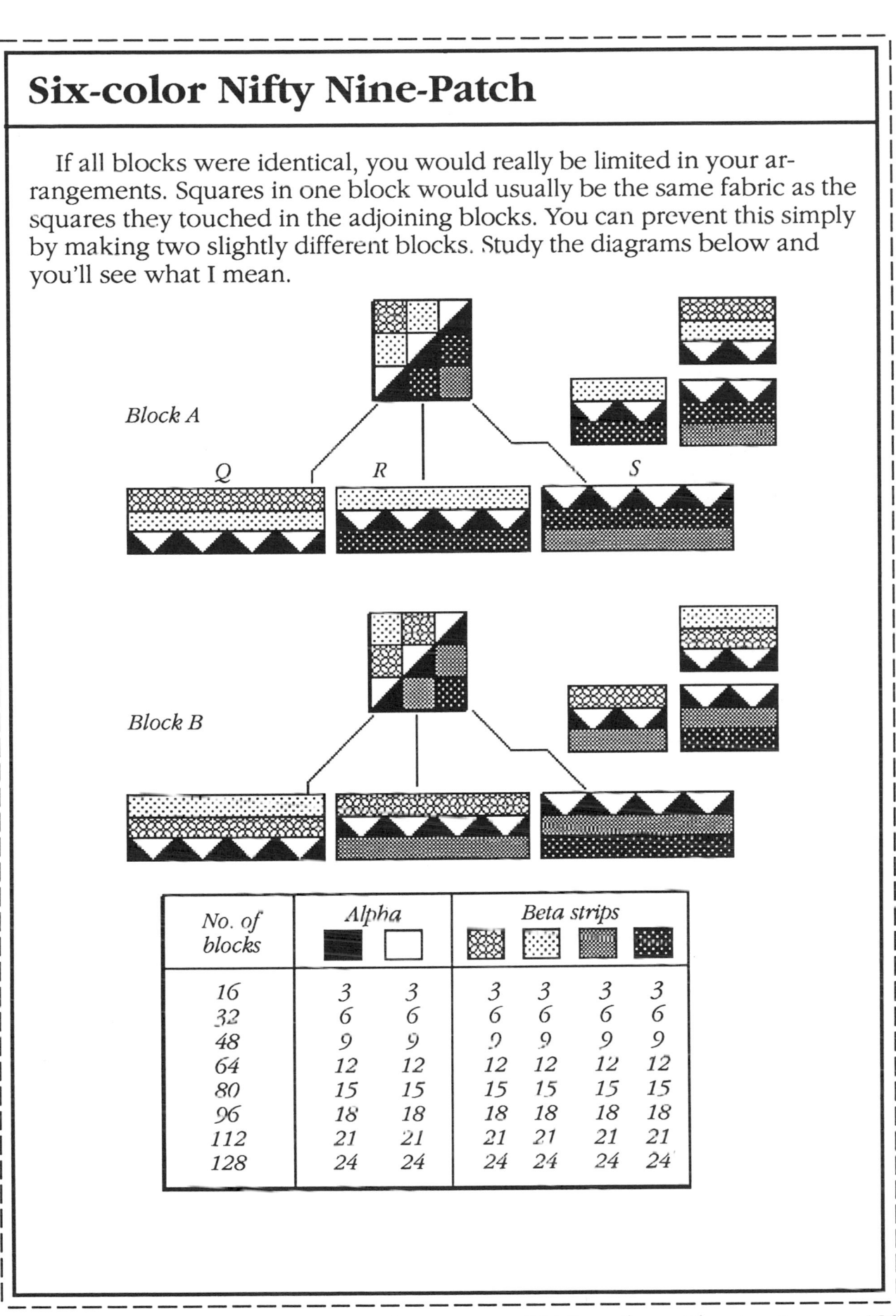

Block A

Q   R   S

Block B

No. of blocks	Alpha		Beta strips			
16	3	3	3	3	3	3
32	6	6	6	6	6	6
48	9	9	9	9	9	9
64	12	12	12	12	12	12
80	15	15	15	15	15	15
96	18	18	18	18	18	18
112	21	21	21	21	21	21
128	24	24	24	24	24	24

Six-color twin throw

This quilt uses forty-eight medium-sized Nifty Nine-Patch blocks. Quilt size is about 62" x 76".

Making this project with low contrast solid fabrics gives an Amish look. You can also get a Southwest Indian look with brighter colors. Using two different blocks gives a nicely balanced project but not mirror-image symmetry.

Fabric needed:

Light triangles and first border: 1-3/4 yds. light

Dark triangles and outer border: 2-1/4 yds. dark

Beta strips (squares): 3/4 yd. each of four fabrics, two dark and two medium light

Backing: 3-2/3 yd.

Batting: 62" x 78"

Binding: about 8 yds.

1. Cut Alpha strips. Cut nine dark and nine light strips 5" x 21". Cut them lengthwise as shown to save long areas for borders.

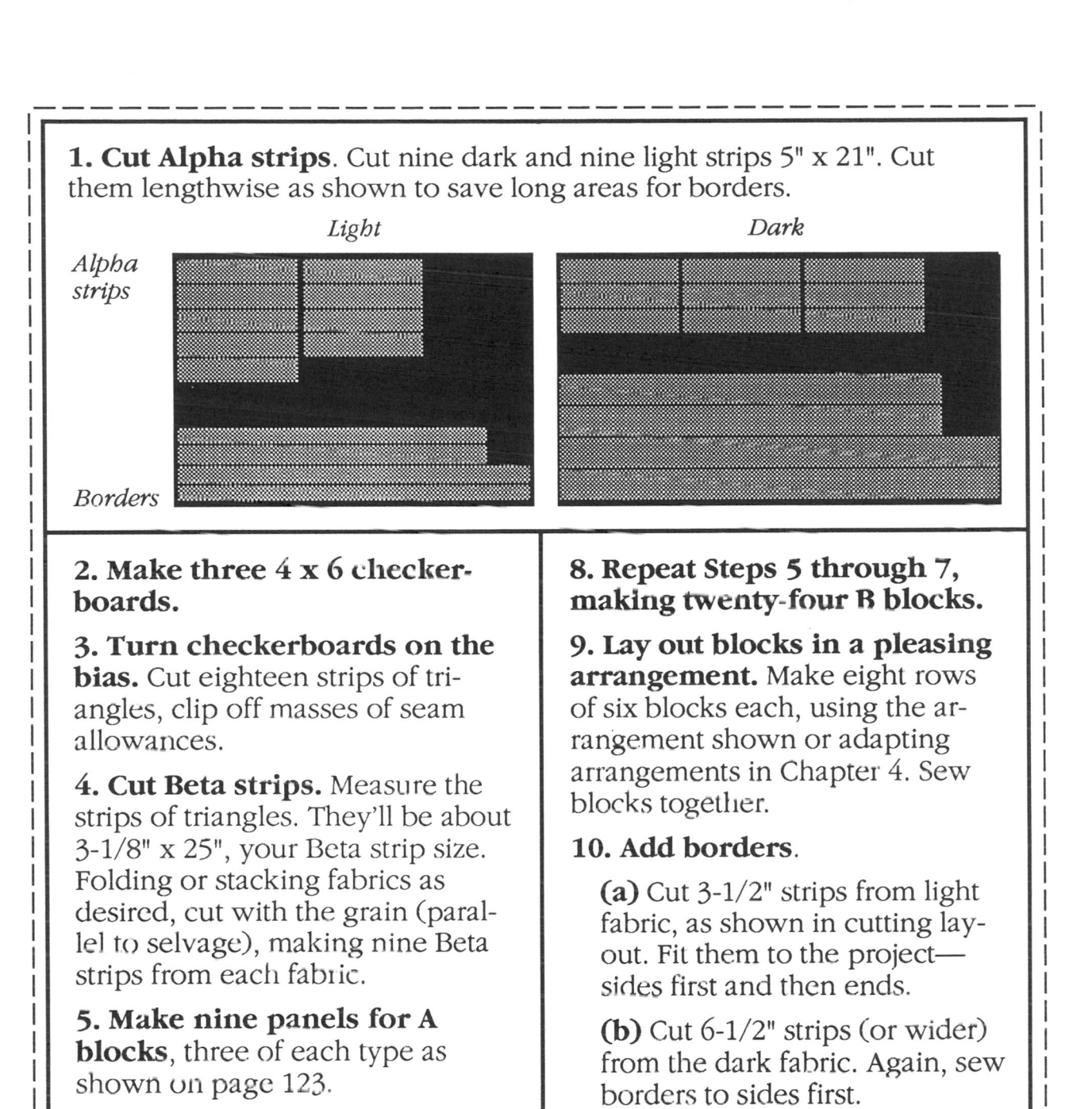

Light

Dark

Alpha strips

Borders

2. Make three 4 x 6 checker-boards.

3. Turn checkerboards on the bias. Cut eighteen strips of tri-angles, clip off masses of seam allowances.

4. Cut Beta strips. Measure the strips of triangles. They'll be about 3-1/8" x 25", your Beta strip size. Folding or stacking fabrics as desired, cut with the grain (paral-lel to selvage), making nine Beta strips from each fabric.

5. Make nine panels for A blocks, three of each type as shown on page 123.

6. Cut panels apart into chains, again clipping off extra fabric at points. Sort chains out into six different stacks according to slant and colors.

7. Make twenty-four A blocks.

8. Repeat Steps 5 through 7, making twenty-four B blocks.

9. Lay out blocks in a pleasing arrangement. Make eight rows of six blocks each, using the ar-rangement shown or adapting arrangements in Chapter 4. Sew blocks together.

10. Add borders.

(a) Cut 3-1/2" strips from light fabric, as shown in cutting lay-out. Fit them to the project—sides first and then ends.

(b) Cut 6-1/2" strips (or wider) from the dark fabric. Again, sew borders to sides first.

11. Complete the project. Make backing, using No. 2 on page 13. Quilt and bind with your favorite method.

Red Hot Squares

I like the effect of red accents with scrap quilts, especially in the center of blocks as they are with Log Cabin. What if we keep the centers of Nifty Nine-Patch blocks **square**, and make those squares red?

Don't let that name dictate your colors; you can just use random colors in the center squares for a softer effect and make up your own name for the project.

Here's how those blocks are made:

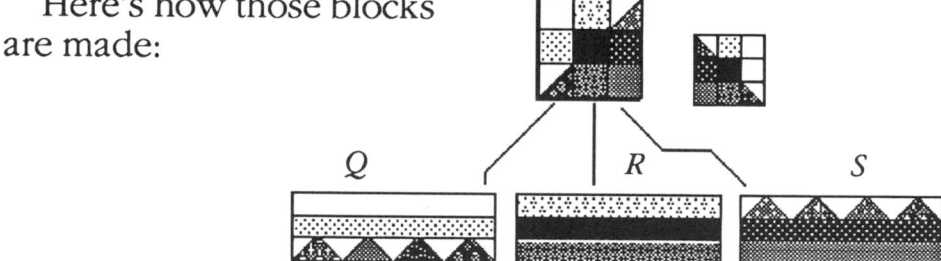

Q   R   S

Red Hot Squares wall hanging

Here is a 36-block wall hanging using small blocks. The project is about 36" square.

Materials needed:

Strips: see Steps 1 and 4

Borders: 1/3 to 2/3 yds.

Backing: 1-1/8 yds.

Batting: about 38" sq.

Binding: 5 yds.

1. Cut Alpha strips. Cut from scraps five dark strips and five light strips, 4" x 17".

2. Make checkerboards. Make one 4 x 4 and one 4 x 6.

3. Turn on the bias. Cut strips of triangles. You will have ten of them. Clip off seam masses at some points.

4. Cut Beta strips. Measure strips of triangles (about 2-1/2" x 20").

(a) For Q and S panels: Cut ten dark and ten light Beta strips.

(b) For R panels: Use Beta-width scraps of any length, equal to two 44" strips of light, two of red, two of dark. Use as many different fabrics as possible.

5. Make Q and S panels, five of each.

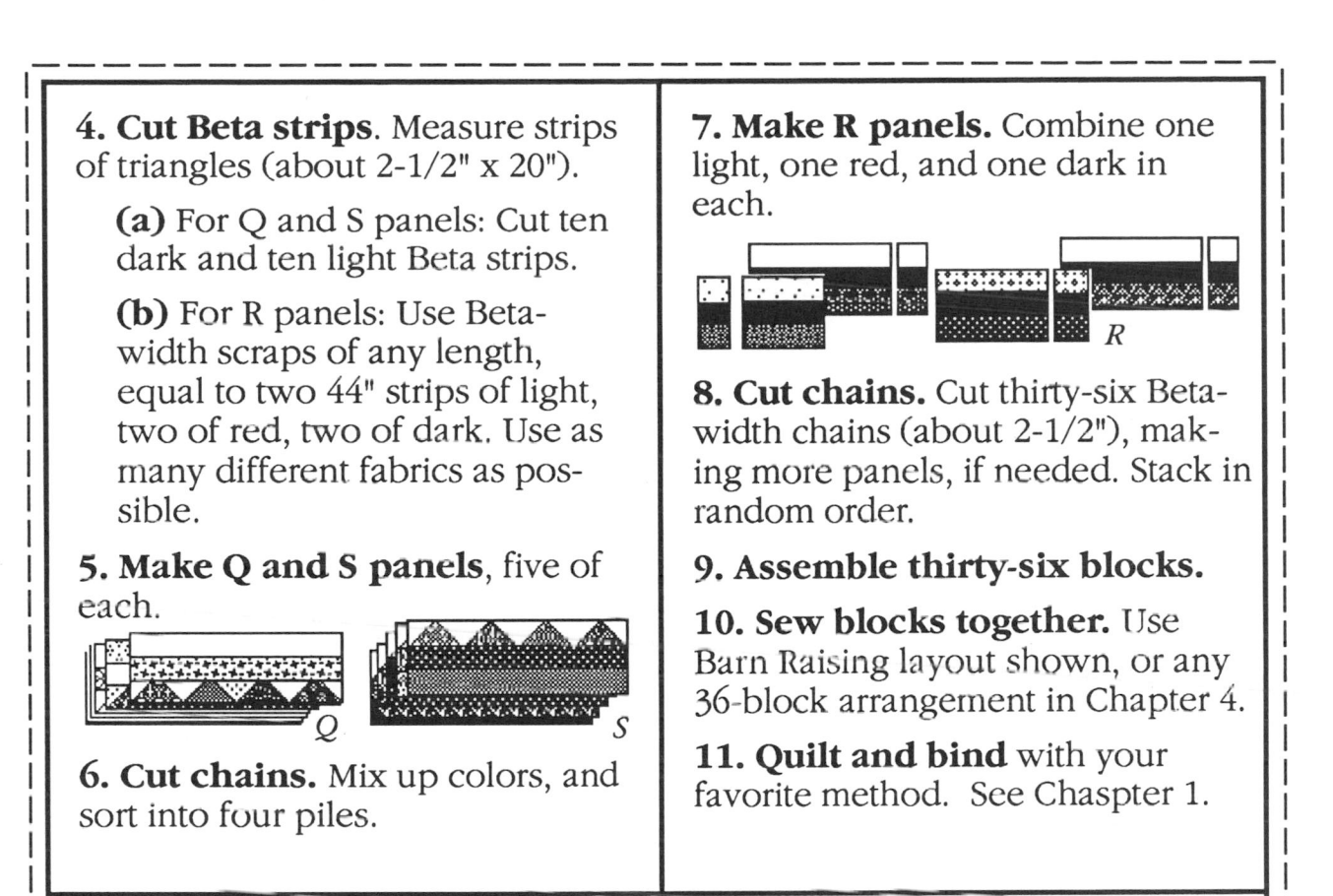

6. Cut chains. Mix up colors, and sort into four piles.

7. Make R panels. Combine one light, one red, and one dark in each.

8. Cut chains. Cut thirty-six Beta-width chains (about 2-1/2"), making more panels, if needed. Stack in random order.

9. Assemble thirty-six blocks.

10. Sew blocks together. Use Barn Raising layout shown, or any 36-block arrangement in Chapter 4.

11. Quilt and bind with your favorite method. See Chaspter 1.

Strips needed for Red Hot Squares

Alpha strips may be 4" x 17", 5" x 21", or 6" x 25". See chart on page 109 to estimate the sizes of the Beta strips.

Number of blocks	Arrangement of blocks	Alpha strips		Beta strips*	
		dark	light	dark	light
16	4 x 4	2	2	8	6
24	4 x 6	3	3	12	9
36	6 x 6	5	5	20	15
48	6 x 8	6	6	24	18
64	8 x 8	8	8	32	24
80	8 x 10	10	10	40	30
96	8 x 12	12	12	48	36
100	10 x 10	13	13	52	39
120	10 x 12	15	15	60	45
140	10 x 14	18	18	72	54
144	12 x 12	18	18	72	54
168	12 x 14	21	21	84	63
196	14 x 14	25	25	100	75

This figure is just an estimate. Half of the total strip length will be used for the R panels and can be odd lengths. Half of those (1/4 of the total dark strips) can be red. One-third of the light Beta strip lengths can be odd lengths.

Garden Path

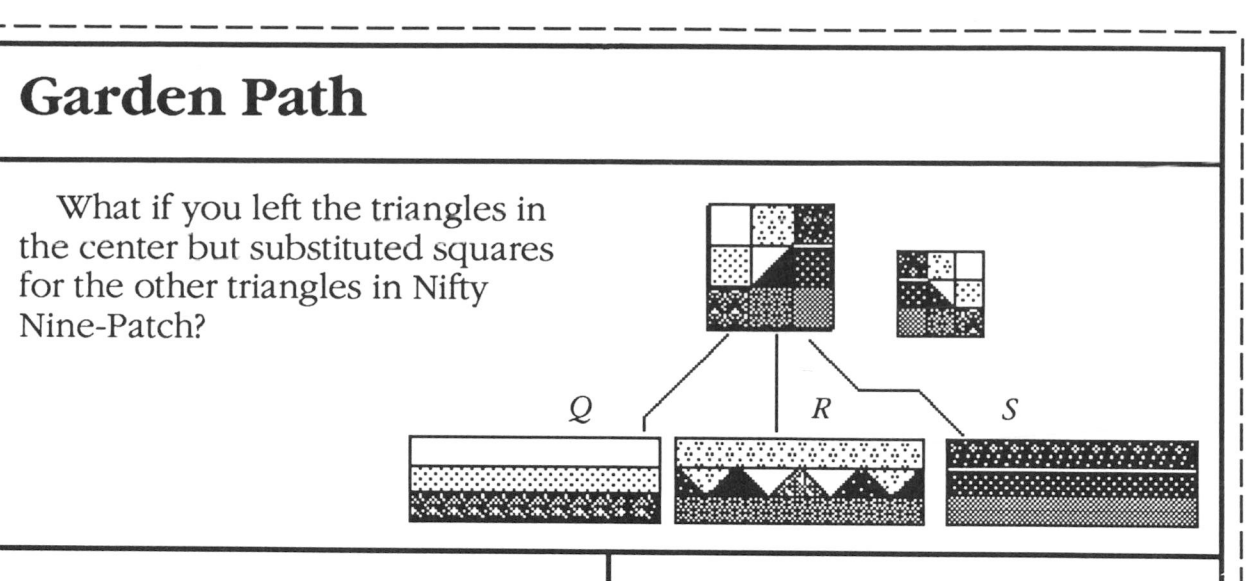

What if you left the triangles in the center but substituted squares for the other triangles in Nifty Nine-Patch?

Q   R   S

This diagram doesn't look like much, so I didn't get terribly excited until I actually tried it. It's a fabulous block! It's extra easy to make since it contains mostly squares. But it's easier to put together than regular squares-only Nine-Patch blocks. The triangles in the center are on the bias, so they have a little give to them, making alignment of seams easier.

Best of all, you get some wonderful curved effects that resemble an old favorite block, Drunkard's Path. I originally called it "Liar's Path" because you could whip up a quilt top in a day and lie about how long it took you to make. But my friend Dorsy, who quilted the wall hanging in the color pages, said that a pretty block like this one needed a pretty name. So I'm calling it Garden Path.

Although you can experiment with other ways to arrange blocks, you'll probably agree that Barn Raising is again the prettiest. Study this diagram to see how it's put together. I'm calling the blocks with an uphill slant **Y** blocks. They are used in the top left and bottom right quarters. The **Z** blocks, which slant "downhill," go in the other corners. Within each section, blocks alternate between those that are upright and those that are upside down.

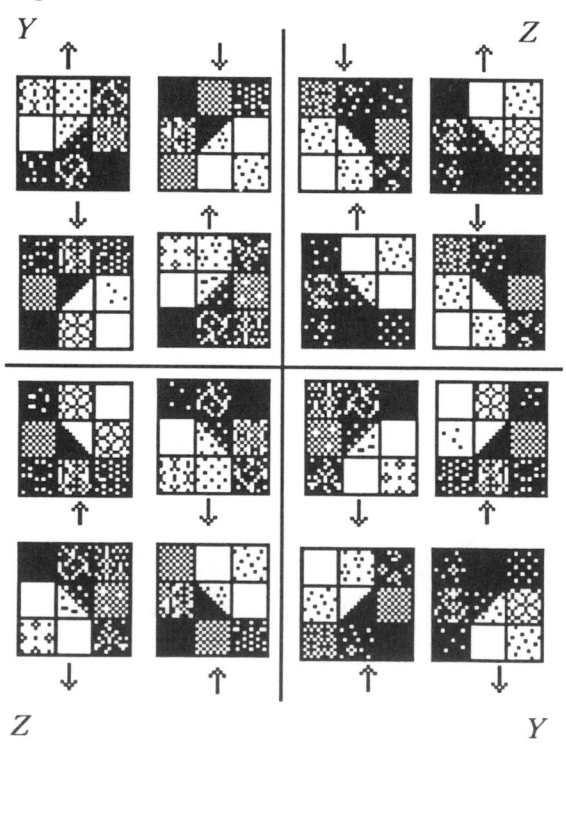

Garden Path baby quilt

Here's how to make the 48-block quilt shown in the color pages. Blocks are small, and the final project measures about 38" x 48", ideal for a baby quilt or wall hanging. A black binding is used, but no other borders (although you can add some if you wish).

Fabric needed:

Strips: See Steps 1, 4, and 6

Switchers: Beta-width squares (about 2-1/2" sq.)

Batting: 42" x 52"

Backing:1-3/8 yds. (more if you add borders)

Binding: 5 yds. (more if you add borders)

1. Cut Alpha strips. Cut from scraps three dark and three light strips, 4" x 17".

2. Make a 4 x 6 checkerboard.

3. Turn it on the bias. Cut strips of triangles. You will have six of them. Clip off the seam masses at some points.

4. Cut Beta strips for R panels. Measure the strips of triangles. They'll be about 2-1/2" x 20". Cut six dark and six light.

5. Make R panels. Sew a dark strip to the dark side of each strip of triangles and a light strip to the light side. Make six panels. Cut chains, mix up, and sort into two piles.

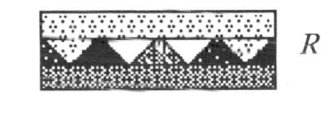

R

6. Cut Beta width strips for Q and S panels.

(a) If using 44" strips, cut twelve dark and six light.

(b) If using scraps: Use any available lengths equal to twelve dark and six light full-length strips.

7. Make Q panels and chains.
Sew together one dark and two lights. Press and cut Beta width chains. Mix up the chains, then stack and count them. Make more, if needed, for a total of forty-eight.

8. Make S Panels and chains.
Sew random dark strips in sets of three. Again, make forty-eight chains, and stack them in random order (some turned upside down).

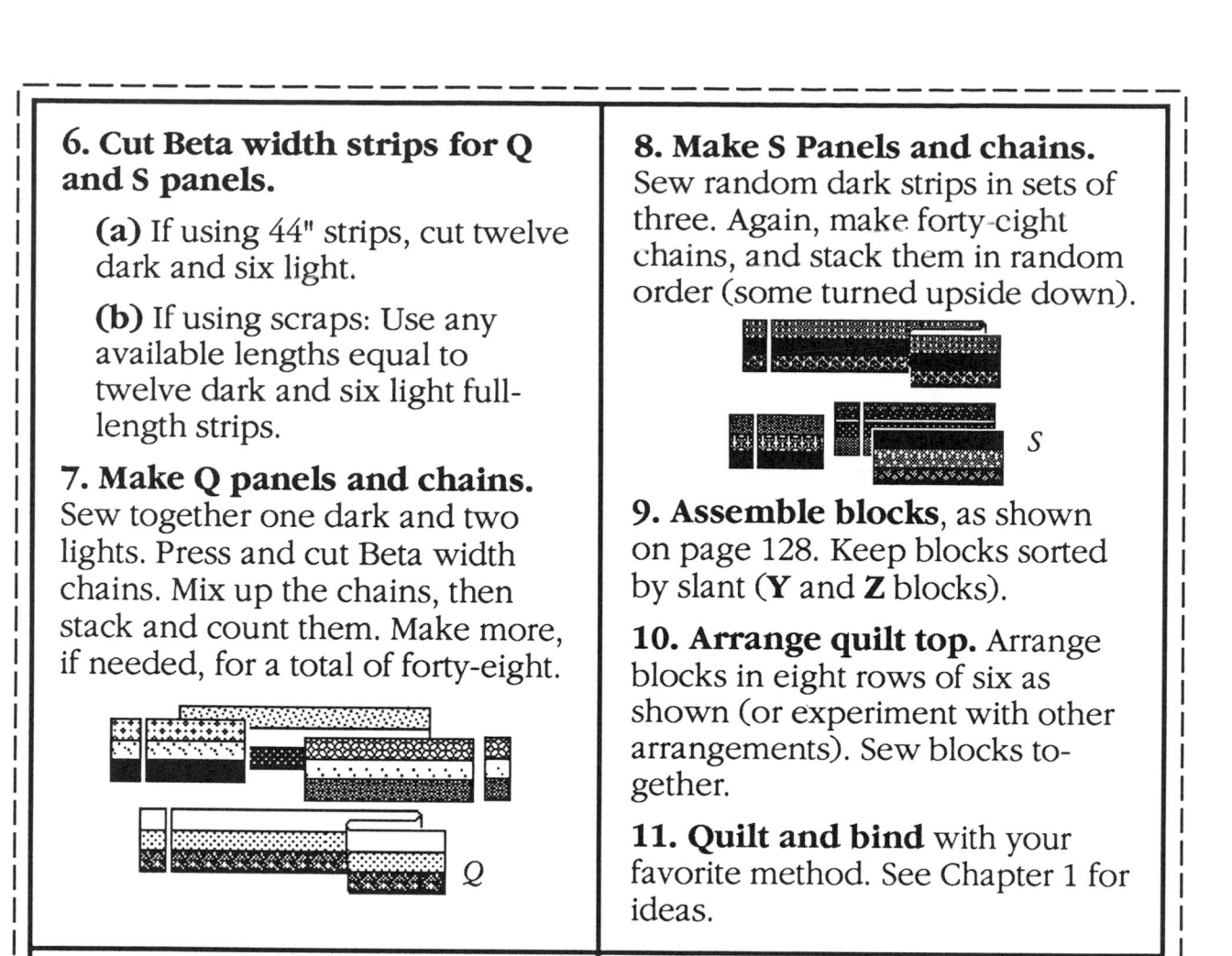

9. Assemble blocks, as shown on page 128. Keep blocks sorted by slant (**Y** and **Z** blocks).

10. Arrange quilt top. Arrange blocks in eight rows of six as shown (or experiment with other arrangements). Sew blocks together.

11. Quilt and bind with your favorite method. See Chapter 1 for ideas.

Number of strips needed for Garden Path

Alpha strips may be 4" x 17", 5" x 21", or 6" x 25". See chart on page 109 for Beta strip sizes.

Number of blocks	Arrangement of blocks	Alpha strips		Beta strips	
		dark	light	dark	light
16	4 x 4	2	2	10	6
24	4 x 6	2	2	15	9
36	6 x 6	3	3	25	15
48	6 x 8	3	3	30	18
64	8 x 8	4	4	40	24
80	8 x 10	5	5	50	30
96	8 x 12	6	6	60	36
100	10 x 10	7	7	65	39
120	10 x 12	8	8	75	45
140	10 x 14	9	9	90	54

*You won't want to cut them all to Beta **length**; you can make Q and S panels from full-length strips or scraps of different lengths.*

Yardage calculations for Garden Path (small blocks)

Use these calculations for 44" strips or fat quarters; you may substitute scraps, of course.

Alpha strips are 4" x 17", Beta strips about 2-1/2" x 20", and blocks are 5-3/4" or smaller.

Blocks	Quilt size (before borders)	A. If 44" strips				B. If fat quarters (5 Beta + 1 Alpha or 6 Beta from each)	
		Alpha width		Beta width			
		dark	light	dark	light	dark	light
16 (4 x 4)	22" sq.	(use short strips only)				(not recommended)	
24 (4 x 6)	22" x 33"	(short strips)		8	5	(not recommended)	
36 (6 x 6)	33" sq.	(short strips)		12	8	(not recommended)	
48 (6 x 8)	33" x 44"	(short strips)		15	9	6	4
64 (8 x 8)	44" sq.	(short strips)		20	12	8	5
80 (8 x 10)	44" x 55"	(short strips)		24	15	10	6
96 (8 x 12)	44" x 66"	3	3	29	18	11	7
100 (10 x 10)	55" sq.	3	3	31	19	12	8
120 (10 x 12)	55" x 66"	3	3	36	22	14	9
140 (10 x 14)	55" x 77"	4	4	43	26	17	11
144 (12 x 12)	66" sq.	4	4	43	26	17	11
168 (12 x 14)	66" x 77"	5	5	50	30	20	13
196 (14 x 14)	77" sq.	5	5	60	36	25	15
224 (14 x 16)	77" x 88"	6	6	67	40	26	17
256 (16 x 16)	88" sq.	6	6	76	46	30	19

Cutting instructions for fat quarters. Cut one 4" Alpha strip from each piece until you have the required number on general chart (you won't cut from all of them). Later cut the remaining parts into Beta strips. With some sizes, you will need to add a few scraps to complete the blocks.

8. Sawtooth Chains

This chapter gives a variety of interesting projects using sawtooth chains. They're easy to make from the strips of triangles you worked with in Chapter 7. Just line them up, with dark triangles all facing the same direction, and cut off sawtooth chains by the dozen.

When people see a panel like this, they often say, "Oh, Flying Geese," but then they notice that the points are blunt. Sawtooth chains need the blunt points for the seam allowances, as we mentioned earlier. You can still make Flying Geese, however. Take a seam down the middle of the Geese to get the points back (which we'll do later in this chapter), or use a different technique to keep the points in the first place (see Chapter 9).

Marking the centers

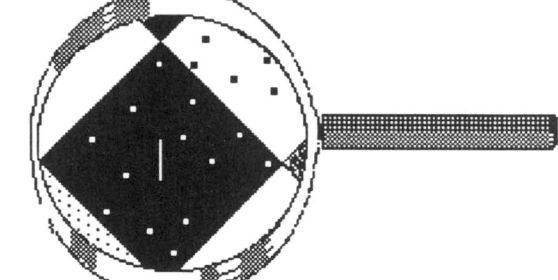

The first requirement with sawtooth chains is a way to keep triangles lined up exactly. You need a mark in the center of each triangle to show where the point of the triangle in the next row should hit.

It's easier to do this marking before you cut the bias panel apart. Just draw lines straight through all squares as shown in the diagram. (There's no need to use disappearing ink, but you might need a white pencil for the dark fabric.) Or cut little slashes, if you prefer. They show up on both light and dark fabric, and on both right and wrong sides of the fabric.

Remember, mark in one direction and cut in the other direction.

Mark

← *Cut*

If a panel is square, like this one, it doesn't matter which way you mark and which way you cut, but be consistent. If you have several panels, cut all strips so they have four large dark triangles and two light half-triangles on the ends (or vice versa). Otherwise, dark triangles won't all line up and point the same direction.

If you accidentally find yourself with mismatched strips like this, just keep the like strips together in their own panels—you'll see what I mean. (Or switch to a different project—see page 141.)

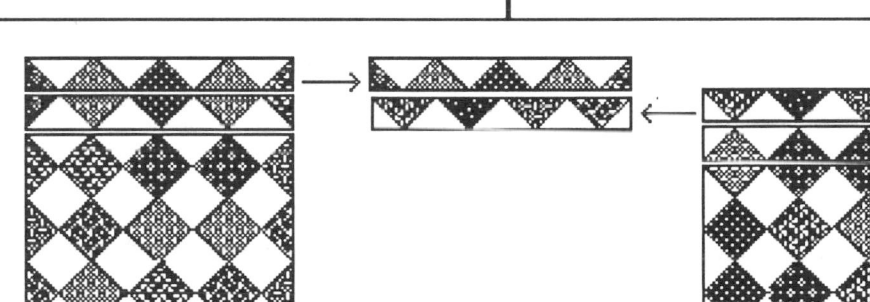

The slant of the triangles

Another important thing about strip-pieced sawtooth chains: The triangles slant up, or they slant down. You'll have an equal number of "uphill" and "downhill" slants, whether you want them or not.

You can't change the slant by turning the chain upside down. You just change the side the dark triangles are on. You can change

the slant by turning the chain on its side, and sometimes that's the perfect solution to a design problem.

Study the directions for the first project whether you want to make place mats or not. Some of the same ideas apply to later projects.

Sawtooth Chains Chapter Eight 133

Place mats with sawtooth borders

Here's a set of six place mats about 13" x 18", using scrap triangles. Each mat uses both uphill and downhill triangles, so everything comes out even. Avoid really light colors and use durable fabric.

Fabric needed:

Strips: see Step 1

Backing and center squares: 2 yds. dark fabric

Fleece: 1-1/8 yd. Thermolam or similar compressed polyester batting (or use odds and ends of leftover fleece, enough to cut six pieces 14" x 19")

Binding: 11 yds. wide bias tape

1. Cut Alpha strips, four light and four dark, but how large? Regular 5" strips make triangles which are a little too large, and 4" strips are too small. So start with strips 4-3/4" x 20" (unless you tend to make wide seams, in which case you can start with regular 5" strips).

2. Make a 4 x 8 checkerboard (remembering to cut cross sections exactly the size of the first strips—4-3/4"). Turn it on the bias (see page 91) and mark centers.

3. Cut strips of triangles. Clip off the masses of seam allowances at some points.

4. Sew five strips together, mixing up strips to get a nice color

assortment. You will probably find you occasionally have to pick out a few inches and adjust things so points line up better. Cut the three leftover strips in two, making six short strips. Piece five of them together into a half-size panel.

5. Cut sawtooth chains. Cut through the center of the blunt points. If they don't line up well enough, pick out a few inches of seam and move the points over a bit. Measure them. They'll be about 12-1/2" long.

6. Cut six center squares. Match the measurement of the chains.

7. Cut backing pieces. Exact size will depend on the size of your center squares. Make the backing pieces one inch wider and six inches longer (about 13-1/2" x 18-1/2").

8. Cut six pieces of fleece the size of the backing fabric.

9. Layer fabric and fleece of one mat for one-step quilting. Spread out the backing fabric, wrong side up, and the fleece, keeping edges aligned. Place the square of fabric, right side up, exactly in the center. Pin through all layers and machine-baste the inside square to the fleece.

10. Sew sawtooth chains in place. Place a sawtooth chain on one side of the dark square, face down, with the light side of triangles along the edge of the square, as shown below. Sew it in place carefully so the seam comes right next to the points of the triangles but doesn't cut them off.

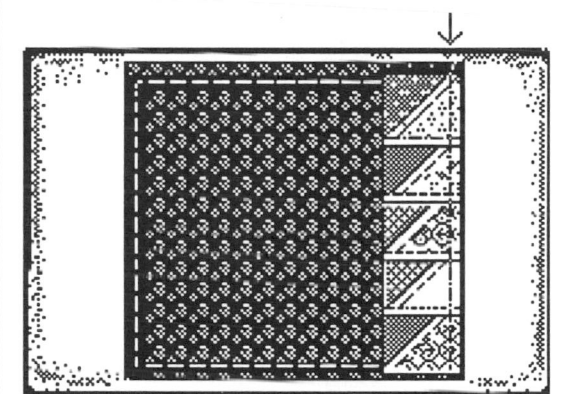

Sew another chain to the other side of the mat—with triangles slanting in the opposite direc-

tion—again with the light side of triangles against the edge. Press chains open and baste along edges.

11. Trim fleece and backing fabric, 1/4" from the edge of the design. Round the corners slightly.

12. Apply binding. Pin it in place and use a zigzag stitch, again being careful to cover the edges of the fabric but not cut off points of triangles. Stitch down the end of the binding by hand.

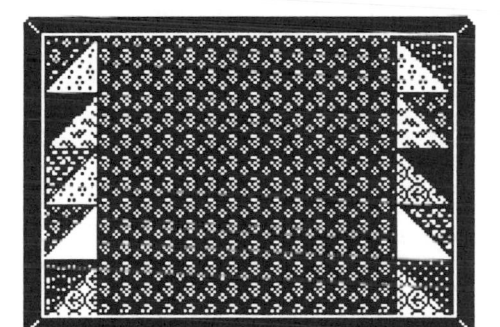

13. Repeat Steps 9 through 12 with all mats. Do decorative quilting in the centers of mats if you wish.

Sawtooth Flying Geese

As mentioned, Flying Geese is featured in Chapter 9, but here's a Flying Geese variation made with sawtooth chains. Instead of wide single-triangle "Geese," these have seams down the middle to restore the points.

Why even use this version with the extra seam? Because the method given in Chapter 9 is quite

strange. Try this version first if you find Chapter 9 baffling. Use Sawtooth Flying Geese for large blocks on everyday quilts.

I'll write up directions a different way this time, letting you choose among three projects. Just "make it up as you go along" with this one. You can use many different combinations of sashing and

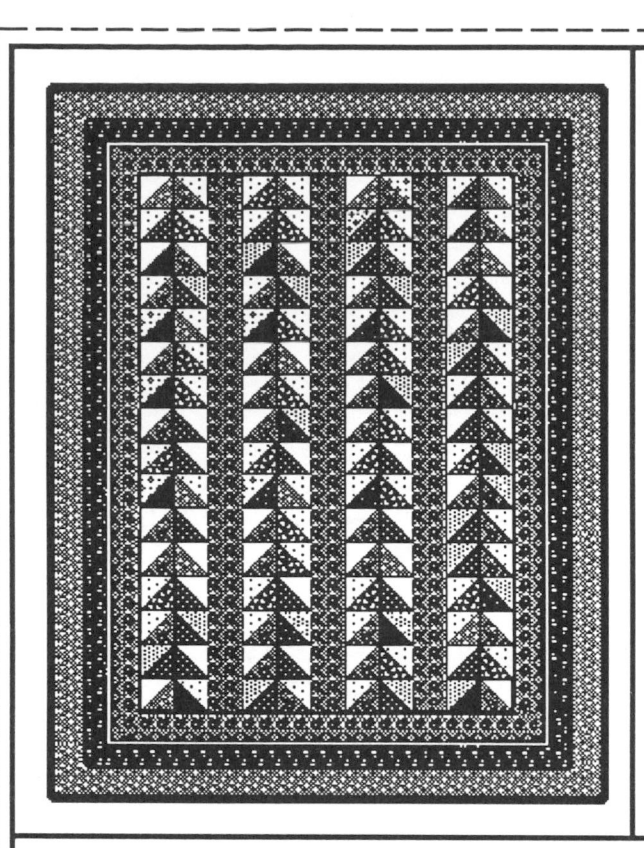

borders to get different sizes of projects and different visual effects. Since each dark "goose" can be considered a complete block, blocks can be very large, made with 6", 7", or 8" strips. Cutting big panels can be a nuisance, so use the largest mat possible.

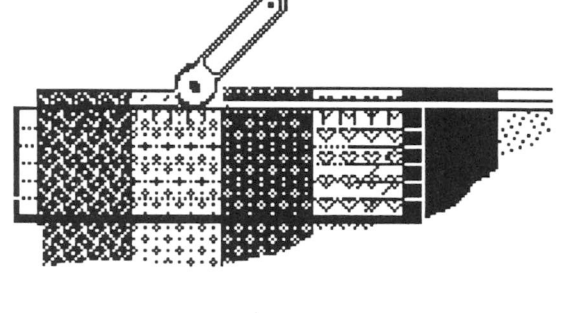

Two ways to make Sawtooth Flying Geese

Variation A. The two sides of each Goose match. The project will look like regular Flying Geese at a glance if small dark random prints are used.

Variation B. The two sides of each Goose are different. There is no accidental matching. See an example of this variation in the color pages.

Variation A:
Flying Geese with matching sides

1. Use 44" strips. Cut this number of strips:

For a large crib quilt: Cut 6" strips, five dark and five light.

For a twin throw: Cut 7" strips,

six dark and six light.

For a double bed throw: Cut 8" strips, seven dark and seven light.

2. Make two 4 x 8 checkerboards. Use the Alpha-strip bypass method described on page 93. Mix up cross sections thoroughly.

3. Turn the checkerboards on the bias. (See pages 89 to 91.) Mark the centers.

4. Cut strips of triangles. Be careful to mark and cut the direction which will give you strips with **four large dark triangles** with two small light triangles on the ends. (If you goofed on this, switch to Variation B instead.

You'll get two-color geese with an occasional match.)

5. Sew strips of triangles together. Mix up the strips to get a nice balance of darks and lights and colors. Matching the points to the center marks, make a panel of sixteen strips. Press the panel carefully, using spray starch to stiffen it because it's very stretchy. If possible, let it sit overnight to ease back in shape if anything was distorted.

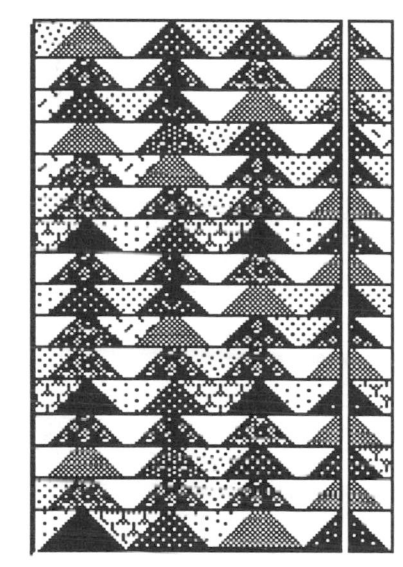

6. Cut sawtooth chains.

7. Reassemble chains in pairs. Join the two adjacent chains right where they were originally cut apart. Pin thoroughly and sew carefully so seams will match up and points will look nice.

8. Join strips with sashing, following guidelines on pages 151 to 153. Decide how you want to quilt the project. One-step quilting works nicely for this project. See pages 16 through 19 for directions.

9. Add borders. Many ideas are given in Chapter 1 and on page 154.

Variation B: *Flying Geese with two-color geese*

These directions guarantee that the two halves of the triangles will never match accidentally.

1. Cut strips. Cut eight light and eight dark strips of regular Alpha strip size:

For a large crib quilt: Use 6" x 25" strips.

For a twin throw: Use 7" x 29" strips.

For a double bed throw: Use 8" x 33" strips.

2. Make two 4 x 8 checkerboards. Don't mix up parts this time—you don't want any fabrics used in both checkerboards. I'll call these two checkerboards A and B.

3. Turn checkerboards on the bias. Mark centers.

4. Cut strips of triangles. It doesn't matter this time where darks and light triangles are— they'll work out okay. Clip off masses of seam allowances at some points.

5. Make sawtooth panels:

(a) Sew the eight strips from panel A together.

(b) Divide the panel to make half-width panels.

(c) Sew the two half panels together end to end to make sixteen rows.

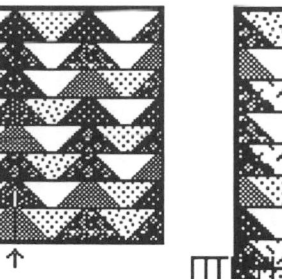

(d) Repeat steps (a) through (c) with strips from panel B.

(e) Press panels carefully. Use spray starch to stiffen them because they're very stretchy. If possible, let them sit overnight to ease back in shape.

6. Cut sawtooth chains.

7. Sew chains together in pairs.
Each time, use a chain from panel A and a chain from panel B. Pin thoroughly and sew carefully so seams will match up and points will look nice.

8. Join strips with sashing, following guidelines on pages 151 to 153. Decide how you want to quilt the project. One-step quilting works nicely for this project. See pages 16 through 19 for directions.

9. Add borders, using ideas from Chapters 1 and 9.

Those are the basic steps, but for either version, there is a lot of room for creativity. I don't think I have ever started a Flying Geese project with preconceived ideas about sashing and border fabrics and project size.

Make the chains of Geese, then try out every suitable fabric you have for sashing. Join chains with sashing, then try out different fabrics for borders, adding as many borders as you want. You can even get creative on the back of the project by using a Flying Geese chain to join two pieces of fabric.

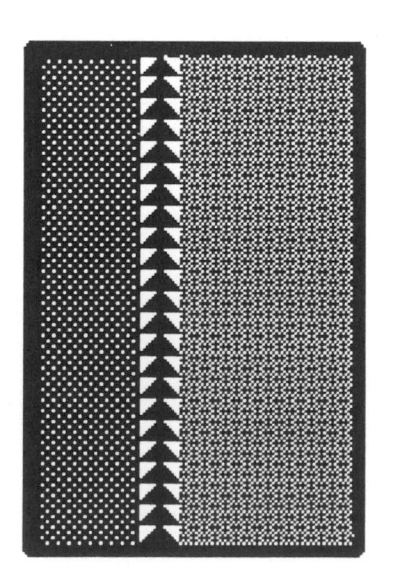

Can you work with smaller triangles than I have given in these projects? Yes, but it's a pain to line up the points. Use the technique in Chapter 9 for smaller triangles. Though the ideas in that chapter are more advanced, the sewing is easier.

Hundreds of Triangles

Once I started making a large Sawtooth Flying Geese quilt. When I had two 8-row sawtooth panels made, I changed my mind. I had already made three similar quilts and decided I wasn't really that interested in making another one. I cut sawtooth chains and sewed them together, making two panels. All the uphill chains were in one panel, and all the downhill chains in the other.

I gave them a diagonal setting and made two cozy quilts somewhat like these:

Designing Hundreds of Triangles quilts	Geese to Hundreds of Triangles.

Designing Hundreds of Triangles quilts

Here's what to expect if you switch from Sawtooth Flying Geese to Hundreds of Triangles. These calculations are for projects starting with eight dark and eight light Alpha strips. All sizes are approximate.

Strip size	Make two triangle panels this size	Allow this area if turned on diagonal	Size of corner triangles
6" x 25"	26" sq.	37" sq.	20" x 20" x 28"
7" x 29"	32" sq.	45" sq.	24" x 24" x 34"
8" x 33"	37" sq.	52" sq.	28" x 28" x 40"

Thousands of Triangles

What if you want to make one big quilt full of triangles instead of two small ones with triangles only in the center? Use twice as many strips (sixteen dark and sixteen light). Mix up cross sections to make four checkerboards, four sawtooth panels, and four panels full of triangles. Then fit them together into one big quilt. (You won't actually have *thousands* of triangles, but you'll have 512, and if you never make any mistakes, you can make them all without any short seams!)

Goodwill quilt revisited

If you make Hundreds of Triangles with large blocks, you will notice that you have one of the two-tone block arrangements shown in Chapter 4.

While you are checking out that idea, look again at the Goodwill quilt in Chapter 4. It was made with large individually cut triangles. Triangles were arranged in the Barn Raising pattern in the antique quilt in the color pages. Could that arrangement be made with strips of triangles instead?

The answer is yes.

Although Barn Raising doesn't use sawtooth chains, it's closely related to what you've been doing in this chapter. It also might give you ideas for switching projects if you goof up and cut zigs and zags that don't match.

How to make Barn Raising with strips

1. Cut strips, twelve dark and twelve light 8" x 25". (Don't use plaids and stripes with any strip projects. They are shown in the antique quilt because that was made with single triangles.)

2. Make four 3 x 6 checkerboards. We aren't putting many squares in each checkerboard because the squares are so large.

3. Turn checkerboards on the bias. They will resemble the 4 x 6 panels on page 91. Mark the centers.

4. Cut apart strips of triangles.

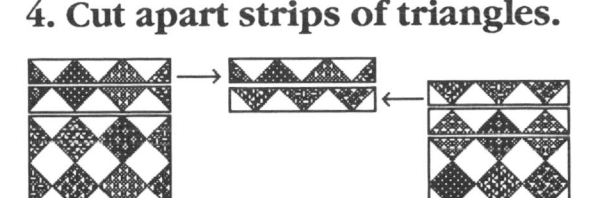

Important: *Cut two panels so they have three large light triangles. Cut the other two so they have three large dark triangles. (That's just the opposite of the rule I gave you earlier—you don't **want** them to line up the way sawtooth panels do.)*

5. Make four zigzag panels.

Drawing from both types of triangle strips, assemble four panels with a zigzag pattern. (These panels aren't the same, even if you turn them upside down. The darks and lights are reversed.) Make two of each type of panel.

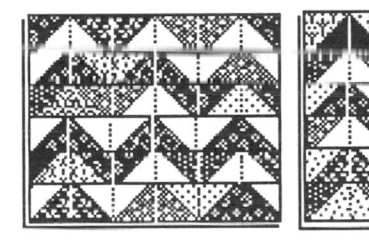

6. Cut chains.

7. Assemble four sections.

Spread out the chains on the bed or floor so you can select the chains that go together to form this pattern. Rearrange to get a nice fabric and color mix. Pin rows together and sew, making four panels again. The design slants in one direction in two panels, and in the other direction in the other two. These are the four quarters that make up the final quilt.

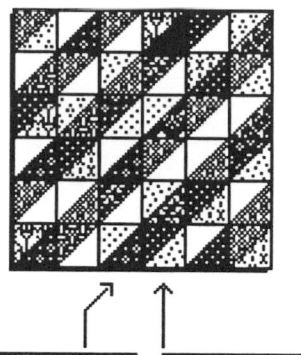

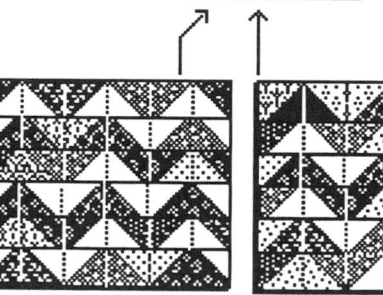

8. Arrange the quilt top like this: Because panels tend to be a little longer in the direction of the final seams, don't turn panels on their sides. Keep all final seams going the same way.

Can you use any of the other arrangements shown in Chapter 4?

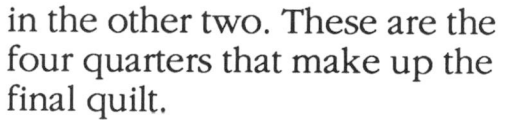

Yes, but I don't have room to show you how. After you have done Fast Patch for a while, you may be able to figure it out for yourself. (For clues, see the Pinwheel and Fool's Square blocks in Chapter 8 of *Fast Patch: A Treasury of Strip Quilt Projects*.)

That project was off the subject; let's get back now to sawtooth chains.

Sawtooth borders

Sawtooth chains make great borders for pillows or quilts. They look best with all the darks toward the inside of the project and all the light triangles on the outside, or vice versa. Then you start getting into trouble, because strange things happen in the corners. The first corner you make is attractive, the second is okay too, but the other two might be downright ugly. So plan ahead.

In *Fast Patch: A Treasury of Strip Quilt Projects*, I show several ways to make corners attractive (see pages 92 and 93). Here is a quick survey of some of the main ideas.

How to make attractive corners

1. Make borders for two projects at the same time.
Have all the "uphill" chains in one project, and the "downhill" chains in the other. This solution is good for pillow borders.

 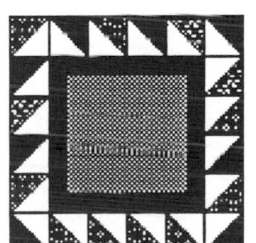

2. Switch direction in the center.
This works great for almost all projects, including large quilts.

3. Use squares in the corners.
This is wonderful for sashing or quilt blocks. Set a single block on the diagonal for an attractive pillow.

My *Fast Patch* book also has detailed information about fitting borders to quilts, including calculations for borders for dozens of sizes of square and rectangular projects. See pages 98 to 101 in *Fast Patch*.

9. Flying Geese

In the last chapter I showed one way to make Flying Geese, with seams down the middle to get the points back. With the version in this chapter, points are never lost—so it's much easier.

This chapter is the last one in the book for a good reason. You need to do some other projects first or you'll be totally baffled. Even quiltmakers who have done a lot of triangle designs with the Fast Patch technique will find some surprising new ideas and some changes in the old rules. So don't even read this chapter unless you've done other projects, at least one from Chapter 8.

After you've mastered this chapter, Flying Geese may turn out to be your favorite speed quilt.

Caution: *Not for faint-hearted patchers!*

How Flying Geese is made

First, I'll review what you've done so far and show what you have to do differently now. When making sawtooth chains, you used panels made from strips like these. The points were lost in the seam. That was okay because you needed the seam allowance you got when you cut through the points.

But for Flying Geese, make strips of triangles like this:

When strips are sewn together, points of the **dark** triangles are intact. Points of the **light** triangles are still flattened because you'll cut there and need a seam allowance.

The dark triangles will be called simply "Geese". Although I'm showing the light triangles as uniformly white, you can make them another pastel color. If you make them from scrap fabrics, the triangle on one side of a Goose will usually be a different fabric from the one on the other side. Look at the sample on the cover to see if that bothers you.

Here are the ways the Flying Geese technique differs from other projects in this book:

1. You need two sizes of strips

The dark strips are of normal proportion; light strips are 3/4" wider because they provide the seam allowances. Cross sections are cut the width of the dark strips.

2. You skip the regular checkerboard

Because of the way the dark squares and oversized light squares are arranged, an ordinary checkerboard would not be possible. It wouldn't have straight edges. Instead you make a **slanting panel**, which I call simply an "S-Panel."

The S-Panel shown here has four cross sections, eight squares each; it's equal to a 4 x 8 checkerboard turned halfway on the bias. This is the size you'll use first, but later you might get into some strange new sizes with five, six, or seven cross sections.

3. There is a different way of marking centers

Although the S-Panel will be turned the rest of the way to the bias later, centers are marked at this stage. Dark squares are marked as usual and light squares get **two** marks.

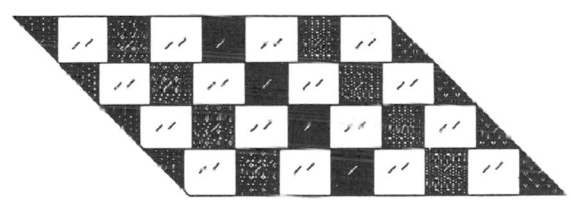

4. The bias panel looks very strange

In fact, if I showed it to you now, it might scare you away from this chapter!

Now, let's start at the beginning and take it step by step.

How to visualize your Flying Geese project

Occasionally it's possible to predict what a project will look like before you cut a single strip. With Flying Geese, it's very easy.

Spread out on a table a long piece of the fabric you plan to use for the light background. It can be just a few inches wide or as much as 22" if you want to use fabric that's still on the bolt. It should be at least a yard long, preferably two or three yards.

Place scraps of dark fabrics on the light background diagonally (starting next to the bolt if you're using uncut fabric). Fold up the light fabric to cover all but a triangle the size you want your Geese to be. Repeat with as many fabrics as possible, removing colors that don't seem right and trying others. Then lay out some strips of potential sashing fabric to complete the effect.

If you plan to use scraps for the light fabrics too, cover some of the folds with other pale colors before adding the dark pieces. Adding the top and bottom borders makes the test even more effective.

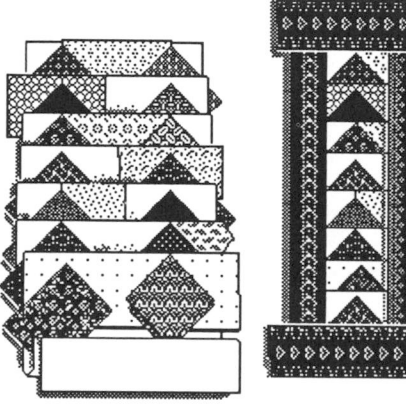

To visualize a quilt with predictable arrangements:

The first project given has you arrange colors in the same order in each chain of Geese. To visualize that, arrange only one row of Geese and the sashing on both sides, then place a mirror along the edge. Mirrors on both sides are even more effective since they reflect endlessly.

Once you choose the background colors and dark colors, you're locked into those, although you can change the total effect by making another little batch of purple Geese—or whatever color you need—and working them into the final arrangement.

But feel free to change your mind about the sashing and borders. Once you get the chains of Geese made, you can just make it up as you go along, adding one border after another. Flying Geese is much more elegant if you use beautiful printed border strips for sashing and borders.

Quilt sizes can vary greatly, depending on sashing and borders, so I'll usually be quite vague about the amount of backing and batting needed.

Flying Geese in an orderly arrangement

Your first Flying Geese project should be this one with four chains of medium-size Geese (Size D, about 4-1/4" wide). There are sixteen Geese in each chain, and fabrics are in an orderly sequence. See the sample in the color pages.

With simple sashing and borders like this, the project will be about 31" x 42".

Fabric needed:

Dark scraps: ten strips 4" x 17", all different (scrap fanatics can get by with eight strips)

Light fabric: 2/3 yd.

Sashing and inner border: 1/3 to 2/3 yd. (or 1 yd. of border print with four repeats of two appropriate designs)

Outer border: 1/2 yard (or 1-1/4 yd. of border print with four repeats)

Backing: 1 yd. or more

Batting and binding: measure finished project

1. Cut Alpha strips. Cut ten dark strips 4" x 17" and eight light strips 4-3/4" x 17".

2. Make two panels. Use five dark and four light strips in each panel, giving you a dark strip at both ends. (Scrap fanatics: Make the second panel with only three dark strips, so it will be light at each end.)

3. Cut cross sections from the first panel: Cut the width of the dark strips, not the light strips—that's very important.

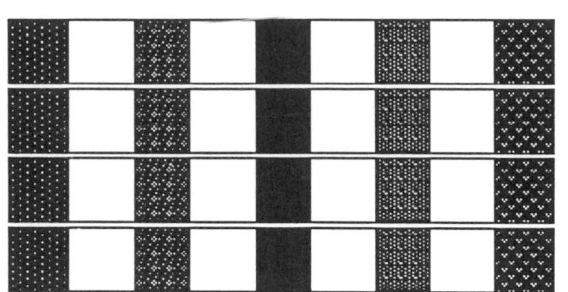

4. Make an S-Panel. Sew the strips together, each time moving the lower layer over one square.

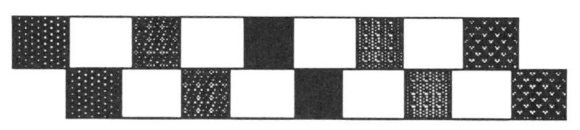

The final seams of the dark squares on upper row line up with the first seams of the dark squares on the lower row. **Pin at that point**.

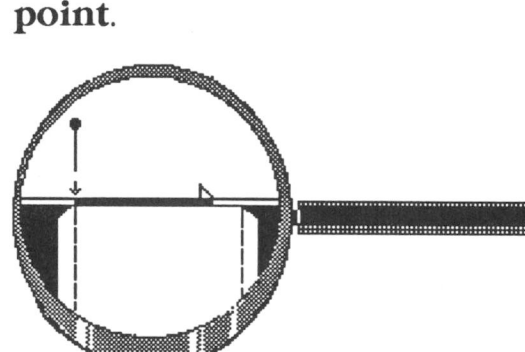

Light squares will overlap because they are wider. The dark squares on the ends are also wider because of unused seam allowances, so they overlap too.

If seams don't line up, correct a seam or (if you can't stand to pick things out) take a tiny tuck in the center of the overlapping light area. Use a safety pin to mark the spot where you cheated to remind yourself to take a closer look at the spot later. You might need to use a wider seam there when sewing strips of triangles together.

After sewing the four cross sections together, cut diagonally through the dark squares as shown to create a triangle on each end. As usual, you cut through the adjoining light square a bit at the edges (see the circles).

Cut exactly at the corner of the light squares; the pieces you cut off will still be attached to each other. If you're a scrap fanatic, you can recycle these triangles in Step 7.

5. Mark centers

(a) Make a template. Cut a square of cardboard or plastic the size of the dark squares. (Measure squares on the inner part of the panel so the unused seam allowances don't confuse you.) Since you started with 4" strips, this square should be 3-1/2". Find the center by drawing lines diagonally both ways. Cut a slit 1/2" long exactly in the center of the template, in one direction only.

(b) Mark the dark squares. Use a razor blade or other cutter to make cuts through the slits in the template. Mark in only one direction, as shown in the diagram. Don't forget the edge triangles.

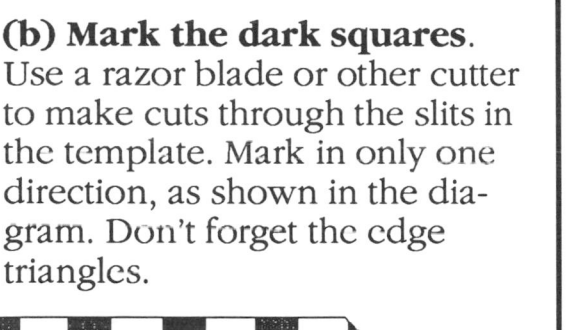

(c) Mark the light squares. These must be marked **twice**, because they have **two** centers. Put the template in the left side of the light square (not including the seam allowance of squares on the edges) and cut a mark.

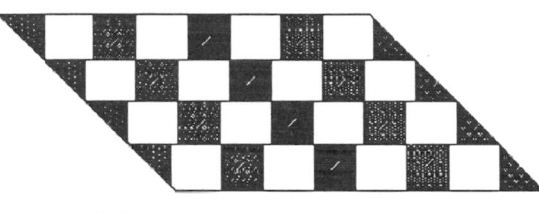

Move the template to the **right** side of the square and mark again.

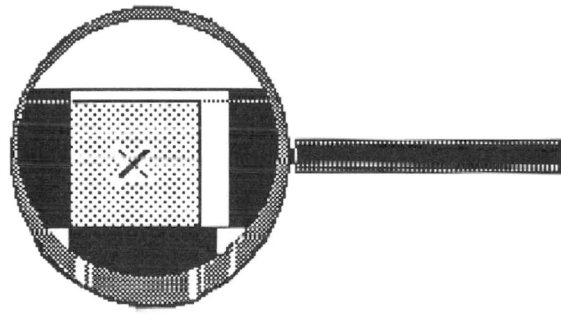

When you cut diagonally in Step 8, both of the light triangles will be marked. (**Don't cut yet.**)

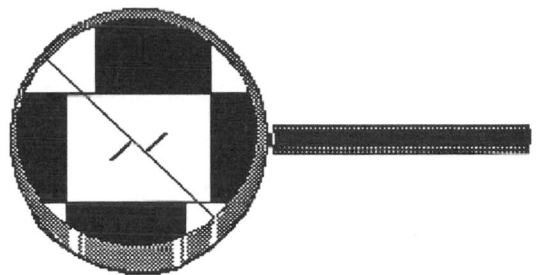

6. Finish turning the checkerboard on the bias. Here's how:

(a) Draw a cutting line. The reason you marked centers early was so you had a guide for this step. Cuts must be at a 45° angle, but the light "squares" aren't square, so you can't just plop the ruler down and cut diagonally across them. Draw a line, starting **inside** the seam allowance (see the circled areas). The line goes to the first center mark, zags over to the **other** center mark, then continues at the correct angle until the next mark, where it zags over again.

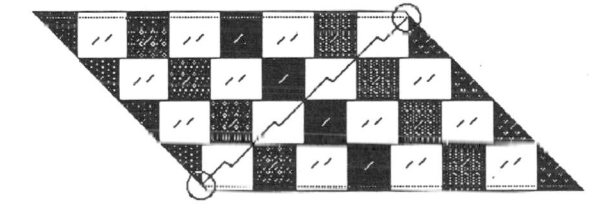

(b) Cut. You'll probably prefer to use scissors instead of a rotary cutter at this stage.

(c) Sew parts together again. See why I say Flying Geese isn't for timid people? The panel looks very strange. But I promise that this Ugly Duckling makes pretty Flying Geese.

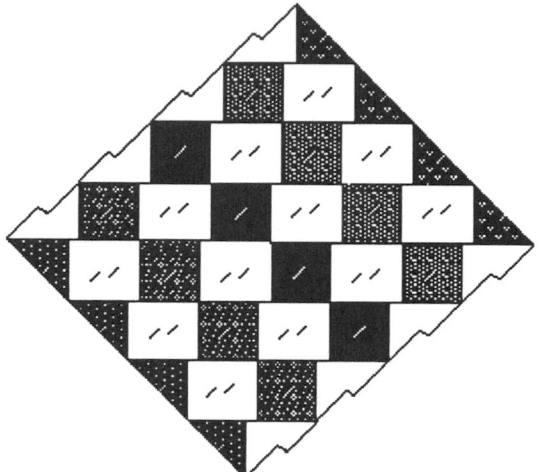

7. Repeat Steps 3 through 6. Make another S-Panel, mark it and turn it on the bias.

Scrap fanatics: After cutting cross sections, you can add a recycled triangle from Step 3 to the end of each section, all slanting the same way, and all triangles on the same end the same color.

Step 3
First panel

Second panel

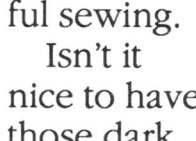

I am a scrap fanatic myself, but the more I experimented with Flying Geese, the less inclined I was to recycle the cut-off triangles. I don't think it's worth the bother.

8. Cut strips of triangles. Using the ruler and rotary cutter, cut as shown. Each panel makes eight strips of Geese. Clip off masses of fabric in the seam allowance in some places.

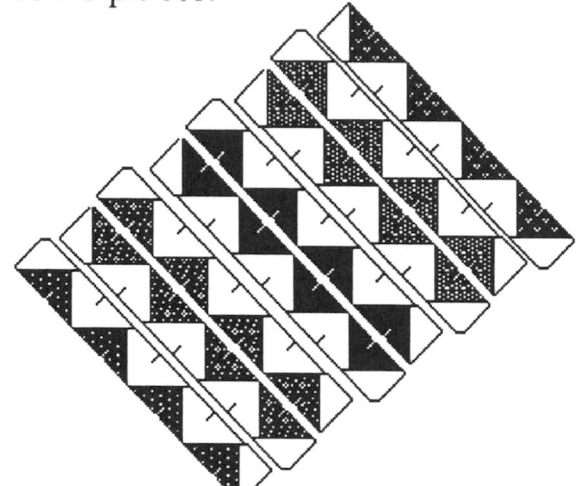

9. Sew chains together. Arrange them in any order that pleases you. Match marks and points as you did with sawtooth chains and sew up one panel of sixteen strips. This is quite an exacting task, so take your time. You're making sixty-four dark triangles and 128 light triangles and sewing them to each other, so there's a lot of careful sewing.

Isn't it nice to have those dark triangles with points intact? It was worth the effort.

This panel is very stretchy, being on the bias. Press it carefully, using spray starch.

As always, check accuracy as you press. Everyone I know has to pick out a seam occasionally. You must have the points of the dark triangles line up well enough that you can place a ruler over the tip of all of them in one straight line. Check the light points too, to see if they line up and see if the points are equally blunt. If any triangles look odd shaped, it's because the bias edge has been stretched or eased too much. Pick out a few inches and straighten it out.

If possible, let the piece set for a few hours to ease back into shape, in case pressing stretched it. While this panel is still flat, measure the length of the panel for Step 12, and make a note of your measurement.

10. Cut through the light triangles. This gives you four chains of Geese. Again, clip off any masses of seams you find.

11. Plan your sashing and borders. Spread out quilt parts and other fabrics and decide how to finish the project. Sashing and borders can be wide or narrow, plain or border print. The same chains of Geese are used in both sketches, but the final effects are quite different.

12. Make sashing. For four chains of Geese, you will need three strips of sashing (or five, if you consider the side borders part of the sashing).

Before cutting it, decide how you want to **mark** the sashing; you have to have a way to keep points of the triangles lined up evenly on each side, especially if sashing is narrow. And you have to have a way to avoid stretching the bias. First find the average seam interval, or height of each dark triangle. (Since you started with 4" strips, triangles will probably be 2-1/8" high—but use your measurement.)

To mark sashing before cutting the strips:

Use this method if you cut sashing from solid fabric.

(a) Cut yardage. Cut a piece a little longer than the chain of Geese and wide enough to divide into all the sashing strips you need, plus a bit for waste. Include the side borders too, if they'll be the same fabric. (Note: When you are doing long projects, you may need to piece the sashing. Do that before doing the next steps.)

(b) Transfer the seam interval measurement to your transparent ruler. Use a piece of masking tape to mark the width—that's easier than looking for the 2-1/8" mark (or whatever) every time.

(c) Draw guidelines. A ballpoint pen is easier to mark with than a pencil because it creates less drag on the fabric. Work on the **wrong** side of the fabric. Leaving a 1/4" seam allowance at the end of the yardage, start marking the fabric, moving along with your ruler **over** the already drawn lines, which line up with your tape mark. When finished, lay a chain of Geese over the fabric to double check the length. When you are sure it is correct, trim off the surplus, again making sure to leave a seam allowance.

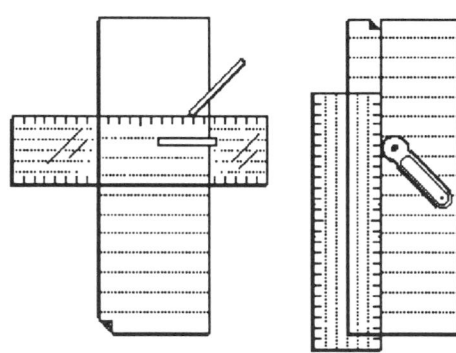

(d) Cut sashing strips. Reposition the tape, or remove it and just use the ruler markings since these can be an easy measurement like 3".

To mark strips that are already cut:

Use this method when using pre-cut strips, such as printed border designs and decorative sashing you create by piecing narrower strips together.

(a) Cut strips. Again, leave them a little longer than you think you'll need. Stack the strips evenly, pin them together in several places, and trim one end. (If you are using a large border print and want the design motifs in the same position on each strip, take extra care to line the designs up before pinning.)

(b) Make a template as wide as the sashing and several inches long. Notch it to mark the seam intervals very accurately, exactly opposite each other on both sides. Don't include the end seam allowances.

(c) Cut notches. Use this template and a razor blade, Xacto knife, etc., to cut notches on both sides of a whole stack of sashing strips at once. Remember to leave a seam allowance at the top and bottom. Keep these marks very shallow, less than 1/4" deep.

Move the template along the stack, overlapping the last section each time, marking as you go. Don't forget the seam allowance at the bottom.

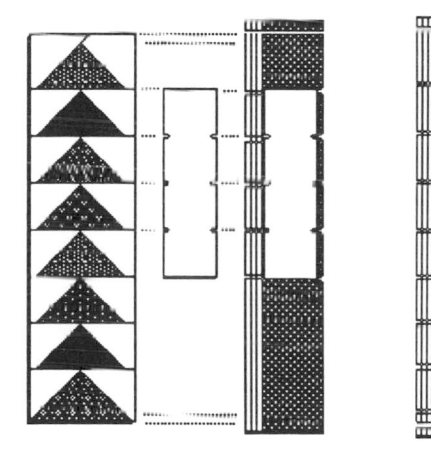

Creating your own decorative sashing

Printed fabric which has three to five repeats of several borders can be very attractive. Unfortunately, it's hard to locate a fabric that has exactly the color and design you need. Border prints can be quite expensive because you have to buy long lengths and seldom use all the different design strips.

You can create some stunning pieced sashing of your own. Sew narrow strips (perhaps of striped fabric or pre-printed borders) carefully to both sides of a wider strip of regular fabric, perhaps one you have already used to make Geese. For an example, see the quilt on the staircase in the color pages.

13. Sew together rows of Geese with sashing between. The hardest part of doing Flying Geese with strips is keeping the bias edges of the chains from stretching. That's why you marked the sashing accurately. Those marks won't help unless you faithfully match the seam lines to them when assembling the project.

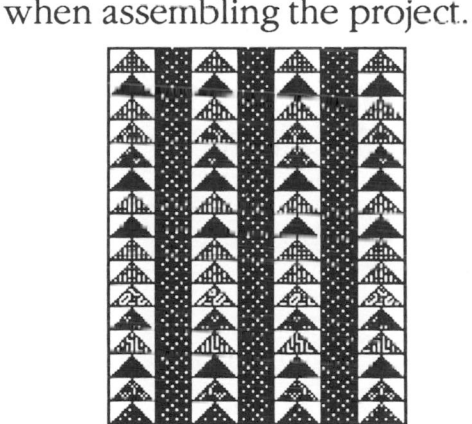

Plan ahead: Will you be mitering the corners of the borders? (See Step 14.) Will you do one-step quilting? (See pages 15 to 19 in Chapter 1.)

Add side borders now if you will be lapping corners. These can be the same fabric as the sashing or a new one. They too must have seam intervals marked to avoid stretching or easing the bias edges.

14. Add borders. Use as many borders as you wish, as wide as you like. What about the corners? Should you miter or lap them?

Miter them if:

(a) You are using a printed border fabric and want an elegant look.

(b) You have plenty of border fabric to use on each edge.

(c) You don't mind a little more work and know how to miter corners (I won't give directions).

(d) You aren't using the one-step quilting technique.

Lap them if:

(a) Borders are a dark print and you can't tell at first glance whether you mitered or not.

(b) Borders aren't long enough to miter

(c) You'd rather make borders quickly and never had much luck with mitered corners.

(d) You will use the one-step quilting technique.

Use a creative solution if:

(a) You're using a border print and realize the effcct of lapped borders would be terrible.

(b) Borders aren't long enough to miter

(c) You'd rather make borders quickly and never had much luck with mitered corners.

(d) You will use the one-step quilting technique.

(e) You have squares of exactly the right fabric to use in the corners. (You might even use pieced blocks.) Squares should echo the colors in the borders and not be so conspicuous that they distract from the Geese, unless you are really creative and know you can achieve an effect you will love.

15. Finish the quilt as you desire. Make backing, and quilt and bind the project, using information in Chapter 1.

Flying Geese in a random arrangement

Now try another small project, this time with Geese in a random arrangement.

(a) Make striped panels. Follow Steps 1 and 2 on page 147. The center dark strips are key fabrics this time; don't have a similar color in that position in both panels.

(b) Cut cross sections. Mix up sections from both panels and reverse some of them.

If you are a scrap fanatic, you might cut the end triangles off some cross sections and sew them to the ones that need them. Make sure you keep these cuts at a 45° angle. See the arrow in the magnified view below? That's the 45° angle line on your ruler. Keep it parallel to the edge of the strip. You cut exactly through the outside corner of the square and cut off a little of the light square on the inside.

(c) Make two S-Panels. Follow directions in Step 4 on page 148. The end colors will be mixed up nicely, but the center dark colors won't be evenly distributed.

(d) Follow Steps 5 through 8. Mark panels, turn them on the bias, and cut strips of triangles.

(e) Do some rearranging at Step 9. When arranging the final chains of Geese, pick out a couple of seams (ones where the Geese weren't quite as accurate). Rearrange chains to get a better effect.

Try other sizes of strips

I give six sizes on the chart on page 163. These are the sizes that would be suitable to these first projects.

Size chain*	Dark strips	Light strips	Size of 16-Goose Width	Length
C	3-1/2" x 13	4-1/4" x 13	3-3/4"	28"
D	4" x 17"	4-3/4" x 17"	4-3/8"	34"
E	4-1/2" x 19"	5-1/4" x 19"	5"	40"

Size is based on 1/4" seams. If seams are even slightly wider, chains will be a few inches shorter.

Double the Geese

Before going on, you may want to try the same steps you have already learned to make a larger project. Use Size E strips. Double the number of strips used in the first projects; start with twenty dark strips 4-1/2" x 19" and sixteen light strips 5-1/4" x 19".

You can make 128 Geese and arrange them two different ways. Use five chains of twenty-eight Geese for a twin throw; chains will be about 70" long. Or use six chains of twenty-one Geese for a shorter and wider quilt. Chains will be about 52" long. Use a random arrangement only.

Going on to larger Flying Geese projects

Flying Geese can be used for quilts of all sizes, with nine or ten chains of Geese, thirty or forty Geese per chain. There are detailed instructions and charts for planning projects on pages 158 through 166. If you don't care how big your project turns out and you'd rather sew than study charts and do calculations, just make it up as you go along.

Here are some shortcuts for large projects. (If you want to "sew along," here are some specifications: The quilt will be the size of the one shown on the stairs in the color pages, a double throw, 63" x 78" after quilting. There are 144 Geese, arranged in six chains of twenty-four, each chain about 65" long. The quilt in the color photo section was made with scraps of all sizes, so it had more variety.)

Make a quilt with 44" strips

As I have mentioned before, you can cut full-length strips and sew them together much faster than the shorter Alpha strips. There'll be less waste, and that's nice since we're trying to find homes for the scraps we already have—not create more!

I won't repeat basic directions since my purpose now is to show you some new tricks. You should have sewn up one of those projects already.

1. Cut strips: Nine dark, 5" x 44", all different, and nine light, 5-3/4" x 44" (cut from 1-1/2 yards of fabric).

2. Sew strips together. Surprise! You can have any number of strips in each panel, as long as you have an equal number of lights and darks. Avoid panels wider than your largest cutting mat, however. Cut cross sections as usual.

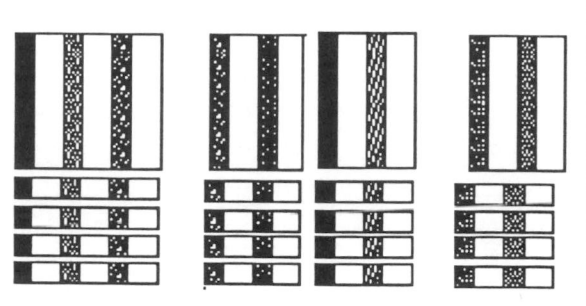

3. Make a super-size S-Panel

Join the cross sections into long chains of squares. Mix up sections to get a random order. It doesn't matter how long chains are—they might be five, ten, or fifteen feet long—as long as they are all the same length.

Make all chains the same length, then sew another dark square on the end of each.

If you have some extra pieces, keep them in case you need them. Two humble leftovers like this make sixteen Geese.

Sew chains together as before and trim the ends diagonally. See the color pages for a photo of this stage.

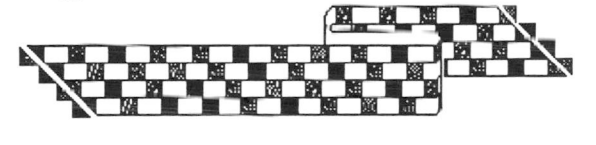

Imagine: The president of your quilt guild comes in now and asks, "What are you doing?" You say, "Making 144 Flying Geese." Then she asks your husband if you have had a psychiatric evaluation lately!

Are all of those seams going to line up? Probably not. (But don't keep taking the work out of the machine and correcting seams or you will feel you need a psychiatric evaluation.) Just take a tuck at the light overlap area when

needed, and keep going. Adjust those spots later, if needed.

4. Cut off ready-made S-Panels.

Cut diagonally through dark squares, every four, six, or eight squares. You automatically get triangles at the edge of all the panels with no waste and no recycling.

If you have only four squares in each section you cut off, it will look like this. Since these squares are large, you may prefer this size if your cutting mat is small.

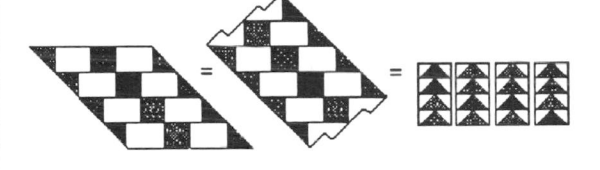

In fact, a panel might have only two squares across, a 4 x 2 panel. That's fine.

The squares in the cross sections (reading across) should not be more than double the number of cross sections (reading down). But even if they are, that's not fatal. Here's a 4 x 10 panel you might make accidentally or deliberately (because you'd rather absorb the extra squares in a large panel instead of having odds and ends).

Here's what it would look like when you finish turning it on the bias, and how to correct the problem.

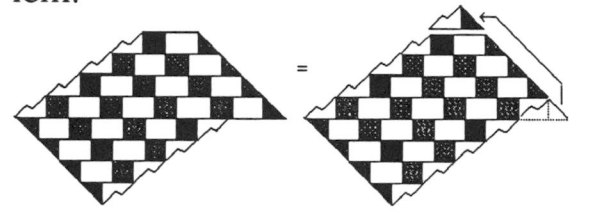

5. Mark centers, turn S-Panels on the bias, and cut strips of triangles. Follow the original directions on pages 148 through 150.

6. Sew strips of triangles together. Since Geese are in random order, it doesn't matter how many strips of triangles you sew together. Keep them short enough to fit on your largest cutting mat. You'll find it handy to have a couple of loose strips or small panels too.

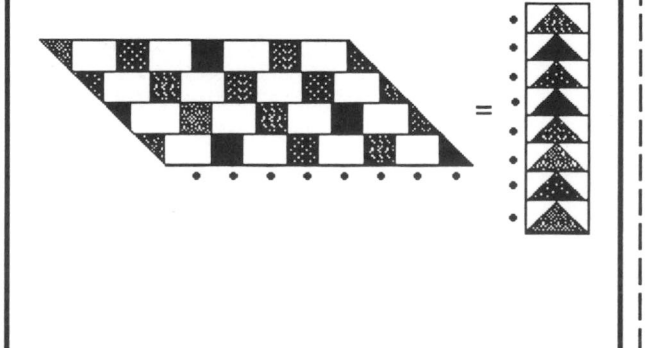

7. Finish the project as usual.

Designing large quilts with an orderly sequence of colors

Your very first project involved keeping an orderly sequence of colors with four chains of Geese. What if you want three chains of Geese—or seven, or ten—all with an orderly sequence? Those can be easily made, too, if you'll take time to learn some more new ideas.

The geometry of S-Panels

Study this diagram to learn how to "read" an S-Panel. First, count the cross sections. There are four in this case. That means that each strip of triangles will have four Geese.

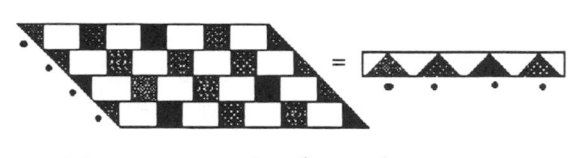

Now count in the other direction. The number of squares in each cross section equals the number of Geese in each chain.

Suppose you want seven chains of Geese in the final quilt top, with fabrics in the same order in each chain. Make S-Panels from seven cross sections.

The method is quite flexible. It doesn't really matter how many squares there are in the cross sections; use a limited number so panels are a manageable size. You don't need to make all the chains at once. If you want ten chains of Geese, make an S-Panel of five cross sections, then a second panel of five, because smaller panels are easier to handle.

If things are getting confusing, don't worry. This page and the charts that follow will make more sense as you get more experience.

Customized Alpha sizes

Use these charts when you want to keep colors in the same sequence in all chains.

To make only three chains of Geese:

Use strips three times as long as they are wide, plus an inch.

Size	Size of dark strips	Size of light strips
A	2-1/2" x 8-1/2"	3-1/4" x 8-1/2"
B	3" x 10"	3-3/4" x 10"
C	3-1/2" x 11-1/2"	4-1/4" x 11-1/2"
D	4" x 13"	4-3/4" x 13"
E	4-1/2" x 14-1/2"	5-1/4" x 14-1/2"
F	5" x 16"	5-3/4" x 16"

Each pair of dark and light strips makes six Geese.

To make four chains of Geese:

Use regular Alpha strips. (This was your first project.)

Size	Size of dark strips	Size of light strips
A	2-1/2" x 11"	3-1/4" x 11"
B	3" x 13"	3-3/4" x 13"
C	3-1/2" x 15"	4-1/4" x 15"
D	4" x 17"	4-3/4" x 17"
E	4-1/2" x 19"	5-1/4" x 19"
F	5" x 21"	5-3/4" x 21"

Each pair of dark and light strips makes eight Geese.

To make five chains of Geese:

Use dark strips five times as long as they are wide, plus an inch.

Size	Size of dark strips	Size of light strips
A	2-1/2" x 13-1/2"	3-1/4" x 13-1/2"
B	3" x 16"	3-3/4" x 16"
C	3-1/2" x 18-1/2"	4-1/4" x 18-1/2"
D	4" x 21"	4-3/4" x 21"
E	4-1/2" x 23-1/2"	5-1/4" x 23-1/2"
F	5" x 26"	5-3/4" x 26"

Each pair of dark and light strips makes ten Geese.

To make six chains of Geese:

Use strips six times as long as they are wide, plus an inch.

Size	Size of dark strips	Size of light strips
A	2-1/2" x 16"	3-1/4" x 16"
B	3" x 19"	3-3/4" x 19"
C	3-1/2" x 22"	4-1/4" x 22"
D	4" x 25"	4-3/4" x 25"
E	4-1/2" x 28"	5-1/4" x 28"
F	5" x 31"	5-3/4" x 31"

Each pair of dark and light strips makes 12 Geese.

To make seven chains of Geese:

Use strips seven times as long as they are wide, plus an inch.

Size	Size of dark strips	Size of light strips
A	2-1/2" x 18-1/2"	3-1/4" x 18-1/2"
B	3" x 22"	3-3/4" x 22"
C	3-1/2" x 25-1/2"	4-1/4" x 25-1/2"
D	4" x 29"	4-3/4" x 29"
E	4-1/2" x 32-1/2"	5-1/4" x 32-1/2"
F	5" x 36"	5-3/4" x 36"

Each pair of dark and light strips makes 14 Geese.

To make eight chains of Geese:

Use strips eight times as long as they are wide, plus an inch. Or use regular Alpha strips and make four chains, then make four more, keeping fabrics in the same order.

Size	Size of dark strips	Size of light strips
A	2-1/2" x 21"	3-1/4" x 21"
B	3" x 25"	3-3/4" x 25"
C	3-1/2" x 29"	4-1/4" x 29"
D	4" x 33"	4-3/4" x 33"
E	4-1/2" x 37"	5-1/4" x 37"
F	5" x 41"	5-3/4" x 41"

Each pair of dark and light strips makes 16 Geese.

For more than eight chains, combine the lengths given on the above charts. Combine four-chain and five-chain lengths to make nine chains, for example. Use the same fabrics each time, of course.

How to plan your own Flying Geese projects

The following steps describe how to make any size Flying Geese quilt. For example, this quilt has eight chains of thirty-six Size F Geese. The size would be about 100" x 114" before quilting. Use thirty-six strips (eighteen dark and eighteen light) 44" long. (Or use nineteen of each to allow for error.) Allow 3-1/4 yd. of light fabric for the light strips.

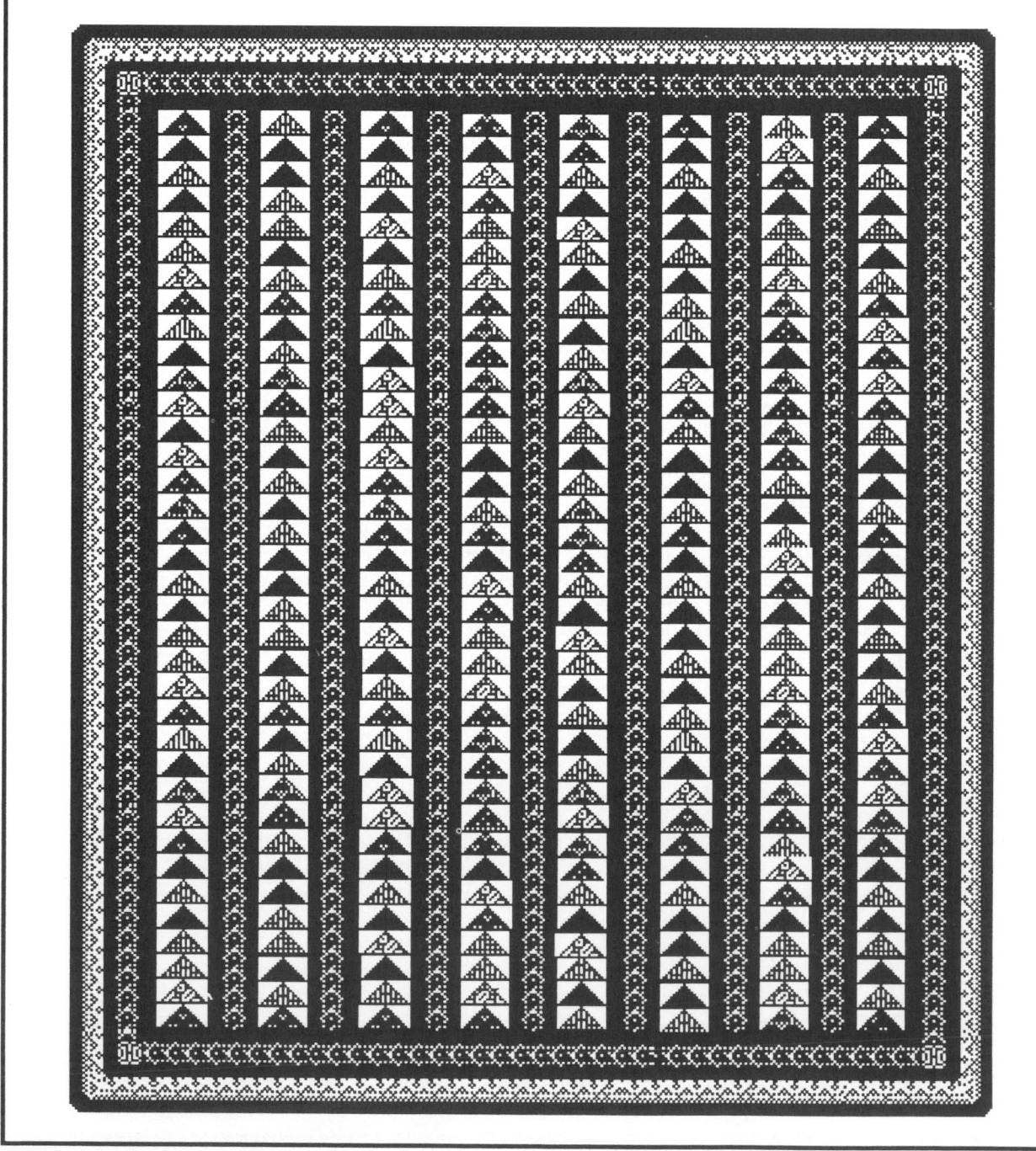

1. Decide how large to make the Geese. As a general rule:

Use Size A for clothing trim and miniatures. In fact, don't use this size at all until you are an expert. It's quite difficult to work this small.
Use Size B and C for wall hangings. Again, these are fairly difficult.
Use Size D for small and medium quilts.
Use Size E for medium and large quilts.
Size F gives oversized triangles, for very large quilts.

Size	Width of dark strips	Width of light strips	Size of Geese Height	Width
A	2-1/2"	3-1/4"	1-1/8"	2-1/4"
B	3"	3-3/4"	1-1/2"	3"
C	3-1/2"	4-1/4"	1-3/4"	3-3/4"
D	4"	4-3/4"	2-1/8"	4-3/8"
E	4-1/2"	5-1/4"	2-1/2"	5"
F	5"	5-3/4"	2-7/8"	5-3/4"

2. Estimate how many Geese you'll need.

This chart will help. Your measurement may be less but probably won't be more. (If your seams average 1/16" wider, your 48-Goose chains will be 3" shorter, for example.) Include a few extra Geese in case your chains turn out shorter than this or some pieces are defective. Remember, the project will be smaller after it is quilted.

Approximate length of Flying Geese chains:

Size	Number of Geese 16	24	32	40	48
A	18"	27"	36"	45"	54"
B	24"	36"	48"	60"	72"
C	28"	42"	56"	70"	84"
D	34"	51"	68"	85"	102"
E	40"	60"	80"	100"	120"
F	46"	69"	92"	115"	138"

Example: *Suppose you want to make a quilt like the one in the artwork on page 162. You want eight chains of Size F Geese, and you'd like the chains to be 100" long. You need thirty-six Geese per chain, a total of 288 Geese. (Add a couple of Geese per chain for good measure, and make that thirty-eight, a total of 304 Geese.)*

3. Decide how many strips you need to make that many geese.

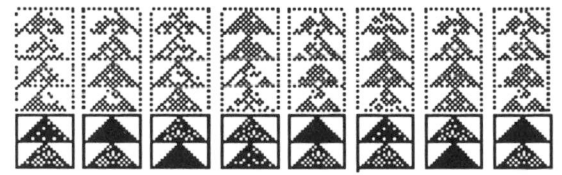

If you want to make a queen-size quilt, don't bother with the math. Just count the Geese in a single chain and allow one 44" strip for each! If you want a quilt with chains of 36 Geese, use 30 strips (18 dark, 18 light). This works whether Geese are in random order or repeat the same sequence. However, you will need to add a few dark strips to avoid having to recycle triangles as mentioned on page 150. And you should allow a few extra strips in case your Geese are a little smaller than expected. The smaller the Geese, the more chains you can make. Here's what you can make from 44" strips:

Size D: ten chains

Size E: nine chains

Size F: eight chains.

If you want to make other sizes of quilts, adapt the directions on page 147 through 156 or make it up as you go along, or (if math doesn't scare you) study the material on page 165.

4. Choose fabrics. Use the visualizing technique on page 146 to decide on a general color scheme.

Dark strips: Use as many different fabrics as possible, especially for small projects. Repeat fabrics on large projects or projects where you want an orderly sequence of colors. Use scraps of all sizes as long as they equal the number of Alpha strips or 44" strips you determined you'd need.

Light strips: You'll probably like the effect better with a uniform background color. Here are some ballpark figures on yardage needed:

Wall hangings: 2/3 yd.

Small quilts: 1-1/3 to 1-2/3 yds.

Medium quilts: 2 to 2-1/2 yds.

Queen size quilts: up to 3-1/2 yds.

You can do some closer calculations if you prefer. See how many 44" lengths you will need and multiply that by the strip width, adding a few inches for waste. Divide your total inches by thirty-six to find yards.

Don't try to make light geese on a dark background until you're an expert on Fast Patch Flying Geese and no longer need the book for basic steps. It would be very confusing to reverse light and dark in all the directions, diagrams, and charts.

cont'd on page 166

Closer calculations for strips needed:

Determine the number of Geese needed. Multiply the Geese in each chain by the number of chains.

Example in the artwork (page 162): *8 x 38 (extra for good measure) = 304.*

If using Alpha strips: A pair of Alpha strips makes eight Geese, so divide the number of Geese by eight and round up to the next even number. You need that many dark strips plus that many light ones. (Add a few dark strips if you want to work with small panels but don't want to recycle end triangles.)

Example: *Divide 304 Geese by eight and get thirty-eight. Cut thirty-eight dark strips and thirty-eight light strips.*

If using 44" strips (Alpha-strip bypass): Divide the number of Geese by this number and round up to a whole number. That gives the number of dark strips. Use an equal number of light strips.

Size	Divide number of Geese by
A	34
B	28
C	24
D	20
E	18
F	16

Example: *You need 304 Geese in Size F. Divide 304 by sixteen and you get nineteen strips. You need nineteen assorted dark strips 4-1/2" wide and 44" long. You also need nineteen light strips 5-1/4" wide and 44" long.*

For projects with Geese in an orderly sequence: Use custom sizes of Alpha strips, as I explained on pages 159 to 161. The rule is simple for eight chains or fewer: **One dark strip and one light strip make two Geese in each chain.** Use the charts to see how long the strips are. The math comes out the same in this case. Nineteen dark strips and nineteen light strips make nineteen pairs of Geese, or thirty-eight Geese per chain.

For more than eight chains, you'll use two shorter strips. If they add up to less than 44" and can share the same 44" strip, that's fine. If they total more than 44", there will be a lot more waste. Cutting will also take much longer, so you might want to change your plans. If you want an extra wide quilt, use wider sashing and borders instead of more chains of Geese.

The maximum number of chains recommended for colors in an orderly sequence:

Size D: ten chains

Size E: nine chains

Size F: eight chains.

cont'd from page 164

5. Design sashing and borders.
I recommend that you make the chains of Geese first, then plan your sashing and borders, unless you have some special fabric on hand and plan the project to fit it, of course. Even if I start with a border print I plan to use and pick colors that match for the Geese, I often find that I prefer a different effect when I am ready to assemble the quilt. (After all, an artist seldom picks out his frame before starting his painting.)

Allow sashing a bit longer than you anticipate the chains of Geese will be. If you will have the same fabric for side borders as was used for sashing, you'll need one more strip than there are chains of Geese. If the side borders will be different, you'll need one fewer strips than there are chains of Geese. If using border fabrics, check to see how many repeats there are of the border you want to use.

Example: *With the project using eight chains of Geese, you find your chains are 99" long. You find a border fabric that has four repeats of a pretty design you would like to use for sashing. You would need two lengths, or 198". Divide by thirty-six and you find you need 5-1/2 yds. Add some for error and get 5-3/4 yds. You decide you can't afford that much today. (After all, you told your family you were using up scraps and wouldn't be buying much fabric.) You have several choices:*

(a) Use different border designs. Buy just one length of the pretty border fabric (make it three yards, allowing length for mitered borders). Use three different border designs. Alternate two of them in the sashing and use another for borders.

(b) Make your own sashing. Sew striped fabric to both sides of strips of print fabric. That's lots of extra sewing, but it might be well worth it.

(c) You can use plain fabric instead of border prints. Buy yardage as long as the chains so you don't have to piece it.

Design Tip: *Add your own creative touches to the project, such as sawtooth borders as shown in the sketch. (Review Chapter 8. If you want triangles the same height as the Geese, you'll need to change strip size to accommodate the seam allowance. Make both light and dark strips the same width, 1/2" wider than the **dark** strips used for Flying Geese.)*

6. Plan backing fabric
Use the information on the chart on page 13. Remember this can be pieced too. Try something creative if you want; see the sketch on page 138.

Wild Goose Chase

Although the most common use of Flying Geese is in vertical chains, they are sometimes used to make borders or quilt blocks.

The most popular is Wild Goose Chase, where Geese are arranged in a diagonal pattern with squares or other motifs where the chains of Geese meet. There can be three, four, five, or more Geese in each chain.

How to plan Wild Goose Chase projects

1. Study the block to see how it goes together.

My approach to designing Wild Goose Chase is based on sets of four chains radiating from a center square (or pointing toward the square).

The dotted line represents the "block" size. It really isn't a separate block because it shares squares with its neighbors, but it helps to know that size. In addition to strips to make the Geese, each set also needs squares and triangles:

(a) One center square which contrasts with the triangles that touch it.

(b) Two small squares to share with neighbors, dark if the center squares are light, light if the center squares are dark. Some must be larger than others because they are cut into triangles and need seam allow-ances. (You might prefer to make templates for the triangles so the grain of the fabric is on the edge of the project.)

(c) Two large background squares to share with neighbors. At least half will be the same width as the length of the chains, but some must be larger because they will be cut into triangles and must have seam allowances. (Again, you may prefer templates for edge triangles.)

To make a Wild Goose Chase quilt:

2. Decide how many Geese you want in each chain. Each pair of dark and light Alpha strips (dark strip four times as long as it is wide, plus an inch, light strip wider) makes one Goose in each chain, so the math is easy. If each chain has three Geese, use three pairs of Alpha strips.

3. Determine your size. Here's what to expect from sizes on page 163.

	Size of Number of Geese per chain*				small squares
Size	3 Geese	4 Geese	5 Geese	6 Geese	
A	3-3/4" (8")	5" (10")	6" (11-1/2")	7" (13")	2-3/4"
B	5" (10-1/2")	6-1/2" (12-1/2")	8" (14-1/2")	9-1/2" (16-1/2")	3-1/2"
C	5-3/4" (13")	7-1/2" (15")	9" (17-1/2")	11" (20")	4-1/4"
D	7" (15")	9" (18")	11" (21")	13" (24")	5"
E	8" (18")	10-1/2" (21")	13" (24-1/2")	15-1/2" (28")	5-1/2"
F	9" (20-1/2")	12" (25")	15" (28")	17-1/2" (32")	6-1/4"

*Chain length ("Block" size is in parentheses)

All sizes are before final seams, but are only approximate! Measure yours.

What about the background squares? Use the **chain length** and cut squares that size. Allow extra for squares which will be cut to make the triangles on the edges.

4. Decide how many sets you want. Multiply the figure from Step 1 by that number. (The example below has four sets of three-Goose chains. Four times three equals twelve, so you'd cut twelve Alpha strips and twelve wider strips. You want medium triangles, so you'd use size D, dark strips 4" x 17", light strips 4-3/4" x 17".) Remember, you may want more of the narrower strips to avoid having to recycle triangles cut off the ends (see page 150).

5. Make chains of Geese. Use any convenient size of panels. Sew together as many strips of triangles as you need Geese in each chain:

6. Cut squares and triangles and work out your arrangement.

(a) Cut **one small dark** and **one small light square** for each set to start with (match the width of the chains of Geese). Cut more squares and triangles after you decide whether they should be dark or light.

(b) Cut **one large square** for each set to start with. These are as wide as the chains are long. Cut more large squares if needed, as well as triangles for the edges. In the example below, the background sections are two different colors. There are many ways to get creative with this project.

(c) Arrange everything into an overall design.

(d) Sew parts together into diagonal rows.

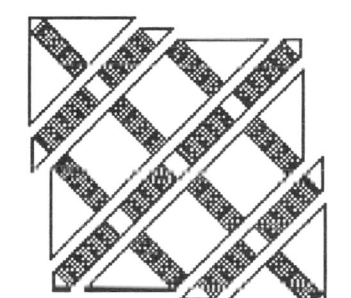

(e) Sew sections together and add borders.

More ideas for Flying Geese

You can also use the Flying Geese chains for many other decorative purposes:

1. Make borders.

2. Make blocks (one is shown below).

3. Make sashing. Flying Goose sashing (below) might be thought of as a variation of Wild Goose Chase, so the information on these last two pages will be some help in calculating those.

4. Make strips to connect panels in **pieced backings**; see page 138.

5. Use in **Strippy quilts**. See page 175 in the Appendix.

6. Use in **clothing decoration**. Make borders for skirts or panels for vests or jackets.

Once you master the ideas in this chapter and the rest of the book, you can design quite complicated projects which you can piece together in hours or days instead of months.

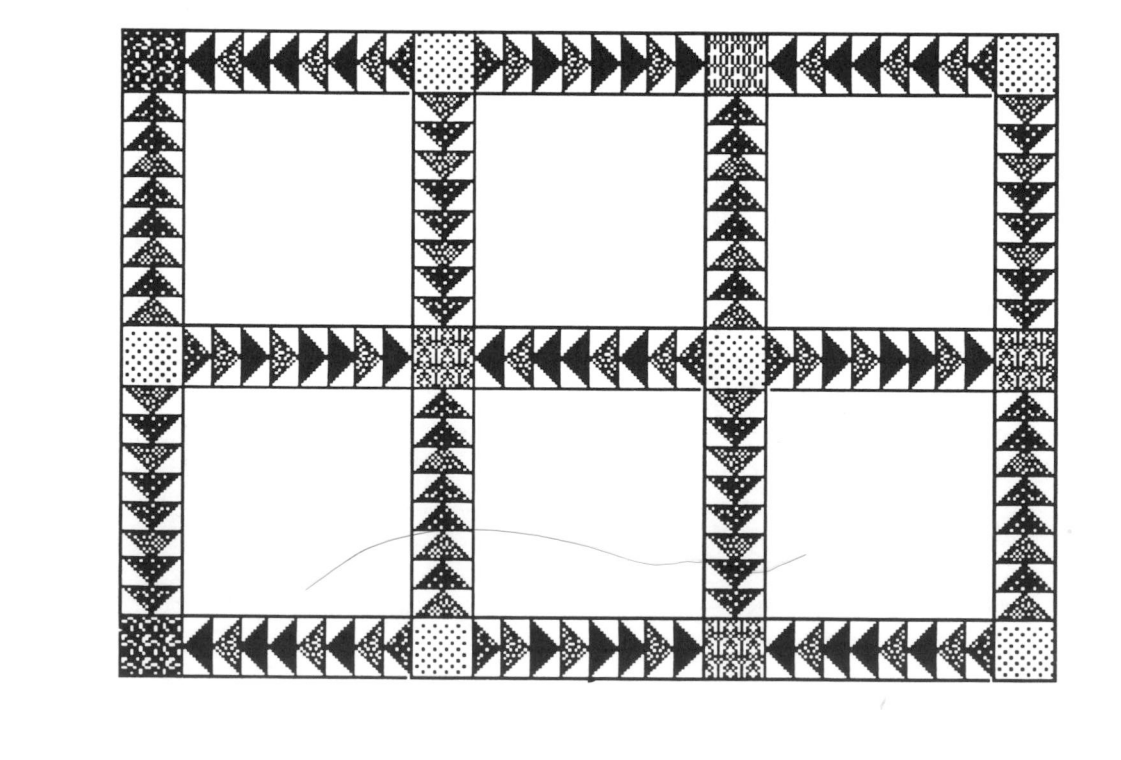

Appendix

Sizes of final triangles

Triangles will be this size after cutting and 1/4" seam allowances. Original strip size is at the bottom of each square.

Connector Triangles and Flying Geese

All others

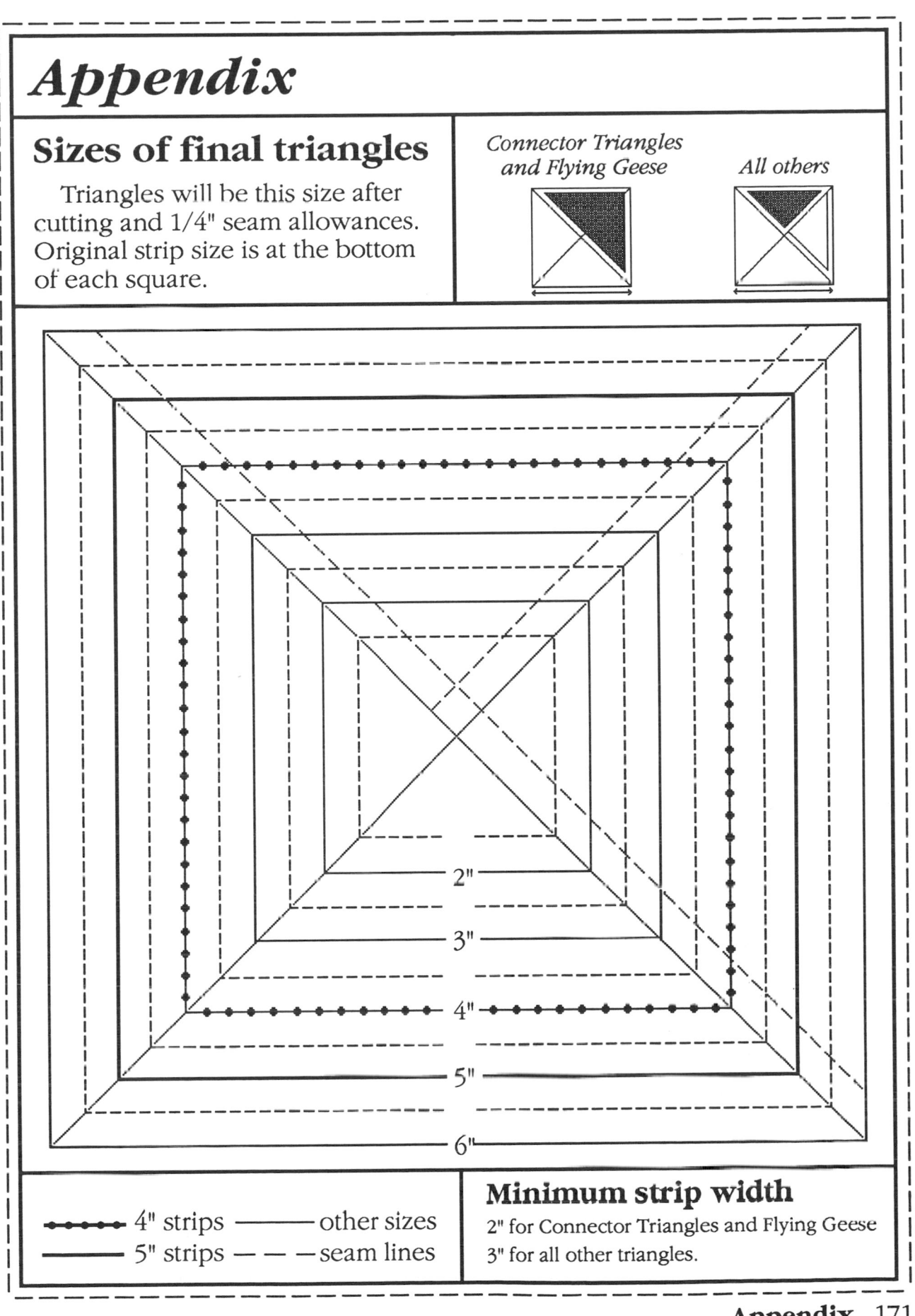

2"

3"

4"

5"

6"

•••• 4" strips ——— other sizes
——— 5" strips – – – seam lines

Minimum strip width
2" for Connector Triangles and Flying Geese
3" for all other triangles.

Common sizes of checkerboards and what they look like turned on the bias

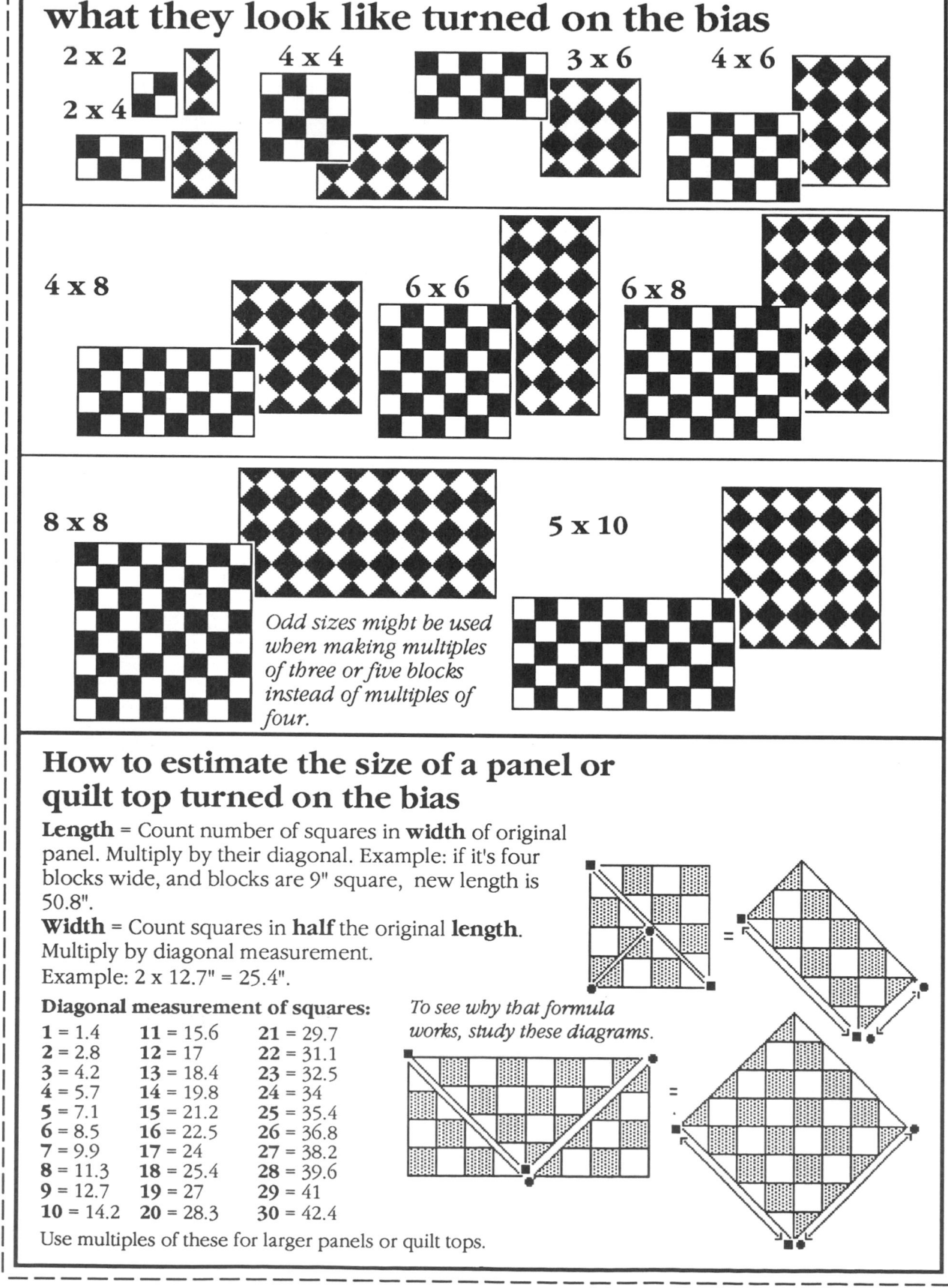

2 x 2

2 x 4

4 x 4

3 x 6

4 x 6

4 x 8

6 x 6

6 x 8

8 x 8

5 x 10

Odd sizes might be used when making multiples of three or five blocks instead of multiples of four.

How to estimate the size of a panel or quilt top turned on the bias

Length = Count number of squares in **width** of original panel. Multiply by their diagonal. Example: if it's four blocks wide, and blocks are 9" square, new length is 50.8".

Width = Count squares in **half** the original **length**. Multiply by diagonal measurement.
Example: 2 x 12.7" = 25.4".

Diagonal measurement of squares:

1 = 1.4	**11** = 15.6	**21** = 29.7
2 = 2.8	**12** = 17	**22** = 31.1
3 = 4.2	**13** = 18.4	**23** = 32.5
4 = 5.7	**14** = 19.8	**24** = 34
5 = 7.1	**15** = 21.2	**25** = 35.4
6 = 8.5	**16** = 22.5	**26** = 36.8
7 = 9.9	**17** = 24	**27** = 38.2
8 = 11.3	**18** = 25.4	**28** = 39.6
9 = 12.7	**19** = 27	**29** = 41
10 = 14.2	**20** = 28.3	**30** = 42.4

Use multiples of these for larger panels or quilt tops.

To see why that formula works, study these diagrams.

Cut-apart checkerboard

Make photocopies of this diagram. Cut different sizes of checkerboards and turn them on the bias, using scissors and removable Scotch tape.

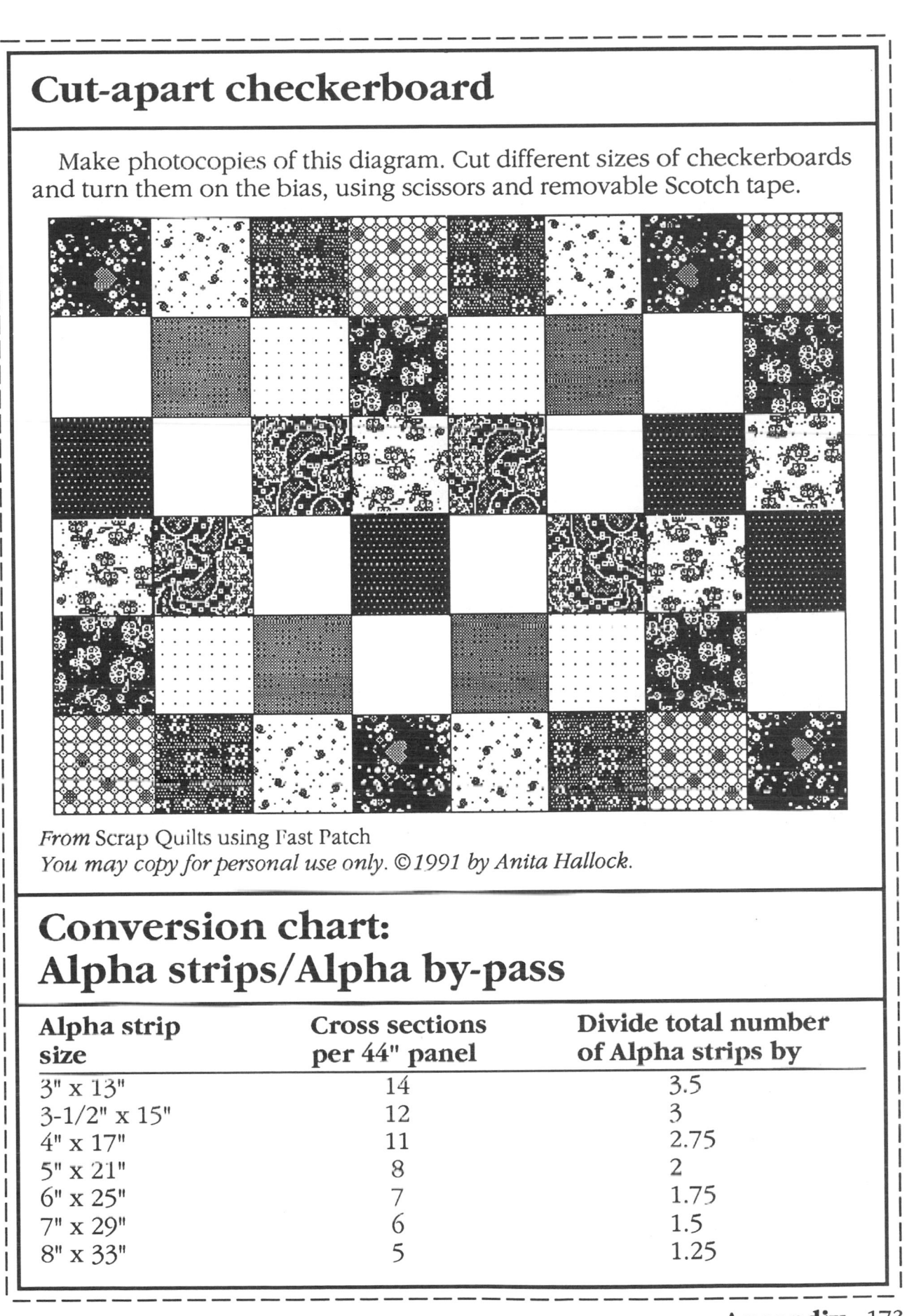

From Scrap Quilts using Fast Patch
You may copy for personal use only. ©1991 by Anita Hallock.

Conversion chart: Alpha strips/Alpha by-pass

Alpha strip size	Cross sections per 44" panel	Divide total number of Alpha strips by
3" x 13"	14	3.5
3-1/2" x 15"	12	3
4" x 17"	11	2.75
5" x 21"	8	2
6" x 25"	7	1.75
7" x 29"	6	1.5
8" x 33"	5	1.25

Cut-apart Flying Geese

This is small, but it will give you some idea of how the Flying Geese S-Panel works. Read the first half of Chapter 9 first, then experiment with scissors, a pencil, and tape. Trim off the end triangles, mark the centers, turn it on the bias, and cut strips of triangles.

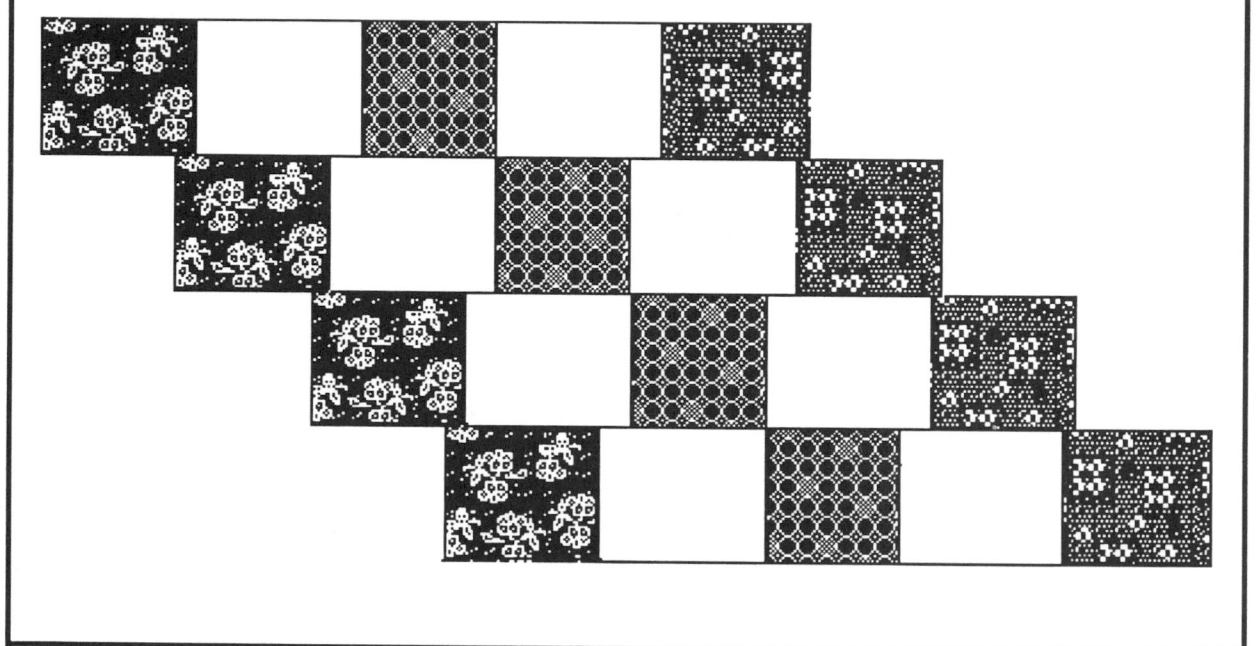

Cut-apart string-pieced panels

Use scissors and Scotch tape to try out ideas in Chapter 3.

From Scrap Quilts Using Fast Patch.
You may copy for personal use only. ©1991 by Anita Hallock.

"Strippy" clip art

Many designs in this book can be adapted to "Strippy" quilts (vertical sampler quilts with strips of many different motifs combined in a creative way). Make several copies of these strips to experiment with Strippy quilt designs, borders, designs to join sections on the back of the quilt, etc.

From Scrap Quilts Using Fast Patch. *You may copy for personal use only.* ©1991 by Anita Hallock.

Other Fast Patch scrap projects

Here are some projects in *Fast Patch: a Treasury of Strip Quilt Projects* which would make good scrap quilts:

Chapter 2: All projects in this chapter could be converted easily; some are already designed for scraps. There are charts for making **Nine-Patch** blocks.

Chapter 3: This chapter is similar to Chapter 6 in this book; the explanations of turning a quilt top on the bias will give further understanding of that process.

Make single Ohio Star blocks one at a time, with all background colors the same, each star a different color, then combine the stars into a quilt top. Try black backgrounds and solid colors for an Amish effect.

Chapter 6: This has a chart for calculating **sawtooth borders** for any size of quilt. Suggestions are made for **Tree** and **Basket** blocks.

Chapter 7: Blocks which would be well suited to scraps are **Nine-Patch/Snowball** combination, **Split Nine-Patch, Maple Leaf, Irish Star, Three-Patch Sampler**, and especially **Hovering Hawks**, which has an **Ocean Waves** look to it when done with scraps.

Chapter 8: Five-Patch blocks which would look best with scraps are probably **Double Irish Chain, Sister's Friend, Crown of Thorns, Handy Andy, Springfield A, Fool's Square,** and **Pinwheels. Wedding Ring** would be especially well suited to scraps.

Recommended Reading

For general quiltmaking techniques

The Complete Book of Machine Quilting, by Robbie and Tony Fanning (Chilton Book Co., Radnor, PA, 1980).

Every Trick in the Book, by Ami Simms (Mallery Press, Flint, MI, 1990).

For more strip-pieced designs:

Fast Patch: A Treasury of Strip Quilt Projects, by Anita Hallock (Chilton Book Co., Radnor, PA, 1989). This includes a five-patch sampler quilt and other projects suited to scraps. Write to author at Box 2, Springfield, OR 97477 for information about other Fast Patch publications.

To use the right thread, needle, and adjustments for your sewing machine:

The Complete Book of Machine Quilting, by Robbie and Tony Fanning (Chilton Book Co., Radnor, PA, 1980), Chapter 1.

Know Your Sewing Machine, by Jackie Dodson (Chilton Book Co., Radnor, PA, 1988), Chapter 1. (This is a general book; this author has written a whole series of books, including brand-specific books.)

Claire Shaeffer's Sewing S.O.S., a compilation of *Sew News* columns by Claire Shaeffer (Open Chain Publishing, Menlo Park, CA, 1988).

Owner's Guide to Sewing Machines, Sergers, and Knitting Machines, by Gale Grigg Hazen (Chilton Book Co., Radnor, PA, 1989), Part 1.

Putting on the Glitz, by Sandra L. Hatch and Ann Boyce (Chilton Book Co., Radnor, PA, 1991).

A Step-by-Step Guide to Your Sewing Machine (Teach Yourself to Sew Better series), by Jan Saunders (Chilton Book Co., Radnor, PA, 1990).

For organizing a group to make scrap quilts:

Friendship Quilts by Hand and Machine, by Carolyn Vosburg Hall (Chilton Book Co., Radnor, PA, 1988).

For other things to do with scraps:

The Fabric Lover's Scrapbook, by Margaret Dittman (Chilton Book Co., Radnor, PA, 1988).

For making quilts with a serger:

Innovative Serging, by Gail Brown and Tammy Young (Chilton Book Co., Radnor, PA,1989), Chapter 12.

Serge-a-Quilt, by Ann Person (Stretch and Sew, Inc., Box 185, Eugene, OR 97440).

Serger Patchwork Projects, by Kaye Wood (4949 Rau Rd., West Branch, MI 48661, 1986).

For more understanding of design and color:

Claire Shaeffer's Fabric Sewing Guide, (Chilton Book Co., Radnor, PA, 1989).

"Color Effects and Harmonies for Quilts," by Judy Martin. *Quilters Newsletter Magazine,* No. 194, July-August 1987.

Color and Cloth, by Mary Coyne Penders (The Quilt Digest Press, San Francisco, 1989).

The Art of Color and Design, by Maitland Graves (McGraw-Hill Book Co., New York, 1951), Chapter 10.

For speed-pieced Log Cabin with limited colors:

Make a Quilt in a Day, by Eleanor Burns. (Quilt in a Day, 1955 Diamond St, Unit A, San Marcos, CA 92069)

Revolutionized Log Cabin Quilt by Roberta Stroud. (1605-C George Dieter, Suite 584, El Paso, TX 79936).

For other speed-pieced quilts:

The Quick Quiltmaking Handbook, by Barbara Johannah (Pride of the Forest, Box 7266, Menlo Park, CA 94026) and other books by that author.

The It's OK If You Sit On My Quilt Book, by Mary Ellen Hopkins. (ME Publications, 18627 Brookhurst St., Ste. 348, Fountain Valley, CA 92708)

Sources of supplies mentioned:

Quilting Books Unlimited *(books)*
1158 Prairie
Aurora, IL 60506

TreadleArt *(books and notions)*
25834-I Narbonne Ave.
Lomita, CA 90717

Clotilde Inc.*(Wonder Thread, other notions)*
1909 SW First Ave.
Ft. Lauderdale, FL 33315

Omnigrid *(rulers and grids)*
3227-B 164th St. SW
Lynnwood, WA 98037

Helyn's Hoops *(Hoop de Deux, shown in color plates)*
911 City Park
Columbus, OH 43206

Index